Crossing Cultures in the Language Classroom

Andrea DeCapua, Ed.D.

New York University

Ann C. Wintergerst, Ed.D.

St. John's University

The University of Michigan Press   Ann Arbor

To my husband, Paul McMahon,
and children, Maria, Lucian, and Geoffrey,
for their love and support

To my mother, Charlotte Wintergerst,
for her love and inspiration

Copyright © by the University of Michigan 2004
All rights reserved
Published in the United States of America by
The University of Michigan Press
Manufactured in the United States of America
⊗ Printed on acid-free paper

2010   5   4

A CIP catalog record for this book is available from the British Library.

Library of Congress Cataloging-in-Publication Data
DeCapua, Andrea.
    Crossing cultures in the language classroom / Andrea DeCapua, Ann C. Wintergerst.
        p.   cm.
    Includes bibliographical references and index.
    ISBN 0-472-08936-6 (pbk. : alk. paper)
    1. Multicultural education.   2. Intercultural communication.   I. Wintergerst, Ann C.
    II. Title.
    LC1099.D39   2004
    370.117—dc22

                                                        2004041172

ISBN 978-0-472-08936-9 (pbk. : alk. paper)

Preface

As we continue our journey into the 21st century, facing the shrinking of our world through technological changes, it becomes quite evident that contact between members of different cultures is on the upsurge. With this increase in cross-cultural contact, there is a greater need to understand ourselves and others as we are shaped by our culture and our language. Teachers are generally those in the forefront of cross-cultural contact, yet they are often ill prepared for dealing effectively with the various issues that arise in cross-cultural communication. It is therefore our intent to make education in cross-cultural awareness accessible to educators working with prospective general education, ESL, bilingual, and foreign language teachers. *Crossing Cultures in the Language Classroom* attempts to balance theory (what research tells us) and practice (what activities show us) specifically for preservice and in-service students in general education courses focusing on the multicultural classroom and for those enrolled in ESL, bilingual, and foreign language teacher training courses. This book is unique in that it combines theory with a wide range of experiential activities designed to actively engage users in the process of understanding different aspects of cross-cultural communication. By the time they reach the end of this book, users will have developed an appreciation for the role that culture and language play in their behaviors, actions, and judgments of others.

We have chosen to use the term *cross-cultural,* rather than *multicultural* or *intercultural,* for various reasons. In the United States, *multicultural* is often synonymous with the ethnic, linguistic, and cultural groups residing here permanently. The focus is on inclusion, that is, on providing equal learning opportunities through the celebration of diverse heritages. The other two terms—*intercultural* and *cross-cultural*—are often used interchangeably, although some argue that there are differences in conceptualization between the two. *Intercultural communication* may be understood to refer to the larger symbolic, perceptual, and situational differences that contribute to differences in the interpretation of and expectations about the meaning and behaviors among people of diverse linguistic and cultural backgrounds. *Cross-cultural* communication may be viewed as referring more specifically to the *study of particular values, beliefs, norms, and ideas of many languages and cultures in order to draw comparisons.* In reality, however, the differences between the two terms are relatively insignificant; both are concerned with communication processes between speakers of different languages and from different cultures. In our quest to provide balance between theory and practice, to introduce basic concepts and ideas, and to encourage users to experience and reflect on the similarities and differences among themselves, we have elected to use the term *cross-cultural* throughout the book.

Acknowledgments

We wish to thank our colleagues, our students, and our workshop participants without whom this book would not have been possible. Their helpful suggestions, useful cultural information, and enthusiastic participation in our field-testing of the activities have been invaluable. Although too many to list, we thank you all.

A special thanks goes out to our editor, Kelly Sippell, for her encouragement and support.

Grateful acknowledgment is made to the following authors, publishers, and journals for permission to reprint previously published materials.

DH Literary Inc. for excerpt from "Miss Manners" by Judith Martin, from *The Washington Post,* January 23, 2002, copyright © 2002.

Dow Jones for excerpt from *The Wall Street Journal,* "When Good Will and Bewilderment Go Hand in Glove," Si Frumkin, 10 August 1992, permission conveyed through Copyright Clearance Center, Inc.

McGraw-Hill for material from *The Big Book of Team Building Games* by J. Newstrom and E. Scannell, copyright © 1998. Reproduced with permission of the McGraw-Hill Companies.

Professor Paul B. Pedersen for adaptation from activity "The Outside Expert."

Sage Publications, Inc. for adaptation from *Bridging Differences: Effective Intergroup Communication, 3rd Edition* (p. 230), by William Gudykunst, copyright © 1998 by Sage Publications, Inc. Reprinted by Permission of Sage Publications, Inc.

Youth for Understanding USA for adaptation of a workshop exercise by Blohm, J. (1991). *Introduction to Cross-Cultural Communication.* Washington, DC: Youth for Understanding International Exchange.

Every effort has been made to contact the copyright holders for permissions to reprint borrowed material. We regret any oversights that may have occurred and will rectify them in future printings of this book.

Contents

Introduction

As a country we are apt to be guilty of great ethnocentrism. In many of our foreign aid programs we employ a heavy-handed technique in dealing with local nationals. We insist that everyone else do things our way. Consequently we manage to convey the impression that we simply regard foreign nationals as "underdeveloped Americans." Most of our behavior does not spring from malice but from ignorance. . . . We are not only almost totally ignorant of what is expected in other countries, we are equally ignorant of what we are communicating to other people by our own normal behavior. (Hall, 1959:iii)

Written more than forty years ago, these words strike an all-too-familiar note. Although in many respects there is greater appreciation of the need for cross-cultural awareness and sensitivity training today, North Americans, used here to include the people of the United States and Canada, still too often blunder their way through cross-cultural situations. Not only do we continue to look at members of other cultures as "underdeveloped North Americans," but often we forget that there might be other ways of "doing"—ways that people of other cultures consider "normal." These different ways may seem alien and even incomprehensible to the average North American. As the world grows smaller through the increased expansion of transportation, commerce, and communication networks (including the Internet), there is even greater contact among people of different cultures. It is becoming rarer for North Americans to isolate themselves from the rest of the world and to have minimal contact with other cultures. Now that we have entered the 21st century and a new millennium, it is even more important than ever that we as North Americans become aware of and sensitive to other cultures, or other ways of "doing." Since teachers are the primary disseminators of knowledge, it is essential that they be both cross-culturally sensitive and cognizant of how to educate others in cross-cultural understanding. It is for these reasons that we have chosen to write this book. It is our expectation that this text, used successfully, will make teachers more aware of themselves as members of a particular culture and will equip them with the skills to better prepare others for living in a multicultural world.

This instructional text is designed for use in three areas:

1. General teacher education courses that address educational issues such as multicultural or ethnically diverse classrooms

2. ESL/bilingual/foreign language teacher education courses

3. Cross-cultural awareness workshops for practicing teachers

In other words, this text is intended for teacher-trainers in master's programs, certification courses, and undergraduate education courses.

Information presented in the text attempts to strike a good balance between theory and practice. The general goals of the book are

- To expand cultural awareness of one's own culture and that of others

- To achieve a deeper understanding of what culture is and the relationship between culture and language

- To acquire the ability to observe behaviors in order to draw conclusions based on observation rather than preconceptions

- To understand and implement observations of cultural similarities and differences

- To develop an attitude of tolerance toward cultural differences

The primary goal of this book is to help teachers become more culturally aware. The book is intended to facilitate the process of **culture learning,** which involves

- Learning about oneself, both as an individual and as a member of one's own culture and subcultures

- Learning about the universal phenomena and specific elements of culture

- Learning about the interaction between culture and communication

- Learning about how to become more observant and more cognizant of culture factors influencing identity questions, behavior, and interaction patterns.

The theory and the practice sections in this book will enable teachers to see how their particular set of eyes influences their understanding of the world around them. Such awareness will lead to increased cultural sensitivity, which, we hope, will lessen instances of cross-cultural miscommunication and misunderstanding. The **theory section** in each chapter acquaints readers with relevant research and information on the chapter topic. Its suggested use is as assigned reading at home, followed by an in-class review of the content through the included questions for study and discussion.

The **practice section** in each chapter allows readers to take part in a variety of experiential activities designed to reinforce the information presented in the theory section of the chapter. The activities are clearly referenced in the theory section, and they should be done in class, following the suggested procedures. The majority of the experiential activities are intended for preservice and in-service teachers in courses or professional development workshops. Those activities adaptable for use in high school, college, and adult ESL classrooms at the advanced level or the intermediate level are signaled by this icon 🏫 . We do not recommend any of the activities be used in K–8 settings. Suggestions for adapting these activities for ESL audiences and their recommended proficiency levels are indicated for each activity (A for advanced, I for intermediate).

The section on **further readings** at the end of each chapter presents key books and articles on the chapter topic. These materials lend themselves quite readily to research reports and further inquiry.

A principal proponent of experiential learning, Kolb (1984) developed a four-stage learning cycle involving experience, reflective observation, abstract conceptualization, and active experimentation. This emotional as well as intellectual engagement leads to reflexivity, self-awareness, critical reflection, and theory development. Since experiential learning is at the core of many teaching and learning situations, one goal of this book is to provide readers with **experiential activities** that engage them in the learning cycle. The majority of the activities presented in the text are designed for next-day implementation—they can be incorporated immediately into the classroom—while a few require minimal advance preparation. All of the activities included were field-tested on our students and in professional workshops nationwide.

We believe that this text will help teachers, both current and prospective, develop the abilities to discern which cultural elements affect communicative interactions, why they affect the interactions, and how they do so. Atkinson (1999:643) posits that "knowing students individually also involves knowing them culturally." Thus, teachers "need to develop *appropriate pedagogies*—approaches to learning and teaching that dynamically respond to that knowledge" (p. 643). All cultural groups are made up of individuals who are products of their culture and language. In other words, to understand people, we must understand their cultural lives.

Each chapter of the book includes the following sections:

- **Anecdote.** The purpose of this section, which is comprised of a brief anecdote related to the chapter theme and a discussion of key issues raised by the anecdote, is to capture the attention and interest of the reader. The use of anecdotes often stimulates readers to recall or reconsider situations where there may have been instances of cross-cultural misunderstanding. Anecdotes encourage readers to reexamine their own assumptions and preconceptions about themselves and others. This section further provides readers with a brief overview for the experiential activities in each chapter.

- **Theory: What Research Tells Us.** This section reviews literature focusing on the chapter theme and offers questions for study and discussion. The intent of this section is to provide readers with a theoretical base for the chapter theme and for the experiential activities included in each chapter.

- **Practice: What Activities Show Us.** In this section, readers have the opportunity to broaden their cultural outlooks through experiential activities focusing on the chapter theme. Each activity is described step-by-step. The types of activity range from those that can be done in the classroom to those to be done outside of class. The various types of activity include observation activities, simulations, questionnaires, and critical incidents, among others. Those activities adaptable for ESL audiences are signaled by an icon, and suggestions for use are provided.

- **Further Readings.** This section provides an annotated bibliography of readings on each chapter topic. The references are from different fields, including communication, language teaching and research, anthropology, and linguistics. The bibliography is not an exhaustive list of materials available under each topic but, rather, a list of major readings related to each chapter theme.

The text is divided into six major themes.

- Chapter 1 is concerned with the issue of culture in shaping our behavior, attitudes, and perceptions of the world. The chapter explores the definition of culture, different aspects of culture, and the relationship between culture and language.

- Chapter 2 continues the examination of what culture is and how culture influences people's behaviors, their social relationships, and their perceptions of the world around them.

- Chapter 3 examines culture shock, its roots, and its ramifications.

- Chapter 4 investigates various aspects of nonverbal communication and cross-cultural differences.

- Chapter 5 considers social roles and expectations cross-culturally. Some of the topics covered include family roles, religious beliefs, medical practices, and women's roles.

- Chapter 6 explores how speakers use language in social contexts and the relationship between language and culture.

An essential question in any book on culture is, which culture should be taught? In second language situations, the answer is generally clear. Students need and want to become familiar with the culture of the host country, including significant regional variations; thus, the role of the teacher is to act as facilitator. The question becomes of greater significance, however, for teachers in foreign language situations. For example, should native speakers from one English-speaking country teaching in EFL situations be expected to impart cultural knowledge about the entire English-speaking world? Should these instructors limit their discussion only to the culture of their home country? Should they focus their discussion only on surface cultural aspects such as holidays and food? Such questions become particularly acute in foreign language situations where the students have limited exposure to the target language culture and where the teachers themselves may not be intimately familiar with the culture or cultures of the language they are teaching.

We firmly believe that the preservice and in-service courses and workshops that utilize this book will find users becoming more aware of themselves, their behaviors and actions, and the role of culture. They will also acquire important skills for developing cross-cultural awareness in others. Since the intended audience of this text is preservice and in-service teachers, the book's focus is on general cross-cultural awareness. Although much of the theory and practice herein has broad cultural applications, this text is focused on a North American cultural perspective and may therefore not be appropriate for settings abroad.

Chapter 1
Introduction to Culture

I. Anecdote: *"Two* sets of eyes"

The concept of culture can be rather ambiguous. People often ask, "What *are* you?" which translates into "What is your cultural background?"

Sook, a Korean-American woman who was frequently teased about her background while growing up, recounts her father's words to her after she came home one day in tears. As her father met her at the door, Sook tearfully said, "Dad, everyone is making fun of the way I look."

Her father took her by the hand and replied, "Let me tell you something, Sook. You are a very special person and a very lucky one."

"I am?" Sook responded in disbelief.

"Yes you are—because you have *two* sets of eyes with which to see the world."

"What do you mean?" Sook asked baffled.

"You are both special and lucky because you see the world through both Korean *and* American eyes."

Although Sook continued to be made fun of, and even at times discriminated against, she realized over and over again how her father's words had empowered her. She felt both proud and lucky to be able to see the world from two different points of view.

Discussion of Key Issues

We all have different eyes with which we see the world. We often react to situations instinctively and interpret situations based on our own cultural "eyes," that is, our cultural influences and conditioning. Most of us do not realize that our values, beliefs, and ways of interpreting the world are not absolutes in the way that the laws of physics are, that they are a part of our upbringing and cultural heritage and vary accordingly. Consequently, our preconceptions and attitudes may often lead us to misunderstand, misinterpret, or even be completely unaware of a sensitive or offensive behavior in cross-cultural encounters.

We need to learn to observe behavior, including our own, more carefully. As we assume, albeit often unconsciously, that our way is the "normal," "natural," "right" way to do things, we tend to react at a gut level to what we perceive as offensive or negative. We are unaware that what has offended us is not the action itself but the fact that the action violated some deeply held belief or value. However, we cannot all expect to become experts in every culture that differs from our own. At the same time, it is an exercise in futility to try to list all the differences in patterns of behavior among cultures. As we become better observers of our behavior and that of others, we will better recognize where potential misunderstandings are likely to occur.

The implications of different cultural expectations in the classroom have been widely discussed (e.g., Heath, 1992; Hofstede, 1986; Park, 1997; Parry, 1996; Richard-Amato & Snow, 1992). For example, when ways of showing respect differ, speakers may unintentionally convey the opposite of what they intended. American teachers expect students to look them in the eye when responding. Yet some cultures indicate respect by avoiding eye contact and lowering one's eyes. American teachers unfamiliar with such a cultural difference in behavior are likely to misinterpret the students' behavior to mean that the students don't know the answer, are avoiding the question, or are even lying. In addition, students accustomed to authoritarian teacher roles may have difficulty adjusting to the informal, interactive teacher roles more common in the United States and Canada. These same students may encounter difficulties in cooperative learning situations where group discovery learning is emphasized and teacher-centered learning is minimal. Even the purpose of working in groups can differ. In some cultures, group work is conceived of as a way of helping each student achieve individually. In other cultures, successful group work results in the efforts of individuals to succeed as a whole.

Chapter 1 is concerned with the issue of culture in shaping our behavior, attitudes, and perceptions of the world. The chapter explores the definition of culture, different aspects of culture, and the relationship between culture and language.

Questions for Thought

- What is culture?

- How does culture influence behavior?

- What are some of the central beliefs and values of your culture?

II. Theory: What Research Tells Us

The Concept of Culture

Culture is pervasive, all-encompassing, and inescapable. The images and messages we receive and transmit are profoundly shaped by our culture. It is the framework through which we understand and interpret the world around us, in that it provides the context for a group of people to understand and interpret the world around them. Defining culture is not an easy task. Culture is a very broad concept for which there is no single, simple definition or central theory. Different fields of study differ in their concept of culture, in their definitions of culture, in their methods of investigating culture, and in the focus of their cultural studies. The many definitions given to the concept of culture have been strongly influenced by research in the fields of linguistics, anthropology, sociology, psychology, and communication.

Within the broader field of linguistics, the subfield of applied linguistics emphasizes areas of study such as language use, communicative competence, and linguistic and social variations of language. While *theoretical linguistics* attempts to understand the underlying deep structure of language or the more abstract and universal features of language, *applied linguistics* attempts to understand language in its social context as used by speakers. The language users in a culture are a crucial variable. They are the source of knowledge of the rules of interaction for their community, as well as the judges of the appropriateness of the communicative event (e.g., Goody, 1978; Grice, 1975; Yule, 1996). Cross-cultural investigations have brought attention to the influence of cultural differences in language use and function (e.g., Beebe & Takahashi, 1989; Boxer, 1993; Meier, 1999; Thomas, 1983).

Anthropology, the science that studies human culture, consists of two major disciplines—physical anthropology and cultural anthropology. *Physical anthropology* is the study of the biological aspects of humankind, while *cultural anthropology* emphasizes the study of human societies around the world. Cultural anthropology focuses on the relationship between language and culture, culture and personality, and the processes of social change and acculturation (e.g., Brislin, 1981; Gudykunst & Kim, 1984; Hall, 1959, 1966, 1983). *Anthropological linguistics* seeks to understand the meanings in communicative interactions within wider cultural practices (e.g., Duranti & Goodwin, 1992; Geertz, 1973; Hymes, 1971). Applied linguistics and anthropological linguistics are closely allied fields that have heavily influenced each other.

The study of human behavior in social groups is the central theme of sociology. *Sociology* deals with such sociocultural variables as age, sex, attitude, and motivation and with such areas as social organizations, descriptions of social groups, and social psychology. In the early 1970s, sociology influenced a shift in the theoretical positions of anthropologists and linguists in relation to such basic concepts as language, culture, and communication. This shift resulted in revised analyses of sociological variables relating to community, social class, and social norms (e.g., Bernstein, 1971; Goffman, 1981; Labov, 1970) and resulted in these variables becoming important elements in studies on language.

Psychology, which studies human perception, evaluation, personality, and cognition, includes the subfield *social psychology,* the study of individual behavior within a social and cultural framework. Social psychologists emphasize how society and, by extension, culture affect personality, motivation, and attitudes. Their focus is on the influence of the individual speaker's personality in conjunction with psychocultural variations in perception, attitudes, and motivation (e.g., Gardner & Lambert, 1972; Giles & St. Claire, 1979; Tajfel, 1984). Cross-cultural social psychologists are particularly interested in studying how sociocultural variables affect human behavior and how these differ and/or remain the same across cultures, with the goal of understanding the relationship between culture and individual behavior.

The field of *communication* stresses perception, physical and social context, interaction, feedback, and cross-cultural variations. Communication studies attempt to gain knowledge and understanding of the myriad factors influencing interaction, why it occurs, and the consequences thereof. Communication is viewed as a process whereby the actual message between speakers is merely one part of the whole communication process. The nature of the communicative exchanges themselves is essential in forming and maintaining meaningful interactions between speakers. Understanding communication entails knowing something about what takes place when people interact, why the interaction is taking place, the effects of the interactional exchange itself, and, finally, what individuals can do to influence and maximize a particular communicative interaction. Cross-cultural investigations have been instrumental in underscoring the impact of culture on communication (e.g., Condon, 1974; Porter & Samovar, 1997; Stewart & Bennett, 1991).

Defining Culture

The term *culture* is a very general concept, composed of a complex system of interacting elements. Culture is universal, multifaceted, and intricate. It permeates all aspects of human society; it penetrates into every area of life and influences the way people think, talk, and behave. Culture is not a characteristic of a single individual but, rather, a "collective mental programming of the people in an environment" (Hofstede, 1980:42). Culture can be viewed as the set of fundamental ideas, practices, and experiences shared by a group of people. Culture can also refer to a set of shared beliefs, norms, and attitudes that are used to guide the behaviors of a group of people, to explain the world around them, and to solve their problems. It can further be defined as "membership in a discourse community that shares a common social space and history, and common imaginings" (Kramsch, 1998a:10). It is the sum of the way of life of any group of people (Kohls, 2001:26). **(See Activity A—Defining Culture)**

How do we identify a culture? The most general answer to this question is that the members of a culture share clearly identifiable traits, patterns of behavior, worldviews, systems of social organizations, and similar value systems. For example, learning to drive is a rite of passage for Americans and reflects the American culture. A garage sale, on the other hand, is something that some Americans like to do but is not illustrative of the type of American culture referred to here. Certainly not all members will exhibit these behaviors or share these values or perspectives to the same extent, but the large majority of them will. These shared matters are what identify the members of a particular culture, such as German, Canadian, Chinese, Malaysian, or Vietnamese. When referring to a culture, it is important to note that any generalizations do not apply to all members. Cultures are not completely homogeneous but heterogeneous, in that within every culture are subcultures or subgroups. Members of these groups share many of the same characteristics of the majority or larger culture but differ in some significant way or ways by virtue of their regional or ethnic background, their sexual orientation (e.g., a gay or lesbian subculture), their work affiliation, their religious convictions and practices, or other significant factors. All members of a larger culture also belong to any number of subcultures. **(See Activity B—Class Begins)**

Moreover, a culture is not static, unchanging, or even homogeneous. A culture is a changing combination of different ambient factors, diverse constituents, and complex elements. Cultures are dynamic, marked by changes in response to new technology, to encounters with different cultures, and to new societal and environmental needs and demands. Cultural change is an ongoing and continuous process. The United States and Canada of the early 21st century are markedly different cultures than the ones of the early 20th century. We need only to point to their radical transformation from early industrial, largely agricultural societies to highly industrialized societies to understand a few of the factors changing what we know as the American or Canadian culture today. We can also point to the influence, in an even shorter time span, of television or film media in changing (as well as reflecting changes in) North American culture. The same holds true of any culture: as society and environment change, so does culture as people adapt to changes in their world.

Enculturation

By its very nature, culture is a teacher. It is a subconscious teacher of the beliefs, values, worldviews, and patterns of behavior of its members. The process of becoming socialized into one's culture begins early in life, through what is known as *enculturation*. Because culture is shared with people who live in and experience the same social environments, enculturation becomes a collective experience (Hofstede, 1980). It is the process of learning about the customs, conventions, and practices of one's society. This process entails learning relevant cultural patterns through family members and interactions in social environments such as peer groups, school, and work. In today's modern world, mass media, particularly television, is an important influence in the enculturation process. Enculturation predisposes members of a given culture to view the world from a particular perspective. Since enculturation encompasses the process of becoming a member of one's society and is in large part a subconscious learning effort, we are generally unaware of the central role that enculturation plays in shaping our worldview.

The culture in which individuals are raised is the most important determinant of how they view and interpret the world. Members of different cultural groups see and interpret events differently; through the enculturation process, they develop attitudes, beliefs, and values that affect the meanings they assign to the world around them. Culture bestows a set of lenses for seeing the world, lenses that influence the way members of groups choose, decipher, process, and utilize information. Consider the anecdote of the elephant and the mouse.

> One day the elephant and the mouse decided to take a stroll when they came to a rickety old wooden bridge over a river. As they crossed the bridge, it began to rattle and clatter. Above the racket, the mouse shouted, "Listen to us stomping together and making this old bridge bang."

From his point of view, the mouse was contributing as much to the noise as was the much larger elephant. Like the mouse, people's cultural lenses will affect the way they construct their realities (de Waal, 2000/2001:66).

Culture also serves as a filter that prompts both the meanings that members of the group assign to social roles, contexts, and communicative behaviors and how they perceive, interpret, react, or are affected by these. According to Hall and Hall (1989:xiv), each culture has "hidden codes" of behavior that, when the culture is viewed from the outside, can rarely be understood without a "code breaker." Even within cultures, members of different subcultures view the world through different lenses. Noted cognitive scientist S. Pinker (1997:173) recounts his experience when visiting an exhibition on spiders at the Smithsonian National Museum in Washington, D.C.

> As I marveled at the Swiss-watch precision of the [spider] joints, the sewing-machine motions by which it drew silk from its spinnerets, the beauty and cunning of the web, I thought to myself, "How could anyone see this and not believe in natural selection!" At that moment a woman standing next to me exclaimed, "How could anyone see this and not believe in God!" We agreed *a priori* on the facts that need to be explained, though we disagreed about how to explain them.

(See Activity C—Old Woman, Young Lady)

A person's culture provides the guidelines for appropriate social behavior and interaction and shapes the expectations its members have in judging the appropriateness of the social behavior and communicative interactions. Since culture provides the framework for its members to both enact and construe meanings, people from different cultures will perceive and interpret others' behaviors in different ways. Because a large part of culture proceeds at a subconscious level, people are usually unable to identify their own cultural expectations, assumptions, and presuppositions until they encounter ones different from their own. An interesting example of this is how Western and Eastern scientists once held contrasting views of great apes. Formerly, Western scientists believed that apes were self-sufficient and lived independent of social groups and ties—in what Jean Rousseau labeled as the world of the "noble savage." Not until about the 1970s did Western scientists change their point of view. Asian scientists, however, began observing great apes from the point of view that, as humankind's closest ancestor, they must have some sort of complex social life. Already in the 1960s, Japanese scientists were able to establish through lengthy and thorough field observations that apes, specifically chimpanzees, live in large social groups with complex ties and memberships. At this same time, Jane Goodall, the premier Western researcher on chimpanzees, was hypothesizing that females and their dependent offspring might be the only ones to exist as social groups.

Culture pervades all areas—arts and artifacts, beliefs, behaviors, ceremonies, concept of self, customs, ideas and thought patterns, ideals, knowledge, laws, language, manners, morals, myths and legends, religion, rituals, social institutions, tools, and values (Kohls, 1984). A distinction, however, has been made between *Culture* written with a capital *C* and *culture* written with a lowercase *c* (Bennett, 1998). *Culture* written with a capital *C* refers to art, literature, drama, classical music, dance, or cuisine. This Culture is often referred to as *objective culture* or *highbrow culture*. It most often encompasses those aspects associated with money, education, and museums, although it is also associated with the more institutional aspects of culture, such as political or economic systems.

Culture written with a small *c* refers to *subjective culture,* to the day-to-day features that define a group of people. This type of culture is psychological in nature, involving people's attitudes, beliefs, and values. Subjective culture also refers to such distinguishing elements as choice of discourse, style of dress, in-group/out-group networks, and norms of interactions. Cultural groups may range from the larger society as a whole; to cultural groups of people within a specific age range, such as Generation X; to employees of a particular corporation; to white, middle-class teenagers; to gang members; to the individuals of a family.

The most important variables that distinguish one culture from another are not easily observable phenomena such as dress, housing, food, or table manners but, rather, the underlying values, attitudes, beliefs, and worldviews that shape how a culture perceives itself and others. Because these elements, which are below the level of conscious awareness, form such a large part of culture, it is difficult for people to describe their own cultural ways without training. Just as native speakers of a language who have not studied language are often hard-pressed to explain the how and why of grammatical structures and language use, so, too, members of a particular culture who have not learned to study culture find it difficult to explain the components of culture and to comprehend how these shape people's perspectives and interpretations of the world.

To better understand the dynamics of subjective culture, Pike (1954) identified two ways of examining culture— *emics* and *etics*. The two terms derive from linguistics, *emic* from *phonemic* and *etic* from *phonetic*. *Emics* refers to the ideas, behaviors, items, and concepts that are culture specific. The emic approach focuses its studies from within the system and examines only one culture at a time. The idea is to discover the structure of a culture and its elements from observation within the system itself. This is the approach generally followed by anthropologists, who prefer to focus on the unique aspects, behaviors, and concepts of a culture.

The approach preferred by cross-cultural researchers, regardless of field of study, is the etic approach. *Etics* refers to those ideas, behaviors, items, and concepts that are culture universal. Rather than focusing on one culture and making the discoveries within one system, the etic approach focuses on studies of more than one culture and from a position outside the system. The idea is to understand what elements hold true across all cultures and times. From an etic point of view, for instance, motherhood is a universal construct. However, how the role of mothers and motherhood is enacted and viewed will differ among cultures—this, then, is the concern of emics. Questions that researchers might ask include the following: What are the responsibilities of a mother? Is she solely responsible for discipline? If not, with whom does she share the responsibility? Does being a mother necessarily entail being the primary caregiver? If not, under what circumstances does this change? What is the role of women who bear no children? Are mothers revered, honored, respected? How is this manifested within the culture? Such questions help researchers understand both the emics (differences) and the etics (universals) of mothers and motherhood. Marriage is another universal construct, but who may marry whom, at what age, under what type of ceremony or ritual, what roles each partner fulfills within the marriage, and how each partner is expected to act differs cross-culturally. This will be discussed at greater length in chapter 5. **(See Activity D—Emics and Etics of Culture)**

Elements of Culture

Culture is the sum of many diverse elements, including beliefs, values, norms, mores, taboos, and attitudes. These manifold elements are an integral part of who we are and why we do what we do. When any or every aspect of these elements is ignored or violated by members of other cultures operating under different sets of expectations, we experience strong emotional reactions.

Beliefs

Beliefs are an individual's convictions about the world, convictions that are shaped by the culture a person is raised in. How strongly individuals adhere to a particular belief depends on the degree to which individuals ascribe certain characteristics to that belief. In other words, the deeper an individual's conviction, the greater the intensity of that belief. Members of a given culture hold strong similarities in their belief system. For instance, whether an individual believes or disbelieves in spirits, visions, second sight, or fortune-telling as sources of knowledge is influenced by that individual's cultural background and experience.

A belief that is held by most members of a culture is called a *cultural belief.* Cultural beliefs include fundamental teachings about what reality is and expectations of how the world operates. Although individuals within a culture group may hold different beliefs, these individuals have relatively more similar beliefs with members of their culture than they do with individuals of different cultures. For example, for most Japanese, gift giving is an important symbolic ritual that is considered a social duty and obligation and a part of everyday life; it is not merely something one does on special occasions such as birthdays or Christmas, as in Western cultures. Japanese employees returning from vacation, for instance, bring everyone in the office a small token gift. In addition, since maintaining harmony or balance in all areas of life is essential in Japanese culture, the recipient of a gift must always be sure to give a gift in return. By offering a gift in return, the original recipient is no longer indebted to the original giver, and harmony is restored. The actual presentation and acceptance of the gift are also important parts of the gift-giving ritual. Gifts are generally carefully packaged and wrapped and are opened before the giver in only certain situations. When the recipient does open the gift in front of the giver, the recipient must be careful not to tear the wrapping paper, cut the ribbon, or appear in any way anxious to see the gift. Once the gift has been accepted, it is important for the recipient to praise the value, while the giver must exhibit humility by downplaying the value of the gift.

The German and Swiss are noted for their punctuality. They pride themselves on their timepieces and on the punctuality of their trains, buses, and airplanes, and they are generally careful about starting meetings, classes, or other activities exactly at appointed times. Latino cultures are noted for a more lackadaisical approach to time. Some Spaniards may be more time conscious than some Swiss, but overall, as a culture, the Swiss value punctuality more highly than do the Spaniards. In fact, when North Americans and Latinos plan joint activities, they will often specify *hora latina* or *hora americana,* which translates as "Latin time" or "American time."

Beliefs regarding the causation of diseases and their appropriate treatment differ across cultures. In some cultures, evil spirits or ghosts are believed to cause diseases, and cures are achieved by appealing to these forces or engaging in specific behaviors designed to counteract the evil influences (Andrews & Boyle, 1995). From a Western standpoint, members from such a culture may engage in "eccentric or abnormal" behavior when they combine modern medical practices with traditional remedies, particularly remedies involving amulets, charms, prayers, or rituals. Also, from the Western point of view, perceived unconventional approaches to medical care are often suspect. Acupuncture, for instance, which has been used successfully in Chinese culture for thousands of years, has only been practiced relatively recently in the West and is still not accepted by all medical practitioners.

Values

Values are ideals or abstract standards, whether good or bad, that members of a cultural group hold in strong affective regard. They are shared assumptions or judgments about what is good, right, and important. They fundamentally influence the behavior of individuals within their cultural context. Values have an evaluative dimension in that they dictate what individuals should or should not do. They provide members of a culture with a feeling of how they aspire or strive to behave. They tend to be the foundation on which individuals base their own decisions and actions and according to which they evaluate the decisions and behavior of others. Cultures that value self-reliance, hard work, and individual effort are more likely to allow for social and economic mobility than are cultures that value birth, family connections, and family wealth. Cultures that place a high value on communal family goals are also noted for their close-knit

families and collectivistic tendencies (see chap. 2). Asian cultures influenced by Confucianism highly value harmony. Members of these cultures
strive to reconcile and integrate conflicts of all sorts—for example, of
ideas, beliefs, or opinions—which also carries over into communication
strategies. Chinese, Korean, or Japanese speakers, for instance, evade
directly saying no (see chap. 6).

Closely related to values are *morals*. Morals are cultural, societal,
and religious guidelines that individuals try to follow in order to promote
certain cultural values. People's values determine which personal morals
they have and, in turn, which morals affect their behavior. Not all members of the same culture necessarily share all the same values and/or
morals, and disagreements or conflicts frequently occur. For instance,
while American and Canadian society as a whole values marriage, cohabitation without legal bonds has become increasingly common over the
past three decades. Although such behavior is in keeping with the morals
of some members of the culture, it is acting against the morals of other
members of the same culture. In this case, both groups share the value of
marriage, but the moral regarding the practice of cohabitation differs.
(See Activity E—Values)

Norms

Norms are the fixed behavior patterns for members of a cultural group.
They are culturally shared notions about what is appropriate behavior.
They may also be described as culturally established patterns of doing
things. Norms govern such behavior as how greetings and partings are
enacted, appropriate classroom comportment, and patterns of respect.
Norms governing the role of children and parents, for example, differ from
culture to culture. Chinese culture emphasizes what children should do
for their parents, whereas American and Canadian culture emphasizes
what parents should do for their children (Hsu, 1981).

Although members of a culture may share the larger norms of their
society, the importance and intensity with which these norms are held
may vary within the culture itself. These variations are often based on
socioeconomic and/or ethnic differences within the majority culture. Cultural norms so pervade thought and action that few individuals recognize
the assumptions governing their behavior. So much of cultural knowledge is subconscious that, until they are confronted with a culture different from their own, people rarely notice that they interpret and talk about

events differently than do people in other cultures. Imagine two friends working for the same employer. The two of them together receive $100 from this employer. In the United States, the two friends would share the money equally. However, in a culture operating under different cultural norms, the friend coming from a family of higher status might receive more money. It would be the duty of the friend of lower status to ensure that the friend of higher status received proportionately more in acknowledgment of the status difference. By the same token, the friend of higher status would recognize receiving the larger share as his or her right by virtue of status. In a different culture, the more skilled friend might receive a greater share of the money in recognition of his or her greater abilities. In still another culture, with strong notions of reciprocity and indebtedness, if one friend had done the other friend a favor in the past, the friend who had received the earlier favor would feel obligated to give the other a larger share of the money to compensate him or her for the earlier favor and to return balance to the relationship (Triandis, 1994).

Norms are generally categorized into two types. *Formal norms,* called *mores,* govern culturally and socially sanctioned behavior and incur social penalties or censure when they are violated. Some examples of North American mores include avoiding plagiarism and respecting private property. The most formal norms or mores are laws that citizens must obey or incur punishment for breaking. These cover such diverse areas as stealing, littering, murder, child abuse, parking in a handicapped space without a permit, or driving while intoxicated. While some of these actions are universally punishable by law, other "crimes" are culturally determined. In Saudi Arabia, for instance, it is illegal for women to drive, and in many Moslem countries, the sexes must be educated separately. *Informal norms,* often termed *folkways,* are culturally and socially preferred ways of doing things, but since they may only be weakly enforced, they incur relatively mild penalties or disapproval when they are disregarded. Examples of informal norms include table manners, playing loud music after a certain hour, offering gifts to bureaucrats to complete requisite paperwork, or requiring young unmarried women to be chaperoned at social functions and/or on dates.

Taboos

Taboos are an important subset of mores. Taboos specify what is or is not permissible. In their strongest form, taboos cover universal prohibitions such as murder and incest. In their weaker form, taboos include such folk-ways as restrictions against eating with the left hand, which foods one may or may not eat, and whether or not one makes eye contact with one's superior. In some cultures, the left hand, used for body functions, is considered unclean. Consequently, eating with the left hand is unacceptable, and passing something to another person with the left hand is insulting. Food taboos, often religiously based, are widespread: Moslems and Jews may not eat pork, and Hindus may not eat any living creature, whether animal, fowl, or fish. To show respect to one's superior in some cultures, subordinates keep their eyes lowered to avoid eye contact. This very action signalizes the reverse in cultures where making eye contact indicates attention and/or respect to one's listener, regardless of social status. Chapter 4 examines more extensively the relationship between nonverbal behavior and societal norms.

Attitudes

Attitudes are emotional reactions to objects, ideas, and people. People learn attitudes within a cultural context. The opinions individuals express and the communicative interactions and other behaviors in which they engage are based in large part on their attitudes and beliefs. The cultural environment to which an individual is exposed helps mold the individual's attitudes and, ultimately, his or her behavior.

Germans, who generally value their leisure time highly, place great emphasis on *Gemütlichkeit,* for which no equivalent term exists in English. It encompasses a feeling of comfort, well-being, and contentment. *Gemütlichkeit* is very much in evidence in the ubiquitous German cafés and terrace gardens, with their comfortable seating, lavish summer floral displays, and general air of coziness. The Germans (generally men) who traditionally meet regularly at the same time and place usually even have what is known as a *Stammtisch,* or "regular table." From the Japanese perspective, a person's business and social lives are not seen as separate or apart. Employees are regarded as part of the company "family" and engage regularly in social activities arranged by their company.

Because the United States has historically been a country peopled by immigrants seeking religious freedom, many newcomers are surprised by the variety of religious houses of worship and the number of Americans attending religious services regularly. Furthermore, again since many immigrants have come to the United States for religious freedom, the attitude toward religion is often more serious in that country than in other countries. In many European and Latin American countries, there is no official separation of state and church, and there is often one principal or official religion; religion is often taken for granted in such cultures.

Since World War II, the Japanese have avoided most public displays of flying or waving the national flag, because of its past associations with militarism and imperialism. A sign that the Japanese attitude toward the national flag is changing was illustrated in July 2002, when thousands of Japanese enthusiastically waved their flag during the home World Cup games, painted it on their faces, and hung it over their clothing.

As the preceding examples illustrate, cultural attitudes affect the behaviors of the members of a particular culture. The potential for beliefs, values, norms, and attitudes to affect intercultural communication is significant. Cross-cultural misunderstandings often occur when participants interact in situations where any of these elements differ. In an earlier example, we discussed how Japanese notions of gift giving differ significantly from Western ones. We mentioned how gift giving is an indispensable practice of everyday life. Even in business situations, Japanese (and members of other cultures) regard gift giving as part of doing business and consider it an essential protocol. Americans and Canadians, however, tend to equate gift giving in business situations with bribery and hence consider it inappropriate or wrong. Such a cross-cultural difference in perspectives has often caused problems for Americans doing business overseas.

Consider also the practice of giving individual gifts on birthdays, a commonly accepted ritual in many cultures. Even where the ritual exists, what the recipient does on receiving a gift varies. In the United States and Canada, the recipient generally opens the gift immediately and offers appropriate thanks and appreciation. In other cultures, such as the Thai or Filipino culture, the recipient puts the gift away with murmured thanks. In such a case, if the gift givers happen to be North American, they are likely to feel hurt by what they, operating under North American cultural norms, perceive as ungratefulness or even disapproval. The Thai or Filipino, on the other hand, operating under a different cultural norm, is accepting the gift graciously. For Thais and Filipinos, opening the gift in front of the giver indicates that that person is more interested in the gift itself rather than in the act of gift giving. To them, it signals a materialistic and avaricious person, not an appreciative one. **(See Activity F—Shared Backgrounds)**

Language and Linguistic Relativity

Language and culture are intimately linked. Culture influences the way speakers perceive the world and how they use language to communicate. Likewise, language influences how speakers view the world and the way in which they communicate. How intricately linked are culture and language? The degree to which language influences human thought and meaning is termed *linguistic relativity*. At one time, most researchers ascribed to the belief that culture determines language, a belief expressed by the Sapir-Whorf hypothesis (Whorf, 1956), which posits that language and thought are so closely tied that language determines the categories of thought open to the speakers of that language—in other words, that a language determines how its speakers perceive the world. Over time, this view, called the "strong" version of the Whorfian hypothesis, has been challenged. Today, most people accept a more moderate, or "weak," version of the Whorfian hypothesis. This moderate approach holds that a language shapes how its speakers perceive the world.

Although native language influences speakers, they are not inextricably bound by the confines of that language and the culture it represents. For example, although English does not distinguish between a formal and informal second-person singular *you,* it still can convey different levels of formality through other linguistic means such as choices in discourse or rhetorical styles. In communicative situations, English speakers may indicate respect through the use of titles with surnames (e.g., "Doctor Smith," "President Jones") and may heighten the formality of a communicative interaction by avoiding colloquial speech patterns. Or speakers may choose to indicate rapport and fellowship by the use of first names and of discourse styles that are less formal. Some languages, such as Chinese or Korean, have elaborate terminology that always indicates a person's position in the social hierarchy. Speakers of these languages are always aware of their own and others' positions in this hierarchy, as they must always employ the titles and speech patterns appropriate to those relationships. Nevertheless, the influence of such language patterns does not prevent members of these cultures from recognizing, accepting, and/or favoring egalitarianism and equality.

Categorization

All languages use categories to organize the world around them. However, what is included or excluded and how the categories are organized is to some extent arbitrary and varies greatly among languages. Every language has categories to describe the members of the nuclear family: mother, father, daughter, son, brother, and sister. Different languages will make finer distinctions between components in categories that have important significance to the members of that culture. In cultures where hierarchy is important, we generally find additional terms to further refine the categories within the nuclear family. Rather than just "brother," languages used in these cultures will distinguish between "older brother" and "younger brother" or "older sister" and "younger sister."

How speakers take advantage of the finer distinctions depends a great deal on need and circumstances. Take color categories for instance. Objectively, while there is only one color spectrum, there are many different ways to categorize colors (Brown & Lenneberg, 1954; Hilbert, 1987; Kay & McDaniel, 1978). The human eye is capable of distinguishing about 7.5 million colors; nevertheless, people do not make anywhere near that many distinctions. Even in a language such as English, which is very rich in color terms (about 4,000), few people aside from artists and interior decorators use more than 40 color terms.

In comparing English with other languages, very different ways of dividing the color spectrum become evident. In some languages, there are only two color terms, meaning "light" and "dark," the simplest color divisions that are found in any language. Rather than having distinct color terms for different colors and hues, these languages require speakers to differentiate shades with phrases like "as dark as the sky at noon." Although speakers of these languages are certainly capable of distinguishing colors, their cultural history has not encouraged the development of extensive color categories. Thus, while a language will reflect the importance of color in a particular culture, the lack of a wide color terminology does not detract from the speaker's ability to distinguish colors. The difference lies in the importance that the culture has traditionally placed on a particular category.

The precision of the vocabulary of a language for a given category reveals the importance of the subject for that culture or subculture. English speakers working in the fashion industry are required to make use of many more words for types of cloth, fabric cut, and colors than the general public is even aware exist. After all, how many outside the fashion industry know immediately what color puce is? Any subculture, which may include, for example, a particular industry, age-group, regional group, or ethnic group, will develop its own specialized vocabulary to identify necessary materials, conditions, and situations. Since language is a mirror, we can learn a fair amount about a culture or subculture by examining the kinds of categorization, words, word sizes, and number of words used in each domain.

Language and Culture

Language is an organized, learned symbol system used to represent human experiences within a geographic or cultural group (Porter & Samovar, 1997:18). In its most basic sense, a language consists of symbols. These symbols—vocabulary—convey essentially uniform meanings among the speakers of the language. The language must also consist of rules—grammar and syntax—so that its speakers are able to manipulate the symbols meaningfully in order to communicate. In the most general sense, language is a symbolic representation of a people. A language encompasses the historical and cultural backgrounds of a people. Language is more than speech; it is a means of identification. Language, like culture, is a lens through which reality is filtered.

Language reflects the worldviews, the thought processes, and the lifestyles of its people; each culture places its own individual imprint on a language. Language is the primary medium for transmitting among its speakers a culture's beliefs, values, norms, and worldview. It functions as a tool for communication and an indicator of a culture's social realities and their manifestations. The norms governing the communicative behavior of each culture, for instance, reflect what is valued by each culture. Silence, or the absence of speech, is highly esteemed in various native American Indian cultures. Different terminology clearly labeling each person's place in the social hierarchy is essential in cultures where status is highly valued and where socially appropriate language must be employed at all times to avoid giving offense and to maintain social balance and harmony. Koreans tend to remain silent when they are upset by someone's actions, while Hispanics or Arabs are more likely to express their agitation verbally. While Korean culture values repressing one's emotions to save face, Hispanic and Arabic cultures value emotional displays.

Language also has influence on the way its speakers perceive the world and in the formation of cultural patterns of thought. Languages contain categories that reflect the conventions of their cultures. Korean and Filipino cultures, for instance, place great emphasis on respect and on an individual's position within the familial and social hierarchy. In Filipino culture, the elders are considered the leaders of the family and are shown great respect. Younger family members are expected to bow to an elder, take the elder's right hand, and gently press the back of it against their own forehead while saying, "Mano Po" (if they are speakers of Tagalog). In addressing an elder, younger family members must always use the courteous title *Po*. Older siblings are also addressed with titles by younger family members: *Kuya* for the eldest son and *Ate* for the oldest girl. Korean is a language noted for its use of honorifics—particles or inflections attached to words used to indicate varying degrees of politeness and the social relationships between speakers and hearers (see chap. 6). Failure to observe these social language rules results in being categorized as an "unperson," or someone for whom a Korean has no concern. Korean-Americans, often bilingual but lacking the nuances of appropriate sociocultural communicative knowledge inherently gained as part of the enculturation process within Korean society, are often chided by their Korean-based relatives for being impolite, rude, and uncaring.

English is spoken in cultures that have relatively little use for rigid hierarchical societies. Thus, it has limited honorific categories. Germans, while not placing as great an emphasis on respect and social position as do Koreans or other Asians, emphasize these conventions more than English speakers do. German (like most European languages) employs the use of two forms of "you" the informal *du* and the formal *Sie*. Use of the two forms is highly conventionalized and marks users' social roles and position with respect to each other. Russia, despite over 70 years of Communist rule, is still very much a hierarchical society, and Russians remain keenly aware of titles and social status.

In short, language is a medium that allows us to gain insights into another culture. In many ways, we can think of language as both a mirror and a window. As a mirror, language reflects that which a culture deems important: it represents, expresses, incorporates, maintains, and constrains the values, beliefs, and attitudes of a culture. At the same time, language is a window that reveals precisely what values, beliefs, and attitudes a culture considers important and how a culture has chosen to realize these truths through the language. Thus, cross-cultural awareness entails becoming aware of both one's own culture and other cultures. It entails becoming cognizant of cultural patterns and practices. It entails learning to recognize the impact that subconscious cultural factors have on our interpretation of the world and of the actions of people around us, as well as discerning the relationship between language and culture. **(See Activity G—Reactions)**

Since cross-cultural communication is the process whereby speakers of different languages operating under different cultural assumptions and coming from different language backgrounds attempt to convey messages to each other, misunderstandings often occur. There is much more to communication than the mere analysis of a verbal message, because this message is the product of the speaker's unique experiences as a member of a particular culture. Each language has its own frames of reference, shared by the members of a given culture through the enculturation that all normal individuals are exposed to as part of the process of growing up. Cross-cultural misunderstandings are often the result of speakers' assumptions that members of other cultures share their frames of reference and norms of social and communicative interaction. To be effective cross-cultural communicators, speakers must be aware of the relationship between culture and language. Such an awareness allows speakers to make predictions of possible areas of misunderstanding and to provide explanations for such misunderstandings when they occur. **(See Activity H—Draw Me!)**

Teaching and Learning Connections

Culture is an integral part of language teaching and learning. As long as there are speakers, there is culture, as culture resides in the users of a language (Meier, 2003; Seelye, 1997). The goal in education is "to translate culture teaching into a culture learning experience for our students" according to Ryffel (1997:34). Teachers can work toward this goal through careful planning of classroom activities, which may reflect their own personal life experiences, and by actually walking students through the varied stages of developing intercultural awareness or cultural sensitivity. A process approach framework for selecting teaching activities, materials, and techniques so that all aspects of intercultural competence are addressed has been suggested by Fantini (1997b:42). His seven-stage outline holistically suggests a process for developing not only course syllabi but also individual lesson plans. The stages include the presenting of new material, practicing it in a controlled context, explaining the grammar rules behind it, using learned material in a less controlled context, exploring sociolinguistic interrelationships, determining their cultural appropriateness, and making intercultural comparisons.

There are noticeable differences among cultures with respect to tolerance of difference, desire for harmony, the importance of social hierarchies, and so on. Cultural awareness plays an essential role in overcoming communication problems or difficulties between members of cultures with divergent or even opposing beliefs, values, norms, and attitudes. In her article Kramsch (1998b) suggests that the teaching of culture needs to emphasize the development of general sociolinguistic competence and social awareness across cultures. She highlights different ways in which awareness across cultures might be developed in the classroom, and she argues that the context of the native language and the new culture must be built on their own terms. Kramsch's first suggestion is to explore the context of student responses to the cultural phenomena with which they are confronted. The teacher, however, should not impose his or her own interpretations. Kramsch further suggests that students need to reconstruct the "context of production and reception of a given text" from within the foreign culture itself (p. 25). An example of this would be what it means to close a door in different cultures.

In short, Kramsch argues that "our purpose in teaching culture through language is not to make our students into little French or little Germans, but in making them understand why the speakers of two different languages act and react the way they do, whether in fictional texts or in social encounters, and what the consequences of these insights may mean for the learner" (p. 27). What appears evident is that native language impacts on second language learners' understanding of a second culture, for their conceptualizations of the new culture are greatly affected by the worldviews, beliefs, assumptions, and presuppositions of their own culture. Therefore, the role of teachers is to help learners become aware of the role of culture in forming people's interpretation of self in relation to others and the world around them and, we hope, to make learners become more tolerant of different "ways of seeing."

Questions for Study and Discussion

1. Define the following terms and provide examples where appropriate: *culture, enculturation, emics/etics, beliefs, values, norms, attitudes*

2. What fields of study influence the concept of culture? Why do you think the authors of this book discussed the different fields of study that have influenced the concept of culture?

3. The authors distinguish between *Culture* written with a capital *C* and *culture* written with a lowercase *c*, and they provide examples of what is meant by each term. What additional examples of *subjective culture* can you include? What makes these part of subjective culture?

4. Discuss the statement "Culture is a set of lenses through which we see the world."

5. Explain *linguistic relativity?* What examples can you provide? Consider how thought is influenced by culture, the role of "categorization" across languages, and what a language's vocabulary tells us about the culture of its speakers.

6. How can you explain the claim that language and culture are inseparable?

7. What values and attitudes from your own culture (or subculture) do you consider most important to teach to students coming to your country? Why?

III. Practice: What Activities Show Us

A. Defining Culture (10–15 minutes)

Culture permeates every facet of society; it influences how people think, talk, and behave. Because culture is so pervasive, it is difficult to present a single definition of it. Just as there is no one culture, there is no one universal definition of culture. Many factors, including cultural background and personal experiences, affect any definition of culture. Fields such as linguistics, anthropology, and communication also impact on possible definitions.

Purpose: To help students become aware of the many definitions of culture

Procedure:

1. Work individually. Write your own definition of culture on a sheet of paper.

2. Compare your definition with that of two or three others in the group.

3. Work in groups of 3–4. Decide on *one* definition of culture.

4. Write the definition on a piece of paper.

5. Be prepared to read your group's definition to the full group.

   Sample Questions:

   • What differences arose in your individual definitions?

   • What were the similarities?

   • What were the common elements among all the definitions?

- Which problems did your group encounter in trying to agree on one definition?

- Why do you think these problems surfaced?

Alternative:

1. On the first day of class, work individually. Write your own definition of culture on a sheet of paper.

2. Without discussion, collect definitions from all the students.

3. On the final day of class, return the definitions.

4. Revise original definitions based on what was learned during this semester.

5. Share original and revised versions.

 A

To adapt for the language classroom,

Procedure: Steps 4 and 5

4. Write each group's definition on the blackboard.

5. Discuss the definitions from the different groups.

B. Class Begins (20–25 minutes)

The need to socialize children into society is universal. Since cultures have evolved in different environments and under different circumstances, they have developed varied means of socializing their young. Many forms of socialization are ubiquitous, yet the structure varies cross-culturally. While all cultures educate their young, how they do so differs. Some cultures send children to formal institutions of learning, other cultures apprentice them to mentors, and still others opt to educate them at home.

Purpose: To show how daily routines are governed by sets of rules and how these rules differ cross-culturally

Procedure:

1. Work individually. Write your response to the following question.

   - How do you know when class begins?

2. Give enough time for everyone to write an answer.

3. Ask for responses, and list these on the blackboard.

4. Work in groups of 3–4. Prepare a set of guidelines for establishing the start of a class.

5. List these guidelines on the blackboard.

6. Hold a group discussion of the guidelines generated.

Sample Questions:

- What is "classroom culture"?

- How is this class different from/similar to other classes you have taken?

- Are the "rules" for the beginning of class explicit or implicit? How?

- From the responses listed on the board, what can we infer about the rules for the beginning of class?

- What differences are there among class beginnings in elementary school, high school, and university classes?

- Is classroom culture a subculture or its own culture? Why?

NOTE: If members from different cultures are in the group, their responses to this activity will illustrate how rituals and routines can significantly differ.

A

To adapt for the language classroom,

Procedure: Steps 4, 5, and 6

4. Work in groups of 3–4. Make a list of cues or signals that tell you class is beginning (e.g., teacher raises voice, teacher enters room, teacher makes eye contact with students, students rise, and so on).

5. Write each group's list on the blackboard.

6. Discuss these lists as a full group.

   Sample Questions:

   • How did you come to recognize these cues/signals?

   • What are the differences and similarities between the cues/signals listed by each group?

   • Are there any differences among the cues/signals in elementary school, high school, and university classes? If so, what are they?

   • How do class beginnings differ between ESL and non-ESL classes, if at all?

C. Old Woman, Young Lady (10–15 minutes)

Culture is a lens that shapes our perceptions and thinking. Cultural conditioning begins in the cradle and is reinforced throughout life, whether in school, on the sports field, or in the workplace. Our cultural framework influences how we interpret events, circumstances, and objects. In other words, it affects our notion of reality.

Purpose: To highlight the extent to which prior conditioning influences what we see and how we interpret the things around us

Procedure:

1. Prepare photocopies of the first two pictures, which depict a young lady and an old woman.

Depiction of a young lady

This page is reproducible.

Depiction of an old woman

Composite of young lady and old woman

This page is reproducible.

2. Make an overhead transparency of the third picture, which is a composite of the other two pictures.

3. Pass pictures of the old woman to participants on one side of the classroom.

4. Pass pictures of the young lady to participants on the other side.

5. Do not tell the group that you are passing out two different pictures.

6. Allow 15–20 seconds to study the pictures. Then, collect them.

7. Project the third picture on an overhead projector.

8. Ask for a description of what is seen on the overhead. Generally, participants that received the picture of the old woman continue to see the old woman when looking at the composite picture, while those that received the picture of the young lady continue to see the young lady.

9. Discuss reactions as a full group.

Sample Questions:

- Which image did you see first projected on the overhead projector?

- What connections can you draw between this brief conditioning exercise and how people's culture and upbringing influence the way they see and interpret the world around them?

- Based on this exercise and your own experiences, can you explain the following statement: "We interpret the world not the way it necessarily is but the way we ourselves are."

D. Emics and Etics of Culture (20–25 minutes)

Learning to identify what is culture-specific (emic) and what is culture-universal (etic) is fundamental to understanding other cultures. An important step in developing cultural sensitivity is learning how to compare and contrast one's own cultural elements or worldviews with those of other cultures. Recognizing similarities and differences leads to greater cultural awareness and to behavior that is more culturally appropriate.

Purpose: To increase understanding of the terms *culture universal* and *culture specific*

Procedure:

1. Work in groups of 3–4.

2. Bring in photos of a marketplace in a third world country, a café scene in Europe, South American schoolchildren in uniforms, a street scene in Asia, and so on.

3. List the culture-specific and culture-universal behaviors and objects that you notice in each photo.

4. As a full group, compare the lists generated by the smaller groups.

   Sample Questions:

   • Which culture universal behaviors can you observe in the photos?

   • Which items are culture universal?

   • Which behaviors are culture specific?

   • Which items are culture specific?

   • Why did you categorize certain behaviors and items as culture universal and others as culture specific?

   • What generalizations can you make from the photos?

E. Values (15–20 minutes on the first day; 10–15 minutes on the second day)

Often, we are only minimally aware of our values—the fundamental ideals important to us—and of how they influence our day-to-day behavior. When we find ourselves in situations where our values are questioned or even challenged, we feel uncomfortable, annoyed, or angry. Becoming aware of one's values and of how these are influenced by a person's culture and ethnic background is an important step in developing cross-cultural awareness.

Purpose: To become aware of the role that culture plays in a person's value system

Procedure:

1. Prepare two copies of the values worksheet (worksheet 1) for each participant.

2. As a full group, briefly discuss the term *values*.

   * How would you define the term *values?*

   * What makes something a "value"?

3. Work individually. Complete one values worksheet by ranking the values on a scale from 1 to 15 according to their importance to you.

4. Have an individual from a different culture or ethnic background fill out a second values worksheet as a homework assignment.

5. Break into groups of 4–6 to compare results in the next class session.

   Sample Questions:

   * Were you able to identify all the listed items as values? Why or why not?

   * How would you explain each value on the worksheet?

   * Was it easy or difficult for you to rank the values? Why or why not?

Worksheet 1. Ranking Values

Age _____   Gender _____

Cultural/ethnic background _____

Rank the values in the following list from 1 to 15 according to their importance to you.

Value	Rank
1. individuality	1. _____
2. work	2. _____
3. freedom	3. _____
4. leisure	4. _____
5. friendship	5. _____
6. prosperity	6. _____
7. family	7. _____
8. education	8. _____
9. health	9. _____
10. love	10. _____
11. happiness	11. _____
12. equality	12. _____
13. self-fulfillment	13. _____
14. social acceptance	14. _____
15. interpersonal harmony	15. _____

- Did the person you asked to rank the values find it easy or difficult to do so?

- How do the different rankings compare? For example, do you see any patterns based on age, gender, cultural background, or other factors?

6. Share the small-group discussions with the full group.

7. In your small groups, eliminate one value from the list. You must reach a group consensus.

8. Discuss the results as a full group.

Sample Questions:

- Which value did your group eliminate?

- Why did your group choose to eliminate this value?

- How easy was it to arrive at a consensus?

9. In your small groups, add a new value to replace the one you eliminated earlier from the list. You must reach a group consensus.

10. Discuss the results as a full group.

Sample Questions:

- Which value did your group elect to add?

- Why did your group choose to add this particular value?

- How easy was it to arrive at a consensus?

Follow-up:

1. Discuss what this activity has shown in terms of the relationship between culture—including subcultures—and value systems.

2. Discuss what you have learned about yourself and your values.

A

To adapt for the language classroom,

Procedure: Step 2

2. As a full group, discuss the term *values.*

- A value is something a person or a group of people believes to be important. A value can influence behavior. For example, if honesty is something that people value, then honest people are more highly regarded than dishonest ones. People will attempt to be honest to gain the respect of others.

Follow-up:

- Write an essay on what you have learned about yourself, your values, and your culture.

F. Shared Backgrounds (15–20 minutes)

Culture shapes its members. It is the key to the formation of its members' constructs of reality and to the development of their repertoires of culturally appropriate behaviors. How cultures differ from each other stems from the relative uniqueness of their social systems. Although a culture shapes its members, people within any culture differ from one another. Thus, members of a culture remain individuals in their own right.

Purpose: To develop an awareness of the influence of culture and personal preferences that help mold individuals

Procedure:

1. As a full group, generate a list of 10–12 personal preferences and interests, such as food, clothing, music, political affiliation, career choices, media preferences, and hobbies.

2. Divide into pairs.

3. Make three lists. In the center write items (e.g., personal preferences, interests, background information) that are the same for you and your partner. On each side write items that are different.

4. Compare the lists and draw overlapping circles to represent how much you and your partner have in common. After you have drawn the circles, shade in your shared area. For example, if two people share many interests, their circles might look like circle A. On the other hand, people who share fewer interests will produce a circle such as B.

Sample circles

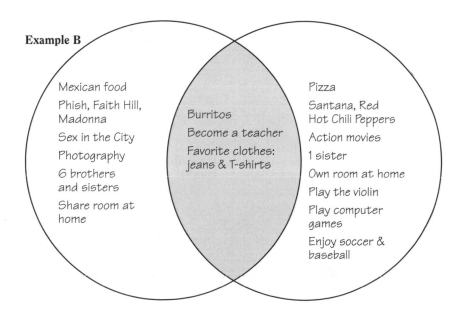

Example A

Leo Di Caprio
Sandra Bullock
Sex in the City
Like cars
1 brother
Grandparents live with me
Like to wear trendy skirts & tops

Favorite food: Chinese & pizza
Puddle of Mudd, Shakira, Pink, Ashanti
Favorite actors: Pierce Brosnan, Jackie Chan, Sponge Bob
I love to go shopping
Want to teach
Soccer fan

Avril Lavigne
Lord of the Rings
Baseball fan
1 sister
Parents divorced
Like to wear jeans & T-shirts

Example B

Mexican food
Phish, Faith Hill, Madonna
Sex in the City
Photography
6 brothers and sisters
Share room at home

Burritos
Become a teacher
Favorite clothes: jeans & T-shirts

Pizza
Santana, Red Hot Chili Peppers
Action movies
1 sister
Own room at home
Play the violin
Play computer games
Enjoy soccer & baseball

5. Compare the circles as a full group.

6. Discuss the implications for comparing cultural differences and similarities.

Sample Questions:

- In what areas do cultures differ?

- Which cultures might have members who share closely overlapping circles? Why?

- Which cultures would probably have members whose circles show fewer overlapping areas? Why?

- What can you deduce from these findings?

G. Reactions (15–20 minutes)

Language is a symbolic representation of how the members of a culture organize, view, and structure their environment. Each culture places its own individual stamp on a language by the kinds of categorization and meaning attributed to its symbols. Language is both a means of communication and a reflection of the social structure of a culture. It affects speakers' perspectives of the world and influences their patterns of thought. Language is the primary tool for transmitting a culture's beliefs, values, norms, and worldviews.

Purpose: To heighten awareness of the relationship between culture, language, and meaning

Procedure:

1. Work in groups of 3–4. Discuss your reactions to the following statements. Have one person in your group record the responses.

- Culture is a pattern of response to customs, language, behavior, and values.

- Culture is about the meaning given to objects, people's behavior, values, and individual roles.

- Language is a vehicle for cultural knowledge.

2. Share the different responses from each group with the other groups.

3. List on the blackboard as many responses as possible.

4. Discuss the responses to see if patterns for categorization can be found.

   • Did the responses fall into any cultural, language, ethnic, gender, or other patterns?

   Sample Questions:

   • Why do you think the responses fall into the patterns you have identified?

   • Which influences shaped the various responses?

   • What conclusions can you draw about the relationship between culture, language, and meaning?

H. Draw Me! (20–25 minutes)

Socialization is the process of forming culturally adept members in a society by training them to adopt certain concepts and values. These culturally savvy members are also individuals with unique personal experiences who bring a priori knowledge to communicative situations. How individuals use this a priori knowledge depends on the demands of the situation.

Purpose: To demonstrate how much of what we do is colored by our prior knowledge and expectations

Procedure:

1. Divide into pairs, sitting back-to-back so as not to see your partner.

2. Provide one partner in each pair with a drawing—for example, geometric shapes, or an unusually shaped dwelling, house, or car. The other partner should not see this drawing.

3. The partner with the drawing should instruct the other partner about the drawing of the picture. The partner drawing the picture should not be told what is to be drawn and should not see the picture. In larger groups, provide different pairs with different pictures. Giving different pairs different pictures allows participants to compare the ease and difficulty of following the directions for completing different types of drawings.

Example geometric shapes for drawing activity

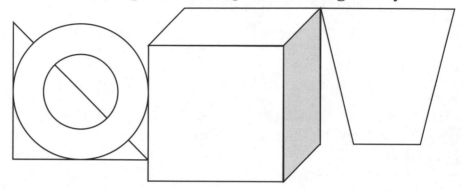

4. Partners who are explaining how to draw the picture may not use words that actually describe the items, must use instructions such as "Draw a straight line about two inches in the middle of your paper," and may answer only yes-no questions (e.g., "Does the line go to the left?") during this activity.

5. After about 5–10 minutes, partners should display the original picture and the new interpretation to the full group. The new drawing is usually significantly different from the original.

6. Discuss what each participant experienced.

Sample Questions:

- If you were providing the instructions, how did it feel not being able to use any body language or nonverbal cues in explaining the drawing to your partner?

- If you were receiving the instructions, how did it feel not being able to observe the body language or nonverbal cues of your partner during this exercise?

- How can you relate your difficulties to those faced by people visiting or living in a culture foreign to them and/or learning a foreign language?

- How did the different pictures compare in the types of difficulty the drawers experienced?

- What role does shared background information play in facilitating communication?

- If your directions or instructions are "clear," why are they often misunderstood?

- How are misunderstandings compounded when dealing with nonnative speakers?

- How does not sharing background information come into play in a classroom situation? Give examples.

> **NOTE:** Participants instructed in the drawing of a picture of a house often say that as soon as they realized what they were drawing, it became very easy to follow their partners' directions. Those drawing a geometric shape generally had much more difficulty producing a replica.

Alternative:

1. Following the preceding directions, one partner instructs the other in the drawing of a picture. This time, the partners face each other.

2. The partner who is drawing may not ask any questions at all.

IV. Further Readings

Articles

Atkinson, D. (1999). TESOL and culture. *TESOL Quarterly, 33*(4), 625–654.

This article offers a reassessment of the notion of culture in the field of TESOL. It takes into account recent work in critical anthropology and cultural studies as well as in TESOL itself. The author infers six principles of a revised view of culture that can inform TESOL research and teaching.

Cooper, E. (1986). Chinese table manners: You are what you eat. *Human Organization, 45*(2), 179–184.

This is a good description of good Chinese (specifically Hong Kong) table manners and of how they often contrast with general European expectations of what constitutes "good manners." Given that so much of how we judge others is based on what we consider "right" and "proper," this article provides an interesting comparison that underscores the subjectivity behind any evaluation of just what is *the* right and proper way to do something.

Hanvey, R. (1987). Cross-cultural awareness. In L. Luce & E. Smith (Eds.), *Toward internationalism: Readings in cross-cultural communication* (2nd ed., pp. 13–23). Cambridge, MA: Newbury House. (Reprint of a 1976 version.)

This is a good introductory article in which the author discusses the complexities of truly achieving cross-cultural understanding. He also delineates what he sees as four different levels of cross-cultural awareness.

Tobin, J., & Friedman, J. (1983). Spirits, shamans, and nightmare death: Survivor stress in a Hmong refugee. *American Journal of Orthopsychiatry, 53,* 439–448.

The authors of this article provide a fascinating look at how traditional Western diagnosis and treatment of typical refugee psychological problems (e.g., survivor guilt, trauma syndrome) are inadequate and at how physicians require different types of diagnosis and treatment when confronted with radically different cultural beliefs and expectations.

Books

Barnlund, D. (1989). *Communicative styles of Japanese and Americans: Images and realities.* Belmont, CA: Wadsworth.

An in-depth exploration of Japanese and American cultures, this book is especially useful for those who want or need a greater background in understanding not only the differences between the two cultures but also what makes each culture what it is. The book is nontechnical and can easily be read by someone with little or no knowledge of this area of study.

Chen, G., & Starosta, W. (1998). *Foundations of intercultural communication.* Needham Heights, MA: Allyn and Bacon.

The authors of this book explore central issues in cross-cultural communication. In addition to discussion of the chapter topic, each chapter includes a minicase discussion of (i.e., a situation that involves a case of cross-cultural misunderstanding) and "research highlights" that summarize the work of an important author as related to the theme of the chapter.

Condon, J., & Yousef, F. (1975). *An introduction to intercultural speech communication.* Indianapolis: Bobbs-Merrill.

This standard text presents a clear introduction to cross-cultural communication. The authors write in an easy-to-read style, using many anecdotes and case studies to introduce and illustrate points. The book's wide range of topics include what it means to gain cultural understanding, an outline and discussion of value orientations, and a description of the arrangements, uses of, and attitudes toward homes in five cultures.

Gudykunst, W. (1998). *Bridging differences: Effective intergroup communication* (3rd ed.). Thousand Oaks, CA: Sage.

The author of this book presents an excellent overview of cross-cultural communication. The book is well organized, highly readable, and packed with useful information about this area of study.

Rogers, E., & Steinfatt, T. (1999). *Intercultural communication.* Prospect Heights, IL: Waveland Press.

This is a very thorough book on intercultural communication. The authors discuss many topics in depth, including the history of the study of intercultural communication and what culture is. Since the authors come from the field of communication, a great deal of attention is paid to communication theory and its application to intercultural communication, with many examples and case studies.

Stewart, E., & Bennett, M. (1991). *American cultural patterns: A cross-cultural perspective* (Rev. ed.). Yarmouth, ME: Intercultural Press.

This book is indispensable reading for those wishing to become more aware of practical issues in cross-cultural communication. The various chapters in the text focus on different areas of cross-cultural communication, ranging from language and cultural behavior to an attempt to organize human cultural patterns into four dimensions.

Triandis, H. (1994). *Culture and social behavior.* New York: McGraw-Hill.

The author of this book approaches culture from the field of social psychology. He focuses on the relationship between culture and social behavior, why we should study this relationship, and cultural influences on social factors.

Chapter Two
More on Culture

I. Anecdote: "Being on time"

The concept of time differs among cultures. Regardless of whether it is an important meeting or just a friendly get-together, culture is an influencing factor in our lives shown by the following anecdote.

I recently received a memo informing me that my department at the university was going to hold a meeting at 2:30 on a Friday afternoon. Since I am always punctual, I made sure to be in the meeting room at least five minutes before the scheduled starting time. To my surprise, no one was there.

At 2:30, I went to the chairperson's office to ask the secretary whether the meeting had been changed. I was told that it had not. I went back to the meeting room and waited. To better understand my dilemma, one needs to know the composition of my department: the chairperson is Italian, and the other full-time departmental colleagues include five Spaniards, three Italians, two French, one German, and two Americans.

The first to arrive after me was one of my Spanish colleagues, followed by the French and the American professors. By 2:40, only a few of us were in the room. As the others, including the chairperson, started trickling in, no one seemed to be bothered that the meeting was already ten minutes late. Everyone was socializing and not concerned with the task at hand. When the meeting finally started at 2:45, two Spanish professors and two Italian professors had still not arrived.

One of my colleagues commented that these professors were always late. I noted that we were not starting on time and added that I had another commitment off campus at 4:30, which I was not going to make because of this delay. Somewhat annoyed, I asked myself, "Why can't my colleagues be on time for a meeting everyone was informed about in advance? This is a formal meeting with business at hand and not just a friendly get-together. Shouldn't such an important meeting start on time?"

You may have guessed that I am the German in the department. The laissez-faire attitude about starting a meeting on time is customary where I teach; surprisingly, it does not appear to be problematic for anyone but me. Is this an example of a cultural clash? Or is this a personal problem?

Discussion of Key Issues

Because members of different cultures have disparate worldviews, they will have diverse understandings of social roles, social relationships, and social and personal obligations. For instance, the latitude accorded the concept of being "on time" varies across cultures. In some cultures, being on time means arriving within 30 minutes of the designated time; in another culture, arriving later than 10 minutes constitutes an insult to the other party. Closely related to a culture's notion of social obligations is the concept of time in general. Time is not as divided, apportioned, carved up, and allocated as strictly and rigidly in some cultures as in others. In Arab and Hispanic cultures, people's relationships and obligations to one another are more important than a more detached notion of punctuality. If a person is on his or her way to a meeting and encounters a close friend, it is of greater importance to spend a few moments with this friend than to arrive punctually for a business meeting. The friend, by virtue of the fact that he or she is a friend and hence a member of one's in-group, deserves such consideration and attention.

As members of a culture, individuals tend to react to situations instinctively and to interpret situations based on their own cultural conditioning, as is illustrated by the introductory anecdote in this chapter. However, since individuals within a culture also differ, it is not always easy to determine whether a behavior is culturally based or part of an individual's makeup.

Chapter 2 continues the examination of what culture is and how culture influences people's behaviors, their social relationships, and their perceptions of the world around them.

Questions for Thought

- What are the principal characteristics of individualistic and collectivistic cultures?

- How do different cultures regard the concepts of time and face?

- What is ethnocentrism?

II. Theory: What Research Tells Us

Individualistic versus Collectivistic

An important dimension that researchers have identified as distinguishing cultures is that of individualism versus collectivism (e.g., Hofstede, 1980, 1991; Triandis, 1988, 1995). Cultures differ in the relative importance its members place on the notion of personal independence and success as opposed to the notion of interdependence and the success of one's group or groups. The basic distinction can be viewed as the answer to the question of how individuals perceive themselves. Do they see themselves as independent persons with very personal goals, aspirations, rights, interests, and desires? Or do they view themselves as members of a complex web of interlocking relationships, the needs and desires of which often supersede those of the individual. The answer to this question indicates where a culture falls along a continuum, with individualistic culture at one end and collectivistic culture at the other end. An important point to keep in mind is that this individualistic/collectivistic dichotomy refers to relative features, not absolutes. Cultures fall within individualistic or collectivistic categories along a continuum, as do the subcultures of a dominant culture. Although the United States has been described as the most individualistic culture in the world (Hofstede, 1980), different ethnic groups within this culture differ in terms of their emphasis on individualism. Nevertheless, Americans, regardless of their ethnic background, are generally more individualistic than members of a strongly collectivistic culture such as China.

How can we describe the features that place cultures close to one end of the continuum as opposed to the other end? *Individualistic cultures* structure social experience around autonomous individuals. In an individualistic culture, individuals view themselves as autonomous, independent of groups, and reluctant or unwilling to subordinate personal goals to those of the group. It is considered weak or unassertive to be overly interdependent on others (Rogers & Steinfatt, 1999:86). Individualistic cultures emphasize self-reliance, individual growth, personal achievement, and satisfaction. Individuals' own desires, personal goals, and particular motivation primarily influence their actions and behaviors in such cultures. Competition among individuals to be the best student, the best worker, the best athlete, and the best of anything is keen. The underlying assumption in individualistic cultures is that each individual has wants and needs and is an authority as to just what these wants and needs are. Independence is encouraged at a young age. Even young children are urged to make their own decisions, and young people leave home relatively early (generally after high school). Family and social ties are important, but the sense of dependence and interdependence takes a backseat to the needs and wants of the individual.

In the enculturation process of their young, individualistic cultures not only promote the fostering of independence but strive to nurture individual achievement, self-expression, and individual or critical thinking. Individuals in these cultures generally make educational and career choices based on their own personal needs and desires, rather than those of their families. Roles and social relationships in individualistic cultures are less rigidly hierarchical and more fluid than in collectivistic cultures, and rules governing social interactions are also less dictated by age and gender roles. The more individualistic a society is, the more the education system of the society emphasizes the right for students to speak up and actively participate in the learning process, especially in secondary and higher education. Individualistic cultures include most northern and western European countries, Australia, Canada, and the United States.

Other cultures structure their social experience around one or more collectives, such as the family, the tribe, the religious group, or the country—hence the term *collectivistic culture*. In such cultures, the goals of the group are valued over those of the individual. Social and familial relationships and networks are primary, extensive, and interlocking. There is a strong sense of reciprocal obligation and responsibility. If someone gives another person a gift or does a favor for someone else, the recipient of the gift or favor is indebted until such time as he or she can reciprocate with a gift or favor of equal or greater value or consequence. Collective and cooperative efforts are prized over individualized efforts.

Collectivists generally view themselves as appendages of their group, whether the family, a social group, a corporation, or other. Unlike individualists, collectivists feel interdependent with members of their group and are willing to subordinate personal goals to those of the group. An individual's needs and wants are established and realized within the context of the group. It is more important to act appropriately than to search for self-fulfillment. The primary motivation is toward the common objectives of the group, whether familial, social, business, or other. Competition takes place between groups rather than between individuals. A collectivist culture promotes interdependence, respect for authority, hierarchical roles and relationships, and group consensus. For example, the Japanese emphasize group affiliation over all other forms of social organization (Caudill, 1973). Negotiations are often conducted by several people who represent a group rather than by a sole representative for the group. Because individuals are defined by their group relationship, an unaccompanied representative is often regarded as someone lacking in status. Japanese children who have spent time abroad in an English-speaking country (perhaps for reasons related to a parent's work) will often avoid using any English upon returning to Japan in order to avoid being different in any way. It is more important to them to be the same as everyone else than to exhibit special knowledge, even in a language class.

In most collectivistic cultures, the family is central. Each person's behavior is determined and constrained by family needs, expectations, and responsibilities; at the same time, members can depend on the family always being there to assist and support in any way necessary to their well-being. Furthermore, a large part of a person's self-identity is established through the family network and concomitant in-groups (see chap. 5). Consider, for instance, the issue of a family-owned business. In the United States, very much an individualistic culture, if a son did not wish to join the family business after completing high school, most school counselors would argue that the son should pursue his career choice and that he need not follow the desires of his family. However, in a collectivistic culture such as China or Japan, if the son chose to disregard the wishes of the family, he would most likely be a major disappointment to his family. He would be seen as wanting to put his personal goals above the larger ones of family and would accordingly be chastised by those around him. In a collectivistic culture, personal goals are to be aligned with a person's responsibilities to the group, that is, self-fulfillment is viewed as something derived from acting based on one's obligations toward the group rather than from making choices based on one's own potential and personal desires. Adherence to the wishes of the family is a matter of duty that transcends personal wishes and desires.

Because of the high value collectivistic cultures place on relationships or networks, they are also cultures where nepotism is rampant, as such behavior is both accepted and expected. It is part of, as well as a reflection of, the network of family and social relationships and group cohesiveness, and it embodies neither negative connotations nor legal implications. Within a worldview that highly honors relationships, it is clearly better to employ those we know and those who have some sort of ties to us than to hire complete strangers. The more collectivistic a culture is, the more its members rely on other people within their group rather than on outside organizations. In China, a person in need of something—whether information, financial assistance, socioemotional support, or otherwise—will turn to someone he knows, who in turn may turn to someone he knows who knows someone. Even in the use of financial institutions, there will be some relationship to a person's in-group. In many cultures, newly appointed officials openly fire all the civil servants under them and replace them with relatives (Pinker, 1997:435). After all, since relatives are members of one's in-group, they are natural allies and will work to ensure your (and their) continued welfare. In the United States, in contrast, it is illegal for most city, county, and state governments to hire someone based on family and social-group ties. There, the term *nepotism* has strong negative connotations and implications, both legal and moral. Indeed, many companies, institutions of higher learning, and governmental agencies in the United States and Canada have formal policies against nepotism.

Another example of differences in perspective between the individualistic and the collectivistic points of view lies in the notion of plagiarism. The idea of intellectual property and the social and legal ramifications associated with plagiarism differ cross-culturally. In individualistic cultures, where the efforts of the individual are encouraged, celebrated, and rewarded, plagiarism is conceived of as the stealing of someone else's thoughts and/or words. In an individualistic culture such as the United States, plagiarizing at a university and/or in a place of business will result in harsh treatment, often leading to dismissal of the one culpable. This contrasts to collectivistic cultures, where there is often both the understanding that words and ideas are to be shared by everyone and the belief that copying the words of another writer shows respect and honor. Given the radically opposing perceptions of self, interactions between individuals from a collectivistic culture and from an individualistic culture can easily result in cross-cultural miscommunication. Members of individualistic cultures are often faced with situations in collectivistic cultures where hiring an employee's family member is accepted and even expected or where a reward is assumed to expedite services or paperwork, practices that may actually conflict with the laws of the company or the institutional home office.

This individualistic/collectivistic dichotomy is also reflected in communicative behaviors. The types of discourse strategies members of collectivistic cultures prefer, for instance, often vary from those preferred by members of individualistic cultures. Lustig and Koester (1993:147) maintain that "people from individualistic cultures are more likely than those from collectivistic cultures to use confrontational strategies when dealing with interpersonal problems; those with a collectivist orientation are likely to use avoidance, third party intermediaries or other face-saving techniques." Members of collectivistic cultures, which value harmony and social relationships, prefer using indirect discourse strategies to minimize confrontation in formal social relationships. They will use what seem to Westerners to be extremely vague and convoluted expressions, so that a message is couched in a web of masterfully polite behavior. Chinese communicate by "beating around the bush," while Americans and Canadians "spell it all out" (see chap. 6). For Japanese speakers, open disagreement is an unpleasant experience. Therefore, to avoid such situations in cross-cultural business negotiations, the Japanese will appoint a middleman to serve as the go-between or the third person to assist in the negotiation process. Such behavior is often disconcerting to members of more individualistic cultures, who expect to be dealing directly with their counterparts and who are not averse to disagreement and may even revel in it.

Polychronic and Monochronic Time

In addition to the dichotomy between individualistic and collectivistic cultures, researchers have also suggested a distinction among cultures based on how they regard time. According to Hall (1983), cultures organize time in two major ways: *polychronic time* (P-time) and *monochronic time* (M-time). In P-time cultures, scheduling of time is of little importance, and many events occur simultaneously. Members of P-time cultures often engage in several unrelated activities simultaneously; doctors in China may treat patients while holding conversations with visiting relatives about separate and often unrelated medical topics, and in Latin America, businesspeople may be interrupted during meetings to conduct personal matters.

The emphasis in P-time cultures is on personal involvement and the culmination of transactions over that of rigid adherence to timetables. Spending time with others is more valued than are strict schedules or punctuality. Meal breaks in P-time cultures are often long and encourage social interactions; conducting any sort of business while eating is often frowned on and regarded as rude. In P-time cultures, a person would avoid cutting a conversation short to be on time for an appointment. Appointments are viewed as approximate, flexible meeting times; people show up late or cancel at the last minute, even when the appointment is important. Such behavior occurs not because members of P-time cultures have no concept of time or punctuality but because these terms have different connotations than they do for members of M-time cultures.

In P-time cultures, the future is often viewed as unknown and unforeseeable; therefore, planning for the future is minimal and rarely cast in stone. Future plans may include caveats such as "God be willing" or "it be God's will," alluding to the belief that the future does not necessarily turn out as one has intended or projected. There is a high tolerance of ambiguity; members of P-time cultures tend to "go with the flow," are flexible with respect to agendas and timetables, and are willing to change course with little advance notice. Navajo Native Americans, a P-time culture, regard time as flowing (rather than as a linear process) and believe that people should live with a focus on the here and now. Planning for the future and carefully scheduling activities are regarded by them as evidence of a person's dissatisfaction and discontentment. Time is not, for them, a commodity to be scrupulously apportioned (Gilliland, 1995).

M-time cultures, in contrast, place a high value on carefully scheduled time, or on the compartmentalizing of one's day. Time is regarded as something dictated by the clock and the hours of the day. Day planners, date books, agendas, and PDAs dominate social and business life in an M-time culture. Time determines and coordinates everything people do, their relationships with others, and their attitudes about the world. There is little tolerance of ambiguity; time is highly structured and organized; planning is sequential, very step-by-step, and concrete. An appointment is something that is either kept or canceled in advance. Members of M-time cultures prefer to focus on one thing or one task at a time, and they separate their time between task-oriented activities and personal or social activities. A business meeting should focus solely on the business at hand, with no interruptions for personal matters; doctor care should focus directly on the immediate medical needs of the patient.

When members of M-time cultures and P-time cultures interact, there is often a culture clash. Germans, Swiss, and North Americans are particularly time conscious. To a North American, "soon" means in the next few minutes, hours, or days, while to a member of an Asian or Arab culture, it may mean three months, six months, nine months, a year, or when people are ready. For an important business meeting scheduled by an American parent company in Chile, the Americans would likely show up just before the hour that the meeting is scheduled to begin. The Chileans, however, would probably arrive from a half hour to an hour later. Suppose the German government were hosting an event for a group of officials from Italy, who they expected to arrive at 7:00 P.M. By 7:30 P.M., the Germans would probably still be the only ones present at the event. Nigerians think nothing of being late for an appointment; rather than regarding punctuality as an individual's responsibility, they see time as a force or entity in itself. Being late is not an individual's fault but, rather, the result of time defeating that person's endeavor to meet an obligation (Enahoro, 1998). In P-time cultures, a person is generally obligated to wait for the other person to show up for a scheduled meeting or appointment, no matter how late that person may be. Not to wait is considered rude and shows impatience. In M-time cultures, the opposite would be true. The late person is considered to be rude and/or inconsiderate for keeping the other person waiting. Punctuality is the responsibility of each individual, and legitimate excuses must be offered to avoid exacerbating the offense when arriving late. **(See Activity A—Cross-Cultural Trivia Quiz)**

Face

In many Asian cultures, the concept of *face* is central. Face is a difficult concept for Westerners to grasp, as there is nothing quite like it in Western cultures. Although the notion of face has been compared to such concepts as pride, dignity, honor, and self-esteem, face is much more complex. It is the embodiment of two central tenets of Confucianism, namely, the essential integration of individuals into groups and the importance of maintaining social harmony. Confucianism emphasizes that individuals exist in interactive relationships with others. Face is related to the social status, influence, and prestige an individual has, and it is realized and sustained through each person's interaction with other members of that culture. Although most relationships are unequal in nature, each individual still has a reciprocal obligation to other individuals. According to Ting-Toomey (1988), face is a person's sense of positive social self-image in a relational and network context. The notion of face is closely related to collectivism; more collectivistic cultures are generally more concerned with the maintenance of face, in that face is closely identified with beliefs regarding group membership and social harmony. Loss of face, therefore, not only entails personal embarrassment or humiliation but also threatens disruption of the larger social harmony.

In all social situations, each person puts forward a certain "face." As long as each person accepts every other person's face, these social situations continue relatively smoothly. The focus of social situations is not each person's face but, rather, the wants and concerns of everyone present. Reciprocal acceptance of face does not imply automatic agreement or positive acceptance of one another; however, it does allow for the development of personal relationships and the transaction of business within a mutually acceptable social framework. In many cultures, the key to maintaining social harmony in social relationships is to accept and respect the need of individuals to maintain face. One's public image must be maintained at all costs, because one represents not just oneself but also one's group, with its complex network of relationships and interdependencies. To lose face is a serious matter that brings shame not only to the individual but also to the family and/or social group. Face reflects people's status and role within and between their groups. It reflects the realities of a culture's social hierarchies, social roles, and power resources and is closely tied to shame, honor, and obligation among its members.

The notion of face is closely related to "Politeness Theory" developed by Brown and Levinson (1978), who propose that speakers in a communicative interaction will choose a politeness strategy based on their perceptions of the threat to their face. The term *facework* has been coined to describe the particular communication behaviors that speakers use to save their own or their listeners' face (Goffman, 1959, 1972; Ting-Toomey, 1985, 1999). In conversational interactions, speakers will choose different communicative patterns in order to maintain their self-image and respect and/or gain the approval or approbation of their hearers. Although the concepts of face and facework exist across all cultures, exactly what is embodied in the notion of face and the particular types of facework behaviors in which speakers engage varies from culture to culture. Both face and facework are dependent on the cultural context in which they occur and can only be interpreted within the framework of that particular culture, as the underlying values governing face and the meanings given to various aspects of facework behavior patterns differ across cultures.

In cultures where face is an essential tenet, elaborate facework is the norm, as maintaining and saving face requires careful balancing among speakers. Saving face, both one's own and that of others, dictates avoiding direct confrontations and favoring indirect communication patterns. Often, what is not said, how something is said, and even the intricate rituals and settings enveloping the communicative exchange are more important than the actual spoken words. In Korea, communicative exchanges are governed by the crucial principle of *nunch'i,* or the ability to decipher and interpret the insinuated or implied nuances of social interactions. Speakers are expected to understand what is not said and to act accordingly. The avoidance of direct communicative behavior allows each participant to avoid situations that could threaten one's face. In Vietnamese, questions are often phrased in a negative form (e.g., "Are you not eating?") so that an affirmative answer may be given (Ellis, 1995). Actually saying "no" is regarded negatively and avoided whenever possible in Vietnamese and other languages where saving face is essential.

In cultures concerned with face, "white lies" are often told to ensure that no one becomes upset, and problematic subjects are alluded to indirectly or avoided altogether. In Vietnam, for instance, if a woman tells another person her husband is dead, it is inappropriate to ask how or when, because she may not necessarily mean physically so. She may mean that her husband has left her and so is dead to her. Saying he is dead allows her to save face (Ellis, 1995). Similarly, Koreans with limited English skills may refrain from letting on how much or how little they understand an English speaker, in order to avoid embarrassment and maintain face (Hur and Hur, 1994).

Most of the research into face and facework can be traced to Goffman's pioneering work on social interaction (e.g., 1959, 1972). Face is highly valued in many collectivistic cultures, given the emphasis on the group and innumerable interlocking social relationships. Wenzhong and Grove (1999:126–127) provide the following anecdote about face in China.

An American teacher in China has filled out an official form of some kind and has submitted it to the authorities at his University. A Chinese clerk loses the form. Time goes by. The American, being efficiency-minded, becomes impatient. He asks the authorities who are dealing with the matter when action will be taken. He is told that the matter has been referred to a higher bureau for a decision, or perhaps that the matter is under review, or whatever. He is not told that the form has been lost. Why? Because losing a form is a type of incompetence, the exposure of which would cause the authorities to lose face by contradicting their implicit claim to be people who can properly handle forms. The American eventually suspects that the explanation being offered is not accurate. If he discovers that the form has actually been lost, he will feel angry because "After all, if I had only been told it was lost, I could have filled out another form and eliminated this interminable delay." *But the authorities were more concerned about preserving face than about the efficient processing of forms or directness in communication.* (Italics added)

In an individualistic culture such as the United States, face as conceived of by the Chinese, with their thousands of years of history under the influence of the tenets of Confucianism, does not exist. The actions of the Chinese in this anecdote are almost incomprehensible for Americans, who, in contrast, are constantly bombarded by messages urging efficiency, honesty, directness, and personal responsibility for one's actions. The Chinese actions were based on the need to preserve everyone's face; the American's expectations, however, were based on achievement or completion of the desired outcome. Chapter 6 will look more closely at face and communication strategies.

Societal Roles

Human behavior occurs in widely different social and cultural contexts. Numerous variables, such as social position, social roles, norms, social control, and social structure, influence human behavior. Although these variables exist across all cultures, the relative importance, classifications, types, interpretations, and responsibilities assigned to different variables vary cross-culturally. *Position* identifies an individual's place in social space. A woman can occupy the position of daughter, mother, or sister in kinship space, of faculty member, committee member, or departmental chairperson in occupational space. It is possible for one individual to occupy all of these positions in a lifetime, often simultaneously. Every member of society occupies various different positions. When individuals occupy a given position, their *role* is comprised of the designated or expected behavior that accompanies that position. Whether a person's role is that of a child, parent, employer, teacher, or senator, that individual's behavior is guided by the role expectations held by others within that same culture.

Through the enculturation process, members of a cultural group acquire requisite socially acceptable behavior. *Social control,* the enforcement of the shared standard of conduct governing the behavior of group members, ensures individuals' adherence to this behavior. Societies vary in how they are structured and in how strict they are in terms of social control. Societal roles have important consequences for the behavior of individuals. Who an individual is, how this individual is related to other members of society, and the status ascribed to or achieved by this individual are important culturally determined roles. Cultures will assign different dimensions and activities to roles. What may be considered women's work or masculine emotions in one culture may be the reverse in another. Hall (1959) points out that great emotion is expected of men in Iran but of women in North American or northern European cultures. In many African and Native American cultures, heavy farm labor and carrying cumbrous burdens are seen as women's work (see chap. 5). **(See Activity B—Proverbs)**

Ethnocentrism

Ethnocentrism is the belief in the intrinsic superiority of one's own culture, language, and/or ethnic group. Because it involves emotions, it is not an intellectual exercise of comparing one culture with another culture. It is a highly subjective, personal, emotional, and (usually) subconscious way of valuing one's own culture above other cultures. The symbols of a cultural group's ethnicity, religion, and the like are objects of pride and veneration. There is the tendency to judge members of other cultures on the basis of one's own personal cultural standards. For example, instead of trying to understand Mexicans within their own cultural milieu, an ethnocentric American attempts to understand them as similar to or different from Americans.

To some extent, everyone is ethnocentric. It is the norm for members of a cultural group to consider their own culture as the standard against which to judge others. In fact, many languages intrinsically convey a sense of ethnocentrism. In Chinese, the word for China means "middle kingdom," as historically the Chinese considered their country to be the center of the world. In the Navajo language, the word for Navajo people, *Diné,* means "the people." By implication, all non-*Diné* are nonpeople or people of lesser status. People living in the United States refer to themselves as "Americans," ignoring the fact that everyone who lives in North, Central, and South America is also American. In the 18th century, when the Dutch occupied Taiwan, the local inhabitants were surprised to see Westerners, with their very different features, and referred to them as *a-dou-a,* which literally translates as "big nose." The phrase became generalized to mean any foreigner, that is, anyone not exhibiting "normal" Asian features.

Ethnocentrism is also reflected in the maps of the world. The Mercator projection, which has been commonly used in North America and

Europe, distorts the size of the continents and countries of the Northern Hemisphere. Greenland appears to be the same size as Africa, yet Africa is 14 times larger. The Mercator projection also makes Europe appear larger than South America. In reality, however, South America is actually twice the size of Europe. Japanese maps center Asia on the map and place the United States and Europe on the edges. In antique European maps of the world and the known solar system, "man" and Earth were always depicted as the center. At that time, Europeans could not conceive of a universe that did not revolve around the world and the people they believed their god had created in his image. **(See Activity C—Cultural Perceptions: *We and They*)**

Although ethnocentrism is a fact of human makeup, there is the concern that it at some point becomes so extreme that members of a particular culture can find nothing to value in another culture. Extreme ethnocentrism results in policies of "ethnic cleansing" (as in Kosovo, Nazi Germany, or the Sudan), according to which people are relentlessly killed in an effort to rid the world of those perceived of as being "different" and, by extension, inferior.

Stereotypes

Stereotypes are overgeneralized, exaggerated, and oversimplified beliefs that people use to categorize a group of people (Allport, 1958). Stereotyping is a psychological process whereby members of one group ascribe characteristics to another group, creating beliefs and expectations about people's behavior, attitudes, views, and demeanors. Stereotypes may be thought of as the mental pictures we have of different groups of people. In North American school systems, Asian immigrant children and teenagers frequently find that they are expected to excel in math, according to the stereotype that all Asians are good in math. Americans are often stereotyped as overweight.

Stereotypes may reflect actual, observed differences in behavior patterns among groups, and they also entail some type of attitude—often, but not necessarily, negative—toward the culture or language in question. Attitudes, which develop early in the enculturation process, are learned from parents and peers, develop through contact with people who are "different," and result from various interacting affective factors. We have had the experience of visiting a hair salon and telling our hairdresser about a recent trip to Dublin. After mentioning that a local acquaintance had taken us to some pubs to experience the pub life, the hairdresser, a member of a minority group that often suffers from negative stereotyping, commented, "They drink like fish there, don't they?"

Stereotypes can be created and perpetuated through the media. Koreans are often regarded as hard workers, sometimes even obsessively so. *Taxi,* a French film released in 2000, portrays two Korean taxi drivers who work as a pair and take turns driving while the other sleeps in the trunk. The stereotype conveyed is that of a people whose sole purpose in life is to earn money, regardless of the social and emotional costs. The American television series *Friends* depicts the antics of a group of mostly single friends living in New York City. These singles in their 20s and 30s live a carefree, glamorous, and rather hedonistic lifestyle, absorbed by their lives and by "major" crises that revolve around themselves, their friends, and their acquaintances, with no concern for the larger outside world and its events. Outsiders often believe that most, if not all, Americans live a similar lifestyle. When the film *Collateral Damage,* starring Arnold Schwarzenegger, opened in the United States, groups of Colombian American protestors surrounded movie theaters in New York City, Los Angeles, and other major cities. They felt that this movie went too far in perpetuating the stereotype of all Colombians as corrupt and involved in the drug trade.

Since people's stereotypes are based on their belief and attitude systems, they affect the way people communicate in cross-cultural encounters. Negative stereotypes may hinder or prevent effective communicative interactions between people of different backgrounds. Americans who have the perception that Arabs are argumentative will tend to approach conversational interactions with the attitude that little negotiation or acquiescence can take place with Arabs. The Americans will be more inclined to make demands than to make requests. The Japanese regard the United States as an extremely informal culture, the opposite of their own. This often results in the inappropriate use of informal language or slang by the Japanese. When meeting the academic dean of an American university, a Japanese student may greet the dean with "Whatcha doing?" Such communicative behavior can be thought to be based on a Japanese speaker's stereotype of the informal American, which may lead the speaker to remain unaware of the more formal greeting required by this social context.

Speakers often resort to negative stereotypes to help explain the behavior of people different from themselves. Rather than attributing different, unusual, or unacceptable communicative and social behaviors to differences in cultural worldviews, norms, values, and mores, speakers will attribute these behaviors to the personality of the other person. **(See Activity D—Stereotype or Not?)**

Attribution

The process by which people explain another person's behavior by referring to their own experiences, values, and beliefs is called *attribution*. According to Heider (1958), people try to make sense of the world around them and to make it more predictable by making inferences about the reasons behind observed behavior. In other words, individuals attempt to "explain" behaviors by attributing causes or reasons to their own behaviors and to those of others. To give meaning to observed behavior, people draw on the personal experiences they have developed throughout a lifetime of living and interacting as a member of their culture. When the experiential backgrounds of people are different, misunderstandings often occur because of differences in perceptions of and interpretations of the actions of the speakers, the social context, and even the physical environment. In cross-cultural situations, people attempt to attribute the behavior of someone from another culture to inappropriate behavior rather than to the adherence to culturally different belief and attitude systems. Discrepancies in attribution may result in misunderstandings, rejection, conflict, and hostility.

Differences in table manners are a case in point. Each culture has clear expectations of what is acceptable and permissible and what is not. Table manners are not merely simple behavior patterns but communicate symbolic messages and encode social events (Cooper, 1986; Douglas, 1975). Learning table etiquette is an integral part of the enculturation process, and members of a culture are generally unaware of just how culture-specific and subconscious table manners are. Yet a person's behavior at the table can make a significant difference in the way one is perceived by others. In some cultures, for instance, it is imperative to show one's pleasure with the meal by burping loudly after finishing. The very same action is highly stigmatized and castigated in other cultures, where burping loudly is indicative of poor taste and bad manners. Another case in point is eye contact. Japanese people do not make prolonged eye contact in negotiating situations. Members of North American and most northern European cultures, who are accustomed to making eye contact with participants in communicative situations, may feel uncomfortable and/or annoyed when negotiating with Japanese.

Differences in manner of dress, nonverbal behavior, and communicative interaction patterns can also lead to false conclusions. Female American and Canadian exchange students in small towns in Latin America at times experience disapproval from their host families for their "fast" behavior. From the host families' perspective, making eye contact with males, going to bars or saloons, and wearing tops with spaghetti straps and/or short shorts are sexual signals for enticing men, rather than part of everyday behavior and dress.

Although less common now than previously, non-Japanese schoolchildren attending Japanese schools have often been perceived as being poor students, troublemakers, or even juvenile delinquents simply by virtue of not having the "correct" hair and eye color. Today, more and more Japanese teenagers dye their hair and wear color contacts, but these teens tend to be regarded warily and to have negative behavior traits attributed to them. Conformity in all areas, including hair, eye color, and uniforms at school and at work, have traditionally been regarded as indicators of harmony and unity in Japanese society.

A student of ours recounts an eye-opening experience she had with a German friend and a case of mistaken attribution.

> The first several times that Dieter and I hung out in New York, I noticed that any time he would pay for something, he always put the money on the counter and never in the cashier's hand. On several of these occasions, I also noticed the cashiers being a little annoyed by him not placing the money into their hands, especially when their hands are out waiting for the money to be placed in them. I became so annoyed with this because in the majority of these occasions, the cashiers were persons of color, and I did not want to interpret it as Dieter's prejudice of not wanting to touch their hands. Moreover, I was doubly offended because I did not know why he was friends with me, since I am a "person of color." I know that when I think about my own Black culture, it has historically been a form of disrespect shown to the "lowly" Black person not to place money in their hands. It was as though they did not want to physically touch his hand as though he was diseased. They always placed things on the counter

so that he had to do the double-duty of picking up every single piece of change they put down, as opposed to if they would have just placed it in his hands to save time.

Later, when I went to visit Dieter in Germany I saw that everyone placed the money on the counter and that there was always a little plastic dish to put the money on. In fact, a couple of times cashiers told me to put the change in the dish and not give it to them so that they could count it faster! It was only then I realized that I was attributing something very negative to his behavior because of my own cultural and ethnic background.

As the preceding anecdote illustrates, our own cultural background subconsciously influences our expectations such that we are often not aware that our judgments are formed not on the basis of objective facts but through attribution.

Culture shock

A common experience that members of one culture have upon entering another culture is *culture shock* (see chap. 3). Culture shock occurs when people interact with members of a different culture and experience the feeling of a loss of control. It occurs when a person's expectations do not coincide with—and indeed conflict with—a different cultural reality. It includes phenomena ranging from mild annoyance to extreme psychological anxiety. Shock is the reaction people experience when they are confronted with the unknown and the different. People respond to specific stimuli in their environment and expect others to behave in culturally appropriate ways that frequently differ from those to which members of the host culture are accustomed to behaving. When individuals are in a different cultural environment and are confronted with people whom they feel behave unpredictably or inappropriately, they feel a loss of control (Hall, 1959, 1976; Triandis, 1994). Because such cross-cultural encounters challenge an individual's subconscious sense of persona, they are a constant threat to one's sense of well-being and feeling of control. **(See Activity E—Different Eyes)**

Factors that foster culture shock include the degree of an individual's sense of ethnocentrism; tendency to stereotype; low levels of similarity in beliefs, values, norms, and attitudes; and misinterpretations of the behaviors and intentions of members from the other cultural group.

Individuals undergoing culture shock experience a wide range of emotions, including frustration, hostility, unhappiness, feelings of isolation and loneliness, anxiety, and homesickness. They filter their cultural experiences in the new environment through a feeling of resentment and alternate between being angry with others for not understanding them and being filled with self-pity (Brown, 2000:183).

Pragmatics and Discourse

Language and communication are more than words and grammar; they are also a reflection of the cultural and social context of the speakers. Language does not occur in isolation; speakers use it to convey meanings that go beyond words. The type of speech (e.g., formal vs. informal), the choice of words, the linguistic forms used to convey messages, and speakers' tone of voice are elements of communication that speakers can manipulate to convey social status, attitudes, politeness, and so on. How speakers convey messages is as important as the actual verbal communication itself. In English, the comment "It's just about lunchtime" can refer to the actual time of the day. It could also be construed as an indirect request for something to eat or as an indirect invitation inviting the hearer to join the speaker for lunch. The actual import of the words can only be interpreted within the context in which they were uttered, yet an accurate interpretation of this utterance is also dependent on speakers sharing the same pragmatic understanding, or rules of speaking. These rules of speaking govern how speakers say what, to whom, when, where, and under what circumstances (Hymes, 1972).

Pragmatics, the study of how language is used in communication, encompasses a broad range of phenomena, including the functions of language, the rules of discourse, and the structure and appropriateness of communicative interactions. Pragmatics concerns itself primarily with the communicative intent of speakers, that is, with what meaning speakers are actually trying to convey to their listeners. The focus is not so much on form but on the import speakers are conveying via the spoken or written word. *Pragmatic competence* is viewed as the ability of interlocutors to participate effectively and appropriately in communicative interactions. This competence generally includes a person's knowledge of such factors as social context; social variables, including status, gender, and age of the interlocutors; and cultural knowledge, including politeness codes and nonverbal cues (see chap. 6). Researchers have contended that learning the organizational rules of a second language is almost simple compared to the complexity of trying to understand the complete scope of pragmatic behavior (e.g., Boxer, 1993; Brown, 2000; Ellis, 1994; Kasper & Kellerman, 1997).

In American English, it is common to end a conversation with "See you later" or "We'll have to get together some time." Such phrases are intended not as actual commitments to meeting the other speaker but, rather, as a way of showing camaraderie and solidarity with that speaker. To actually arrange a meeting, speakers must engage in a series of steps, which allow either speaker to withdraw at any point from making an actual commitment (Wolfson, D'Amico-Reisner, & Huber, 1983). Nonnative speakers unfamiliar with the underlying meaning of such utterances and/or the negotiation processes involved are likely to take such utterances at face value (see chap. 6). Then, when native speakers do not show commitment to what the nonnative speakers have interpreted as actual engagements, the nonnative speakers become offended, hurt, and/or insulted, which often leads them to negatively label Americans as insincere. **(See Activity F—Critical Incidents)**

Chinese speakers often greet each other with "Have you eaten?" Native speakers of English, accustomed to "How are you?" are taken aback and unsure of how to respond to this question. For Chinese speakers, the phrase "Have you eaten?" provides a way of showing concern and consideration toward their listeners. It has a pragmatic or social meaning that cannot be taken literally; however, when they use this phrase in English, the cultural and social contexts underlying the pragmatic meaning no longer apply, and the listeners will misinterpret both the intent and the meaning of the utterance. Because so much of communication is part of the cultural and social context of the speakers, the opportunities for cross-cultural misunderstandings and misinterpretations are great. The rules of speaking vary greatly across cultures, across ethnic groups, and across speech communities. **(See Activity G—Simulation: The Milapalanders)**

High/low context

The anthropologist Hall (1976) has distinguished between two broad types of cultural communication styles, high context and low context. While these are broad generalizations, research indicates that cultures tend to fall along a continuum of high context versus low context (e.g., Gao & Ting-Toomey, 1998; Okabe, 1983; Yoshikawa, 1988).

High-context communication occurs in cultures that emphasize communication through the context of the social interaction (e.g., speakers' social roles, gender, age, status, and other variables deemed important by the culture) and the physical environment in which the interaction is taking place. High-context communication makes extensive use of subtle nonverbal behaviors—including pauses, silences, the use of space, and avoidance of eye contact—to convey a message. Much of the actual message is left unsaid or implied, and it is up to the speakers to understand the implicit information being imparted. The message itself is dependent on the context within which it is being delivered, and it can only be understood or interpreted within that context. Hall notes that high-context communication styles tend to be found in homogeneous cultures, such as China or Japan, with a long shared history. In such cultures, there is enough shared knowledge, values, and background to allow for speakers' tacit sharing and exchange of information.

Low-context communication takes place in cultures that stress communication via explicit verbal messages. Communication is regarded as an independent act performed between speakers and their listeners. Speakers and listeners are seen as autonomous individuals whose relationship to one another is primarily derived from and defined through verbal messages. Although social context and physical environment influence communication in low-context cultures, the primary responsibility for ensuring that listeners correctly receive and interpret verbal messages rests on speakers. Direct verbal modes of communication are preferred, and elaborated messages are the norm. It is up to speakers to ensure effective communication by conveying their messages as clearly, as thoroughly, as logically, and as persuasively as possible. Low-context communication styles are generally found in more individualistic cultures, such as Italy or North America, as these tend to focus more on the individual and to have less of a common history.

Nonverbal Behavior

When communicating, speakers use more than spoken words to convey meaning. A great deal of information is expressed nonverbally. Indeed, some researchers have suggested that what speakers communicate nonverbally exceeds what they communicate verbally and more accurately reflects speakers' actual feelings, emotions, and thoughts (e.g., Hall, 1959). The most important part of a communication may not necessarily be what speakers actually say but how they convey that message through body language (kinesics), eye contact (gaze), the use of interpersonal space (proxemics), or other nonverbal cues. While all speakers exhibit some sort of nonverbal behavior, how much and what types they use and in which situations they use it vary cross-culturally.

In general, individualistic cultures allow greater use of and have a greater range of nonverbal behaviors, while collectivistic cultures encourage more restricted exhibition and use of nonverbal behaviors. Moreover, each culture has its own specific nonverbal behaviors, which can be misunderstood or misinterpreted by members of other cultures who interpret these nonverbal behavior patterns according to the rules and norms of their own culture. Cultural competence is clearly more than merely understanding the intricacies of bowing in Japan, the inappropriateness of accepting food with the left hand in Saudi Arabia, or any other "foreign" nonverbal behavior. It is first and foremost the ability to recognize our own cultural orientations and those of others and the impact that these differences have on our intercultural interactions (see chap. 4).

Cross-Cultural Communication Difficulties

Communication and culture are inextricably linked. Language and culture are inseparable (Hall & Hall, 1989; Risager, 1999; Ting-Toomey, 1999). No culture exists without some form of communication. Although some cultures may not have written forms of communication, all have verbal forms. Communication is a process between two or more speakers that involves feedback, verification of messages, mutual understanding, and corroboration of intent. Cross-cultural communication involves contact between individuals who identify themselves as distinct from one another in such cultural terms as underlying values, worldviews, and social organization. Since communication is the sharing of meanings and the negotiating of outcomes, speakers of different cultures must learn to successfully negotiate shared meanings that result in positive outcomes in a communicative interaction.

Effective cross-cultural communication depends on speakers' awareness of the language and culture of each other. Because communication involves much more than just the exchange of words, speakers must also be aware of the larger social picture of any social interaction. Such knowledge allows speakers to understand better the responses of speakers from another culture in specific communicative situations. For cross-cultural communication to occur with a minimum of misunderstanding and a maximum of information exchange, understanding one's own culturally influenced behavior and thought processes and those of the speakers of the other culture is essential. This entails both perceiving the similarities and differences in other cultures and also recognizing the constructs of one's own culture, or as Hall (1966) puts it, our own "hidden culture." **(See Activity H—The Grapevine)**

Cultural differences in the ways in which speakers of different cultures communicate can create barriers to effective communication. Associated behaviors such as stereotyping and prejudice increase barriers in cross-cultural communication. To promote effective cross-cultural communication, speakers need to explore their own and others' cultural beliefs, values, norms, and communicative styles to avoid misunderstandings and misinterpretations. For speakers to be able to function, they need to learn how to assess the communicative setting of different cultures and their concomitantly different social systems. Without cross-cultural awareness, speakers will find it difficult to communicate with people of other cultures, because they will interpret communicative interactions solely from within the framework of their own culture.

Take, for instance, the notion of *conflict*. Conflict among human beings—whether petty disagreements among siblings or larger clashes between nations—is normal. However, the acceptability and pervasiveness of conflict varies from culture to culture. In English, the mere term *conflict* inherently carries a negative connotation, and much effort is expended in the United States to avoid or contain conflict, whether in interpersonal relationships, in the workplace, or among social and/or ethnic groups. Throughout elementary and secondary education, workshops and classes are offered to help students learn conflict management and conflict resolution. In Greek culture, however, conflict is not considered necessarily wrong, bad, or harmful. Conflict often provides Greeks with stimulation, personal satisfaction, a chance to build self-esteem and self-identity, and the opportunity to strengthen in-group relationships and solidarity (Broome, 1999; Tannen & Kakava, 1992). **(See Activity I—Knowing Another Language)**

To communicate effectively requires certain knowledge—including, but not limited to, speakers' knowledge of social roles and relationships, perceptions of personal and cultural identity, and the communicative goals of an interaction. Since cultural knowledge is built up through years of socialization and enculturation, a newcomer cannot expect to learn everything there is to know immediately. Successful cross-cultural communication is an intricate process, an essential part of which is learning how to observe, evaluate, interpret, and, when necessary, emulate the behavior of others. Once individuals have learned how to gather and process appropriate cultural information, it becomes easier for them to avoid cross-cultural communication misunderstandings (see chap. 6).

Teaching and Learning Connections

The impact of cultural background and tradition on teaching and learning in classrooms throughout the world is rather revealing. Classroom research by Scollon (1999) has shown that different participation structures exist in the classrooms of Chinese students in Hong Kong compared to those in Western classrooms and that these differences are attributed to differing philosophical assumptions regarding communication, teaching, and learning. Her work suggests that Western and Chinese teachers and students have a different way of negotiating their roles within these frameworks. For example, when a teacher is teaching, the Chinese student's role is that of listener. When the physical movement of a teacher indicates that class is over, the Chinese student assumes the role of bystander. In neither case is the Chinese student's role that of participant. Thus, Western teachers of Chinese students must understand the contrasting traditions of Confucian and Socratic discourse and the impact of these differing traditions on teaching and learning practices. Otherwise, teachers may misinterpret the lack of feedback by Chinese and other students influenced by Confucian discourse traditions as an indication that students are unreceptive to the teachers and their lessons.

Improved intercultural communication occurs when we approach other cultures with a frame of mind that is open and free from unbending and biased perceptions or stereotypes. Since human beings have a psychological need and tendency to categorize, they apply their preconceptions either to everybody or to just one person. When individuals oversimplify, overgeneralize, or even exaggerate, they are no longer successful communicators. They have created an inaccurate picture of those with whom they are interacting, and subsequently problems arise. Alerting students to the pitfalls of such comments and guiding them through focused activities to help them avoid these hazards will be beneficial. Generating in students an even greater awareness of the varied components of culture can be achieved through introspective readings, role plays, explorations of mass media, and other resources. Through such means, students will be better prepared for their encounters with other cultures, whether in the classroom, the society, or the world.

Questions for Study and Discussion

1. Explain the differences between individualistic and collectivistic cultures. What original examples can you provide?

2. We describe the term *nepotism* as carrying a negative connotation and as referring to a behavior regarded as a vice in American and Canadian cultures. Do you agree with this assessment? Does this and related terms carry the same meaning in other cultures you are familiar with? Why or why not? Can you think of any other terms that have different connotations cross-culturally?

3. Your neighbor has just informed you that he has received three job offers since graduating college, all through the help of his uncle. How would you react to your neighbor's news? Why do you think you might react this way? Which cultural values do you think would influence your reaction?

4. Identify the major differences between polychronic and mono-chronic time. Which type of time applies best to you? When you consider yourself within the larger context of your culture and/or subcultures, would you consider your concept and use of time a reflection of your culture? Why or why not?

5. What does "saving face" mean? When, in your experience, has it been important to save face? What conflicts have you experienced between your notion of saving face and the notions of others?

6. Reflect on the statement "To some extent, everyone is ethnocentric." What personal examples can you provide to support this statement?

7. Define stereotypes. What are some stereotypes, both positive and negative, that people have about members of other cultures? Give actual examples.

8. Explain attribution. How are differences in table manners a case in point? Imagine you are at a formal dinner. How would you hold your eating utensils, where would you place your napkin, how would you eat your soup, and how would you indicate to your host that you had had enough to eat? How did you learn what is "right" or "proper" and what isn't?

9. Discuss Hall's (1976) high-context and low-context communication styles. How do they differ? How would you describe your communication style? Why?

10. Give three suggestions for promoting effective cross-cultural communication. Discuss why and how you think these suggestions would be helpful.

III. Practice: What Activities Show Us

A. Cross-Cultural Trivia Quiz (15–20 minutes)

When individuals attempt to function effectively in another culture, they often encounter cross-cultural adjustment strains. These strains range from having to learn new culturally appropriate behaviors to having to make decisions about situations without adequate cultural information. Being culturally unaware often leads to inappropriate or unexpected behavior that results in cultural misunderstandings.

Purpose: To increase understanding of cross-cultural differences

Procedure:

1. Prepare copies of a cross-cultural trivia quiz. Use the quiz provided here (quiz 1) or make up your own.

2. Pass out the quiz and ask the participants to respond to each item with *true* or *false.*

3. After everyone has finished, discuss the responses.

   Sample Questions:

   • Did you choose *true* or *false?* Why?

   • What underlying cultural values or beliefs influenced your choices?

   • In which cultures would the responses differ? Why?

Quiz 1. Cross-Cultural Trivia

True   False   1. Tipping a certain percentage is an appropriate—indeed, expected—action for certain types of service, such as taxi transportation or table serving.

True   False   2. Saying "maybe" often means no.

True   False   3. Showing up an hour or so after the appointed time is appropriate.

True   False   4. Students should not question their teachers.

True   False   5. Great concern for personal hygiene manifests itself in elaborate daily rituals involving the cleansing of various areas of the body.

True   False   6. Handing someone something with the left hand is inappropriate.

True   False   7. Smiling is a way of signaling embarrassment or releasing tension.

True   False   8. Group cooperation and mutual help are encouraged and expected in many classroom activities but are condemned and often punished in test-taking situations.

True   False   9. Corporal punishment in the classroom is acceptable.

True   False   10. When you attend a dinner party, it is appropriate to bring your host a gift of wine.

 I, A

To adapt for the language classroom,

Writing a Cross-Cultural Trivia Quiz

- Since the purpose of cross-cultural trivia quizzes is to address different areas of potential cultural misunderstandings, you may want to develop your own quiz choices based on your students, their language proficiency, and your teaching situation. For example, if there are concerns at your school regarding respect or tolerance, you may want to develop questions on this topic.

Cross-Cultural Triva Quiz: Teacher Choices Intermediate/Advanced
Shouting out the answer without waiting to be called on by the teacher is not acceptable.
When participating in group work, the oldest male student should be the one to present the results to the rest of the class.

- Alternatively, you may choose to adapt the quiz choices provided by simplifying the language.

Cross-Cultural Trivia Quiz: Adapted Choices
Hitting students with a ruler in the classroom is acceptable.
OR
Teachers can hit students with a ruler when they are not behaving.

- In preparing a cross-cultural trivia quiz, it is important to focus on choices that reveal underlying values, beliefs, attitudes, and norms.

Discussion of the Quiz

1. In the United States, service workers expect and often depend on tips of 15–20 percent of the total bill. In some cultures, tips are automatically included in the total bill; in others, no tip at all is expected; in others, a tip of 10 percent may be more appropriate.

2. In collectivistic cultures, members generally avoid face-threatening situations by employing strategies that avoid confrontational or direct language such as saying no.

3. Time is relative. Hall (1983) distinguishes between mono-chronic and polychronic time. Northern European cultures (including North America) focus on doing one thing at a time and adhering to a timetable; hence, they are monochronic. Many other cultures focus on involving people and finishing transactions rather than on adhering to a timetable; they are polychronic.

4. In some cultures, teachers are viewed as authority figures and experts in their field. Students never question or challenge their teaching by asking questions.

5. In some cultures, such as the United States, people are sensitive to body odor and regard it as extremely offensive and unacceptable.

6. In some cultures, the left hand is reserved for body functions and is never used for serving, eating, or passing things.

7. Cultures use laughter and smiling for different purposes.

8. In many cultures, group work on tests is viewed not as cooperative work but as cheating or plagiarism. In other cultures, helping friends or colleagues is an acceptable practice because you are assisting members of your group.

9. In some cultures, corporal punishment is regarded as a form of abuse. In others, it is looked on as an appropriate means of discipline.

10. Some cultures expect gifts in such situations; others do not. Related issues include what kind of gift is appropriate and what the approximate value of the gift should be.

B. Proverbs (15–20 minutes)

Proverbs are timeless. They have existed in many languages for centuries. In a few words proverbs capture the essence of what a culture holds important. Proverbs teach truisms or important cultural values that are passed from generation to generation. Understanding the meaning of a proverb means gaining insights into a culture, its value system, and its people. It is just as important to remember that while thousands of proverbs reflect specific cultural values, just as many proverbs address universal values.

Purpose: To understand how proverbs reflect cultural values

Procedure:

1. List about 10 American proverbs on the blackboard. Choose proverbs that reflect cultural values (e.g., "Haste makes waste"); avoid proverbs that express axioms (e.g., "The acorn does not fall far from the oak").

2. Explain that a proverb is a short, stylized folk saying expressing a truth, fact, or cultural value.

3. Instruct participants to write down the values that they see being taught by these proverbs. Allow 5–8 minutes.

4. Share results.

5. Prepare a new list of proverbs from other cultures (elicit student input if possible).

6. Instruct participants to write down the values that they see being taught by these proverbs. Allow 5–8 minutes.

7. Share results. Compare and contrast the second list of proverbs with the list of American proverbs.

   Sample Questions:

   • How could these proverbs affect classroom learning?

   • What do proverbs tell us about ourselves and about our values?

Sample American Proverbs

Proverb	Value Represented
Time is money.	Importance of time
A stitch in time saves nine.	Foresightedness
Early to bed and early to rise makes a man healthy, wealthy, and wise.	Industriousness, work ethic
A penny saved is a penny earned.	Thrift
An apple a day keeps the doctor away.	Foresightedness
Two wrongs do not make a right.	Honorableness, honesty
The early bird gets the worm.	Diligence
God helps those who help themselves.	Self-reliance, independence
Turn the other cheek.	Forgiveness
Waste not, want not.	Frugality
What is good for the goose is good for the gander.	Equality
It is not whether you win or lose but how you play the game.	Fairness
People who live in glass houses should not throw stones.	Being nonjudgmental, fairness
A fool and his money are soon parted.	Wisdom
They that dance must pay the fiddler.	Responsibility

Sample Proverbs from Around the World

Proverb	Provenance
The man who has bread to eat does not appreciate the severity of a famine.	African: Yoruba
The sheep separated from the flock is eaten by the wolf.	Turkish
An ox with long horns, even if he does not butt, will be accused of butting.	Malayan
One "no" averts seventy evils.	Indian
In a closed mouth, flies do not come in.	Spanish
As you cooked the porridge, so must you eat it.	Russian
If I keep a green bough in my heart, then the singing bird will come.	Chinese
He who puts up with insult invites injury.	Yiddish
Dwell not on thy weariness; thy strength shall be according to the measure of thy desire.	Arabic
The nail that sticks up is hammered down.	Japanese

- Are you familiar with other proverbs—from your own or another culture—that deal with the values under consideration here?

- Why are proverbs so timely?

- Do you know of any proverbs that you feel no longer reflect cultural values? Explain why.

Alternative:

1. Choose proverbs that reflect axioms rather than values. For example, the proverb "Let sleeping dogs lie" suggests that people should not disturb the status quo.

 I, A

To adapt for the language classroom,

Procedure: Step 5

5. Ask students to suggest proverbs from their cultures, and discuss these proverbs. In case students are unable to come up with their own, the teacher should have a list of proverbs from around the world. Some suggested Web sites for gathering proverbs follow.

   http://www.afriprov.org/

   http://www.creativeproverbs.com/

   http://www.famous-quotations.com/asp/origins.asp

   Sample Questions:

   - What do proverbs tell us about ourselves, our values, and our cultures?

   - Are there similarities in proverbs across cultures? If yes, what are they? If not, why not?

Alternative:

- The alternative is not recommended for the classroom.

C. Cultural Perceptions: *We and They* (5–10 minutes)

Stereotypes are stumbling blocks in cross-cultural communication that prevent individuals from objectively evaluating each other and the surrounding cultural context. Stereotyping can lead to false cultural hypotheses and problematic cross-cultural interaction. Stereotypes are blanket generalizations that attribute group characteristics to individuals based on their cultural membership. Although the individuals of a culture share certain core beliefs, assumptions of reality, and patterns of behavior, stereotyping devalues individuals and avoids recognizing their worth.

Purpose: To explore the influence of cultural assumptions on our understanding of others

Procedure:

1. Read Rudyard Kipling's poem *We and They*.

We and They
by
Rudyard Kipling

Father, Mother, and Me,
Sister and Auntie say
All the people like us are We,
And every one else is They.
And They live over the sea,
While We live over the way,
But—would you believe it?—They look upon We
As only a sort of They!

We eat pork and beef
With cow-horn-handled knives.
They who gobble Their rice off a leaf,
Are horrified out of Their lives;
And They who live up a tree,
And feast on grubs and clay,
(Isn't it scandalous?) look upon We
As a simply disgusting They!

. . . .

We eat kitcheny food.
We have doors that latch.
They drink milk or blood,
Under an open thatch.
We have Doctors to fee.
They have Wizards to pay.
And (impudent heathen!) They look upon We
As a quite impossible They!

All good people agree,
And all good people say,
All nice people, like Us, are We
And every one else is They:
But if you cross over the sea,
Instead of over the way,
You may end by (think of it!) looking on We
As only a sort of They!

2. Work in groups of 3–4. Discuss the reactions to this poem.

3. As a full group, compare and contrast the comments generated.

   Sample Questions:

   • What cultural elements (e.g., what values, beliefs, norms, mores, and attitudes) are addressed in the poem?

   • How does Kipling convey ethnocentrism? For example, what kind of word choices does he use?

   • How do our cultural attitudes affect how we perceive people from different cultures? Write on this subject for 4–5 minutes.

4. Reflect on an experience you had that challenged your cultural assumptions.

5. In groups of 3–4 share your reflections.

D. Stereotype or Not? (15–20 minutes)

How we ascribe characteristics to different cultural and ethnic groups and what these characteristics are depend largely on our beliefs, attitudes, values, expectations, and worldviews. The perceptions that we develop of others in the lifelong enculturation process can be both positive and negative; these perceptions continue to be reinforced by our interactions with others.

Purpose: To gain a better understanding of stereotypes held in our own culture and in the cultures of others

Procedure:

1. As a full group, discuss the following list.

Mexicans	Italians	Californians	Japanese	Germans
Nigerians	Buddhists	New Yorkers	Parisians	South Africans
Chinese	Arabs	Brazilians	Iranians	British
Moroccans	Australians	Russians	Colombians	Vietnamese

Sample Questions:

- What stereotypes are associated with each group of people on the list?

- Where do these stereotypes come from?

- Based on your knowledge of different cultures, do you know if these stereotypes differ cross-culturally? For example, do Chinese have the same stereotypes of Italians that Moroccans do?

2. List at least three examples of stereotypes. These may be quotations, oversimplified concepts, opinions, media images, and/or anecdotes based on personal experience. They do not have to come from within the United States or Canada. Discuss the following points.

- Why you feel each example conveys a stereotype

- Which (if any) cultural variables are involved

- The role each example plays in maintaining and/or perpetuating stereotypes

- How obvious/subtle the stereotyping is

- How each example reflects a (sub)culture's values, beliefs, ethnocentrism

E. Different Eyes (15–20 minutes for first session; for second session, 3–5 minutes per participant)

Societies have different cultural artifacts. Generally, when we think of cultural artifacts, we think of such things as buildings, clothing, jewelry, and eating utensils. Such artifacts are obvious and readily apparent to outsiders, who have little difficulty in recognizing and accepting differences in architectural or clothing styles. Yet there are other artifacts of common everyday use found in one culture that are enigmatic to outsiders. When exposed to such artifacts, outsiders are oblivious to their use and may even find them shocking.

Purpose: To illustrate that what may be obvious and mundane to someone in one culture may be completely puzzling to someone from another culture

Procedure:

1. Read the following paragraph written by a German. It describes an item the Germans received in American care packages sent after World War II.

2. Guess what item the writer is describing. The answer appears at the end of this activity.

There were . . . one-handed American boxing gloves [in the box]. On their back they had a kind of pocket that was obviously designed for a hand. There were spaces for fingers and the whole thing fit like an enlarged, padded, expanded palm. The elongated fingers were attached to one another by a system of strings and, furthermore, the gloves could be worn on one hand only—there were no pairs. We tried everything—there was nothing that made any sense. Finally, frustrated we decided that . . . boxing was done one-handed, palm open, and by trying to slap the opponent's face while wearing one of these gloves. We even tried to stage . . . "boxing" contests, but it never really caught on. (*Wall Street Journal,* Monday, August 10, 1992, A14)

3. Choose an item of common everyday use.

4. Describe it as an archaeologist who discovers this object 200 years from now. The writing should mimic the style of the preceding reading.

Alternatives:

- Bring in various objects most likely unfamiliar to the group. Ask participants to describe the objects and their possible uses. Items that have worked successfully include a decorated Mexican beater for preparing hot chocolate, an egg punch from Germany for puncturing eggs before boiling, a slide rule, a French poultry wing cutter, and a Chinese earwax cleaner.

- Ask participants either to choose an item they have encountered from another culture or, if they are from another culture, to describe an object from their culture as in step 4 and have the others attempt to guess the use or purpose of the artifact. Items that have been used include Japanese handkerchiefs an American believed to be oddly shaped scarves, oranges served at the end of a Chinese wedding banquet to indicate its end, and finger bowls for rinsing fingers at the table.

Follow-up:

- Read and comment on the following article, which portrays an "exotic" culture from the point of view of an anthropologist.

  Miner, Horace. 1956. Body ritual among the Nacirema. *American Anthropologist, 58,* 503–507. (Reprinted in *Crossing cultures,* by Henry Knepler & Myrna Knepler, Eds., 1987, New York: Macmillan.) Available on the Web at http://www.stanford.edu/~davidf/nacirema.html.

A

To adapt for the language classroom,

Procedure: Steps 3 and 4
This activity lends itself well to a writing exercise. Teachers can have students work on this individually or in pairs.

3. Bring in an item of common everyday use such as a can opener (either electric or manual), an electric toothbrush, a pepper mill, or a cell phone.

4. Ask students to write a paragraph of 5–10 sentences about this item. They should pretend to be an archaeologist who discovers this object 200 years in the future.

Alternative:

• Ask students to describe an object from their own country that is most likely unfamiliar to other members of the class. Students should try to guess what that object is used for.

ANSWER: The answer to step 2 is a baseball mitt.

F. Critical Incidents (15–20 minutes)

The following critical incidents are exercises focusing on an area of cross-cultural conflict or miscommunication. The situation described in each incident presents a problem related to differences in cultural values and beliefs. There are no right or wrong answers in this exercise; the point of the exercise is to stimulate thought-provoking discussion based on the incidents. The goal of considering critical incidents is to increase awareness of and sensitivity to cultural differences and to recognize differences between personal and cultural beliefs.

Purpose: To expand awareness of differences in underlying cultural values and beliefs

Procedure:

1. Prepare different sets of two to four critical incidents. How many sets you prepare will depend on the total number of participants (e.g., for a group of 12 participants, prepare four sets).

2. Break into small groups.

3. Pass out the sets of critical incidents, and ask participants to brainstorm possible solutions.

4. As a full group, discuss the critical incidents, possible solutions, and the cultural values underlying the areas of cultural conflict.

5. Discuss how some of the critical incidents relate to participants' experiences.

6. Write your own critical incident. Share this with a partner or the full group.

Critical Incident 1

There are several students in your class with body odor. A number of other students have complained about this to you. In addition, a number of other students have made disparaging remarks about these particular students.

Critical Incident 2

A student had been acting out in class, so you sent home a note about this problem to the parents. Several days later, you discover that the student has marks all along his arms and neck. Apparently, his parents physically punished him for misbehaving in class.

Critical Incident 3

The students in your class range from 18 to 50 years of age. Several of the older students have indicated to you that they think they should be in a more advanced class because they are older and that they don't like working with such young students. At the same time, several of the younger students have let you know that they find it very uncomfortable to be in class together with older students.

Critical Incident 4

Several Middle Eastern students who are outspoken and combative are in your class. There are also several Asian students who never seem to be able to speak up before they are interrupted by the Middle Eastern students.

Critical Incident 5

Giving tests seems to be your most frustrating classroom activity. No matter what you have said about plagiarism, many of your students seem to work hardest at cheating.

Critical Incident 6

An Asian student in a mainstream class was having difficulty understanding the teacher. One day, after class, the student went to the teacher to ask him to please slow down the pace of the class. The teacher responded that he really could not do this but that he would try to help her. In the next class, the teacher announced that the student was having problems in class and asked whether anyone could lend her some notes to copy from. The Asian student was mortified and felt she could never face the teacher or her classmates again.

Critical Incident 7

Professor Jones is discussing Roberto with a colleague. Professor Jones states that she cannot connect with Roberto, perhaps because they have nothing in common. She comments, "Roberto is getting a C in the course, which is good for him; it is a difficult class." Professor Jones also expresses concern that Roberto does not take advantage of office hours.

Critical Incident 8

A group of foreign students attend a basketball game at the college where they are currently studying. While watching the game, the referee makes what they consider a bad call, so they start whistling loudly. A young professor turns to them and says, "Hey, what's the matter with you?" Two of the students reply, "Nothing, what's the matter with you?" The professor replies, "I'll see you two at the dean's office at 8 A.M. Monday morning." The students he addressed begin to laugh. The young professor then adds: "I was only kidding before, but now I mean it. You better be there Monday morning."

Discussion

Critical Incident 1
Cultures view body odor differently. Some cultures believe that members of meat-eating cultures exude a very offensive body odor compared to vegetarian cultures. Members of some cultures place a high value on heavily perfumed bodies, whereas others find that practice distasteful.

Critical Incident 2
In many societies, corporal punishment is regarded not as child abuse but as an appropriate and accepted means of discipline. In the United States, however, such punishment is looked down on and, in some cases, even regarded as illegal.

Critical Incident 3
In many cultures, age commands respect. It is inconceivable in such a culture to promote a younger employee over an older one, regardless of ability. Likewise, it is difficult to mix large ranges in age-groups in language classrooms, because of potential face-threatening situations, particularly when younger students perform better than older ones.

Critical Incident 4
Appropriate classroom behavior and attitudes toward teachers and fellow students vary greatly among cultures. What may be viewed as re-

spectful in one culture may be considered disrespectful in others. Students considered reserved in one culture may be considered uninvolved in another. Students considered verbal in one culture may be looked on as aggressive in another.

Critical Incident 5
In the English language, *cheating* is a value-laden term that connotes dishonesty. In some cultures, cheating is viewed not as a dishonest act but as an obligation of a member of a group to help the other members of the group. It is another way to assist your group by beating the system (the adversary).

Critical Incident 6
The notion of face, or how others regard one, is of key importance in some cultures. Members of such a culture go to great length to avoid drawing attention to themselves or their actions. Direct actions and confrontations are avoided, and indirect strategies are preferred.

Critical Incident 7
A common problem is the feeling of distance between people of different cultures. People with this problem find it difficult to accept others and may also have low expectations of nonnative speakers' academic abilities because of their accents and relative lack of language facility.

Critical Incident 8
There are several issues at play here. For one, the foreign students may not have recognized the young professor as being a professor. It is very likely that he was dressed down and looked like an older student. In many countries, professors do not attend college sports, if these even exist. For another, there is the matter of appropriate language. The foreign students may lack the communicative competence to recognize that the reply "Nothing, what's the matter with you?" is inappropriate in this situation. Finally, in some cultures, laughter indicates embarrassment rather than rudeness or mockery.

 I, A

To adapt for the language classroom,

Writing Critical Incidents

- Since the purpose of critical incidents is to heighten cross-cultural awareness, you may want to develop your own incidents based on your students, their language proficiency, and your teaching situation. Alternatively, you may choose to adapt the critical incidents provided by simplifying the language or altering some of the conditions, as in the example that follows.

Critical Incident 1 Adapted

There are several students in your class who smell bad. Some students are complaining about them to you. Other students are saying unkind things about the bad-smelling students.

G. Simulation: The Milapalanders (25–30 minutes)

Although basic concepts are universal, cultures view these differently. This leads members of cultural groups to behave in a manner that outsiders may find inconceivable, irrational, or diametrically opposed to what they consider sacred. Very few people understand that culture serves as a road map for behavior. Culture influences and structures members' perceptual processes such that they develop culturally motivated frames of reference. Problems in cross-cultural communication are caused by conflicting frames of reference.

Purpose: To experience miscommunication based on a lack of shared customs, traditions, and values

Procedure:

1. Divide the full group in half. Try to have an equal number of males and females in each group.

2. Leave the room with one-half of the participants. This group will be "the visitors."

3. Give this group the background information and instructions that follow, orally.

Group 1: The Visitors

You have been hired by the board of directors of a major philanthropic organization to go to Milapaland for the purpose of determining how the foundation can best help the people of that underdeveloped nation. The foundation has large resources—monetary resources, technical resources, and expertise—and is willing to do whatever it can to help Milapalanders improve their lot. Specifically, your job is to find out from the Milapalanders what they think is needed most for whom and where; among their needs are, for example, more schools in rural areas, family planning programs, nutrition improvement for children, health programs for impoverished families in urban and rural areas, medical services, scholarship awards for young Milapalanders to study technical fields abroad, more development of heavy industry, and so on.

---

4. Have "the visitors" remain outside the room, where they cannot hear what is said in the classroom.

5. Return to those in the classroom. This group will be "the Milapalanders."

6. Give this group the background information and instructions that follow orally.

Group 2: The Milapalanders

A group of information seekers has come to your country on behalf of a major philanthropic organization to determine how best to help your nation. Unfortunately, the information seekers do not know the following rules of conduct for your culture, which restrict how, when, and to whom you are able to give information.

Milapalanderan Rules of Conduct

1. Yes/no questions must always be answered "yes."

2. Males are only allowed to interact with females if the former are older than the latter.

3. Females are only allowed to interact with males if the former are younger than the latter.

4. Milapalanders never look their interlocutors in the eye. The appropriate positioning of the eyes is to focus on something to the right of and past the speaker's face.

5. Milapalanders always indirectly respond to wh-questions *(who? what? when? where? why? how?)* with a story about nature, dead ancestors, god, outside forces, and so on.

6. Milapalanders greet people of the same sex by shaking the other person's hand with both of their hands several times.

7. When both groups are clear about their roles, invite "the visitors" back to the classroom.

8. Let the two groups intermingle with one another for about 8–10 minutes.

9. When the time is up, ask "the visitors" to report what they learned about the Milapalanders and their needs.

10. When "the visitors" have finished, ask "the Milapalanders" to respond to the comments of "the visitors."

11. Discuss the comments of the two groups.

Sample Questions:

- What did those who were outsiders to the Milapaland culture experience?

- What did those who were Milapalanders experience?

- How did you feel during the activity?

- What did you find strange and/or difficult? Why?

- Why did misunderstandings and/or misinterpretations occur?

- How do we develop explanations for people's behavior?

- How would you apply this experience to your own past cultural encounters?

- What insights have you gained from this exercise in terms of your interacting with people of other groups/cultures?

- What from your experiences in this activity can you extrapolate to cross-cultural communication in general?

Alternatives:

- If the group is all of the same sex, rules 2 and 3 of the Milapalanderan rules of conduct can be altered to reflect age—for example, a younger female can never address an older female first.

- If the group is very large, divide into three groups. Have one group not participate in the simulation but act as observers and notetakers. They can then add their observations during the discussion.

Adapted from an activity entitled "The Outside Expert" by P. Pedersen.

H. The Grapevine (30–35 minutes)

Personal experiences and cultural background shape people. Culture frames how they see and interpret the world. Communication is more than the mere exchange of messages. Messages and responses to them occur in cultural contexts and are uttered by people with unique experiences. People can better understand the behavior and reactions of others if they realize that what they hear and see is filtered through cultural lenses.

Purpose: To gain an awareness of how events are filtered through one's language and cultural experiences

Procedure:

1. Ask for five volunteers and assign each volunteer a number from 1 to 5.

2. Have four of these volunteers step out of the room to an area where they cannot overhear what is taking place in the classroom.

3. Turn on a tape recorder and read the sample reading that follows or a similar reading to the one volunteer who has remained in the room. The story itself is not important. You may choose a story of your own, as long as it includes opinion (e.g., "I thought," "I felt") and information that can lead to generalizations and stereotyping.

4. Turn off the tape recorder.

5. Have volunteer 2 return to the room.

6. Ask volunteer 1 to repeat word for word what he or she heard read to him or her. As he or she is speaking, record what he or she says.

7. When he or she finishes, turn off the tape recorder and call in volunteer 3.

8. Continue these steps until all of the volunteers have been called in, have listened to the reading, and have repeated it.

9. Play back the entire tape recording.

10. Discuss the differences in the recorded segments.

Sample Questions:

- What were some of the major differences among the segments?

- What role did memory play in the accuracy of the segments?

- What role did interpretation play in the accuracy of the segments?

- What kinds of interpretations of the material in the reading did you hear?

- How can you explain the differences among the segments?

- What role did language facility play?

Sample Reading

I was at Grand Central Terminal in New York City during rush hour on a cold, wintry day. Several people were milling about the information booth—most dressed in heavy coats and boots, some glancing impatiently at their watches, some chatting on their cell phones, and others, I thought, annoying us with their headphones blasting rap music.

Several policemen were standing by the arrival gates. Two commuters walking quickly to a departure gate came by me swinging heavy briefcases and, I felt, arguing rather loudly, while several young teenagers at a magazine stand looked angry. A little girl, wearing a blue hat and red mittens, was holding her mother's hand and crying.

Some commuters were rushing to catch the next train. I realized that my train was about to leave, so I started to run. I saw a police car drive by the train station. Someone said, "Slow down; don't be in such a hurry."

 A

To adapt for the language classroom,

Procedure: Step 3

3. Turn on a tape recorder and read the excerpt provided or another like it to the one volunteer who has remained in the room. Students are encouraged to take notes.

I. Knowing Another Language (15–20 minutes)

Language is more than an arbitrary system of symbols. It is a reflection of the culture of its people. Language and culture are interlocking relationships rather than separate systems; therefore, acquiring another language entails acquiring another culture. Communicating effectively across cultures necessitates understanding more than the surface messages of the language. Communication mandates understanding the broader cultural context within which the messages are conveyed.

Purpose: To broaden understanding of what it means to know another language

Procedure:

1. Work in groups of 3–4. Respond with specific examples to the following questions.

   • Why do people talk to each other?

   • What does it mean to know another language?

   • What does language learning encompass?

   • What is the role of culture in language learning?

2. Share the different responses as a full group, listing on the blackboard as many responses as possible.

3. Discuss the responses.

   Sample Questions:

   • Why do you think you and others in the group produced such different/similar responses?

   • How did your personal experiences influence your response?

   • After listening to some of the other responses, would you change your original responses? Why or why not?

IV. Further Readings

Articles

Fantini, A. (Ed.). (1995). Language, culture, and world view [Special issue]. *International Journal of Intercultural Relations, 19*(2).

   This special issue is a collection of articles by authors from different languages and cultural backgrounds. The varied perspectives of the authors attempt to present those connections between language and culture that together constitute an individual's worldview.

Friday, R. (1989). Contrasts in discussion behaviors of German and American managers. *International Journal of Intercultural Relations, 13,* 429–446.

Although this article is ostensibly about German and American managers, much of what Friday describes is applicable to more general discussions about people of the two cultures. An important point the author makes is how differing expectations about such matters as topic, content, and style of rhetoric can lead to misinterpretations or misjudgments.

Furnham, A. (1989). Communicating across cultures: A social skills perspective. *Counseling Psychology Quarterly, 2,* 205–222.

The author of this article examines what it means to be a socially competent individual and discusses the communication skills lacking in those judged socially inadequate. He extends this analysis to newcomers in a foreign culture, whom he likens to socially inept communicators. The article discusses culture shock, business sojourner experiences versus student and immigrant experiences, and major types of cultural differences in behavior.

Johnstone, B. (1989). Linguistic strategies and cultural styles for persuasive discourse. In S. Ting-Toomey & F. Korzenny (Eds.), *Language, communication, and culture* (pp. 139–156). Newbury Park, CA: Sage.

This article presents an interesting look at examples of rhetorical style and cultural expectations. Examples from western European and Arab countries as well as from Iran illustrate how interlocutors' choice of the strategy they view as appropriate for a given communicative interaction tends to be based on cultural influences.

Books

Bennett, M. (Ed.). (1998). *Basic concepts of intercultural communication: Selected readings.* Yarmouth, ME: Intercultural Press.

This book is a collection of classic and contemporary articles on intercultural communication. The different reading selections include a wide variety of topics, such as different communication patterns among cultures, differing cultural assumptions and values, and culture shock.

Berry, J., Poortinga, Y., Segall, H., Marshall, H., & Dasen, P. (1992). *Cross-cultural psychology: Research and applications.* New York: Cambridge University Press.

The authors of this book compare and contrast cultures on such issues as child development, personality, and perception. They examine different types of research strategies for conducting cross-cultural research and address methodological concerns. The text concludes with a discussion of the applications of research findings across cultures. Many helpful diagrams and illustrations are included.

Brislin, R. (1981). *Cross-cultural encounters: Face-to-face interaction*. Oxford: Pergamon.

This book is a classic in the area of cross-cultural communication. The author investigates such basic issues as how individuals' attitudes and personality traits, their group membership, and group dynamics impact on communication. He also discusses evaluating and coping with different types of cross-cultural communication situations.

Damen, L. (1987). *Culture learning: The fifth dimension in the language classroom*. Reading MA: Addison-Wesley.

This is an excellent teacher-oriented text containing a comprehensive discussion of various issues in cross-cultural communication. The author systematically presents theory and practice on integrating culture into the language classroom. Each section concludes with questions for study and discussion, as well as a culture learning exercise.

Fantini, A. (Ed.). (1997). *New ways in teaching culture*. Alexandria, VA: TESOL.

Part of New Ways in TESOL Series II—Innovative Classroom Techniques, this book offers a collection of articles and activities that present effective ways to include culture in ESOL teaching. In addition to innovative classroom activities, it provides conceptual background essays and an annotated bibliography.

Gudykunst, W., & Kim, Y. (1997). *Communicating with strangers: An approach to intercultural communication* (3rd ed.). New York: McGraw-Hill.

This text provides a broad overview of important theory and research in intercultural communication. After the authors introduce and examine the basic processes of intercultural communication, they move on to issues of building understanding between people from different cultural backgrounds and with different patterns of communication.

Hall, E. 1959. *The silent language*. New York: Doubleday.

Hall, E. 1966. *The hidden dimension*. New York: Doubleday.

Hall, E. 1976. *Beyond culture*. New York: Doubleday.

Hall, E. 1983. *The dance of life: The other dimension of time*. New York: Doubleday.

These four books are generally considered classic works in the area of cross-cultural communication and should be read by anyone even remotely interested in the topic. They are highly readable, nontechnical works that can be enjoyed and understood by the layperson. *The Silent Language* is an excellent introduction to the area of culture and behavior. *The Hidden Dimension* focuses on perceptions of space among different cultures. *Beyond Culture* expands on the material covered in the two previous books. *The Dance of Life* discusses the concept of time in various cultures.

Hofstede, G. (1991). *Cultures and organizations: Software of the mind.* London: McGraw-Hill.

This book covers Hofstede's theory of the five dimensions of national cultural differences. Although somewhat technical, it is an important text in the field of cross-cultural communication. The author includes a section on the implications for education.

Samovar, L., & Porter, R. (Eds.). (1999). *Intercultural communication: A reader* (9th ed.). Belmont, CA: Wadsworth.

Samovar, L. & Porter, R. (Eds.). (2003). *Intercultural communication: A reader* (10th ed.). Belmont, CA: Wadsworth.

This is an invaluable introductory guide to the field of cross-cultural communication, with articles written by widely known experts. It covers a wide variety of subjects, including the links between culture and identity, the relationship between culture and language in communication, and communication processes from cross-cultural perspectives.

Seelye, N. (1997). *Teaching culture: Strategies for intercultural communication* (2nd ed.). Lincolnwood, IL: National Textbook Company.

This practical hands-on textbook is intended to provide foreign and, to some extent, second language teachers with techniques for introducing their students to the culture of the target language within the context of their language study curriculum.

"Everyone is kneaded out of the same dough
but not baked in the same oven."

Yiddish proverb

Chapter 3
Culture Shock

I. Anecdote: "Culture shock abroad and at home"

We typically associate culture shock with experiences overseas but as this anecdote illustrates, culture shock can occur at home, too. The author's personal experience confirms this.

I remember the first time I heard the term *culture shock.* I was taking an advanced Spanish course in preparation for my junior year abroad. It seemed like such a strong, negative term for what I had imagined was going to be a wonderful experience. I simply couldn't imagine how I would ever experience culture shock. I certainly wasn't going to be one of those people who go to live in a new environment and over time confront a clash in values between oneself and the host country. I, of course, was "different." I couldn't imagine my going through the U-curve of adjustment—first a honeymoon stage where I would be euphoric and find everything wonderful; then a gradual descent into "the depths," where I would revile just about everything having to do with the host country; and finally a regular ascent to a plateau of adjustment and acceptance of the different culture. After all, I had lived abroad before as a child and grew up in a bilingual, bicultural household.

The reality, however, turned out to be quite unlike what I had expected. I, like all my other compatriots, went through culture shock. There was a period where the Spanish could do little that I considered right, there was little about the culture I liked, and I valued little about the country. Luckily, like most people, I came through that stage of culture shock to a new appreciation of myself, of Spain, and of the Spanish culture.

Several years later and perhaps somewhat wiser, after having lived overseas in different countries, I had learned what culture shock was all about, and I even considered myself somewhat of an expert on it. Not only had I gone through it myself a few times, but now I was helping foreign students in the United States work through theirs. I definitely thought I knew what culture shock was about. If I had been asked to describe it in a nutshell, I might have summarized it as what occurred when there was a clash between one's own, often unconscious values and ways of behavior and those of the people of another country.

Then I got married. I married an American like myself, or so I thought, until our first Christmas as a married couple together. Then I experienced culture shock in a new and unexpected way, one that returned annually with the Christmas holiday season for the first five or six years of our marriage.

My husband grew up celebrating on Christmas morning when everyone ripped open their gifts in great confusion and commotion. I grew up celebrating on Christmas Eve when we each opened up a gift one at a time, with time off in between for indulging at an elaborate smorgasbord. (Santa Claus came while my mom took us kids out driving to look at Christmas lights.) For us, Christmas morning was reserved for our Christmas stockings. (Yes, Santa made two trips to our house.)

My husband grew up with one large meal on Christmas Day, served rather casually on holiday paper plates and napkins. After all, why should anyone have to slave in the kitchen on this holiday? I grew up having a smorgasbord on Christmas Eve, a special brunch on Christmas morning, *and* a special Christmas dinner served on my mother's best dishes, crystal and silver. After all, holidays are for using one's best.

I questioned whether *his* celebration could even be deigned a celebration. He questioned how *my* celebration could be considered anything but tedious. We argued these points back and forth for many years, until we reconfigured Christmas to be a combination of both "cultures."

Discussion of Key Issues

Culture shock can occur everywhere. It certainly is not necessary to move to an esoteric or very different culture to experience it. It simply takes place whenever one faces a contradiction between ones' own values, beliefs, and assumptions and those of the person or people surrounding one.

The more different or the more esoteric the unfamiliar culture is, the greater one's culture shock is likely to be.

In essence, culture shock is a combination of unfamiliar stimuli and a loss of familiar signs, signals, practices, and customs of social intercourse. The first stage of coming to a new culture is one of great excitement. Everything is new, different, and fascinating. The second stage is not nearly as exciting. What was previously fascinating is now irritating, annoying, or offensive. At this point, many people feel homesick and depressed. They may doubt their reason for traveling abroad, berate their host culture, and isolate themselves. Luckily, this stage passes, and people entering the third stage begin to feel more comfortable. They begin to understand and appreciate the values of their host culture, without feeling like they are sacrificing their own. By the fourth and final stage, the individual has adjusted to the extent that he or she feels a part of the new culture.

We know when culture shock takes place, but how does it manifest itself? Essentially we can say that culture shock entails feelings of stress and feelings of emotional and even physical upset. Typically, people experiencing culture shock will begin to adopt negative attitudes toward "the others" and will spend a great deal of time complaining about how "they" ("the others") are doing things wrong.

Chapter 3 examines culture shock, its roots, and its ramifications, as well as how it can become part of a positive learning experience.

Questions for Thought

- How would you define culture shock? Have you ever experienced culture shock? If so, how would you describe your experience?

- What are the causes of culture shock?

- What are some aspects of culture shock?

II. Theory: What Research Tells Us

Defining Culture Shock

Learning to live in a new and different environment is both exciting and stressful. The newcomer's first reaction is one of excitement, and there is often a sense of euphoria. Gradually, however, this feeling wears off, and the newcomer is left feeling vaguely dissatisfied, irritated, angry, and frustrated. Culture shock has set in.

Culture shock is the phenomenon individuals commonly experience when they are confronted with the realities of a different cultural environment. The phrase *culture shock* is used to describe the feelings of individuals when they encounter different social norms, values, beliefs, and ways of doing. The anthropologist Oberg (1960) who initially introduced the concept of culture shock, defines culture shock as the distress of newcomers to a different culture experience as a result of being confronted with an environment in which their familiar signs and patterns of social interaction are no longer valid. According to Taft (1977) culture shock is the result of the feelings individuals experience when faced with discrepancies between the demands of a particular situation and their resources for dealing with that situation. Culture shock has been described as "phenomena ranging from mild irritability to deep psychological panic and crisis" (Brown, 2000:183). For Winkelman (1994), culture shock is a multifaceted phenomenon, which individuals experience due to various forces they encounter when they come in contact with a different culture.

The circumstances initiating culture shock and individual reactions to culture shock depend on a number of factors. These factors include the degree of difference between the individual's culture and the new culture, an individual's prior cross-cultural experiences, the individual's preparedness, the social support networks available to the individual, and the psychological characteristics of the individual (Furnham & Bochner, 1986). In addition, the greater the cultural distance between two cultures is, the more likely it is that the newcomer will experience a greater degree of culture shock. In other words, when the underlying philosophies, worldviews, and cultural values of the new culture and the individual's own culture differ significantly, newcomers are likely to face more adjustment problems (Furnham & Bochner, 1982; Stephen & Stephen, 1985; Torbiörn, 1988). Social support networks—whether provided by members of the new culture, members of the home culture, or a mix of both—are frequently cited as an important factor in easing the transition process.

People who have had prior experience living in another culture will often have fewer adjustment problems, although this is no guarantee. Newcomers who had relatively few difficulties adjusting to one new culture may find themselves facing greater-than-expected culture shock when immersed in another culture, because of cultural distance and/or the lack of social support networks available to them. Furthermore, each culture is governed by its own philosophical framework and has its own cultural values, meaningful signs and symbols, communication styles, rules for social interaction, and inventory of socially appropriate behavior, any or all of which may differ significantly from any previous culture the newcomer has been exposed to.

Although certain individual characteristics seem to predict less culture shock, no definitive conclusions have been reached with respect to personality traits. Nevertheless, there is general agreement that individuals exhibiting high tolerance for ambiguity and less of a predilection toward stress do better in new cultural situations. The greater an individual's tolerance for ambiguity is, the less severe his or her culture shock is likely to be (Gudykunst, 1998; Kohls, 2001; Marx, 1999). A person's tolerance for ambiguity influences his or her ability to function in different cultural environments and under different cultural expectations. Other studies indicate that motivation and low dogmatism are positive psychological characteristics in such contexts (Taft, 1985). In short, the degree of culture shock and the length of the shock experience depend in large part on an individual's personality and psychological makeup. **(See Activity A—Defining Culture Shock)**

Stages of Culture Shock

Culture shock is manifested in various stages. Oberg (1960) proposed a four-stage model of learning to live in a new culture. The first stage is the *honeymoon phase.* During this stage, newcomers are fascinated by the new culture. They love the food, the scenery, and the people, and they are interested in seeing and doing as much as possible. For many, there is a sense of extreme well-being. They are open to new experiences and inclined to reserve judgment, focusing instead on the positive aspects in the culture. This stage is also referred to as the *tourist phase,* as this is the stage usually experienced by people who stay only briefly in other cultures, whether for leisure travel or for business.

Gradually, however, these positive feelings begin to change. Then, the newcomers enter the second stage, *culture shock*. This is the stage where people begin to feel overwhelmed and confounded by the new culture and experience a growing sense of disorientation and unease. This stage is associated with feelings of anger, hostility, frustration, unhappiness, homesickness, and even physical illness. Six main aspects of culture shock have been identified (Oberg, 1960).

- Newcomers suffer strain as they try to adapt.

- They feel a sense of loss and deprivation with respect to friends, status, and social and professional roles.

- They feel rejected by and/or reject members of the other culture.

- They feel confused with respect to their values and self-identity.

- They feel distress, anxiety, and even outrage at and/or disgust by foreign customs and routines.

- They feel helpless in handling or being able to cope with situations in the new environment.

The second of the four stages, culture shock, is the most unsettling and the most detrimental to cross-cultural sensitivity. Culture shock is precipitated by the anxiety that results from unfamiliarity with the signs and symbols of social behavior in a different culture. Culture shock of an American has been described as follows:

> Initially, things in the cities seem quite similar. There are horns blaring and people hurrying along talking into cell phones. There are hotels with hot and cold running water, fax machines, and computer hookups. There are theater districts, neon lights, Internet cafes, and tall buildings with elevators. There are some people who speak English and even the occasional billboard or other advertisement in English. But shortly the American realizes that underneath the layer of familiarity, there are great differences. When someone says "yes," it often doesn't mean yes at all, and when people smile it does not necessarily mean they are happy or pleased. When the American tries

to be gracious and polite, his actions may be interpreted as just the opposite; when he tries to be friendly, his overtures are not accepted. People tell him they will do things and then they don't. The longer the American stays in the new culture, the more baffling it becomes. (Adapted from Hall, 1959:35)

As people begin to deal with their feelings and attitudes toward the new culture and to understand the new and distinct realities of that culture, they enter into the *adjustment* or *acculturation stage*. In this stage, people start to function well in the new culture. Their feelings are now a compromise between those in the honeymoon stage and those in the culture shock stage. They begin to see the good and the bad aspects (the pros and cons) of their old and new cultural realities and to weigh their options accordingly. Individuals are learning how to adjust and adapt to the new cultural context. They learn to function according to the norms and values of the new culture, and they begin to understand how others interpret the world around them.

During this stage, people develop the problem-solving skills for living in and dealing with the new culture. Individuals' negative reactions and responses decrease as they recognize that problems are the result of cross-cultural misunderstandings, best resolved by learning to understand, accept, and adapt to the realities of the new culture. The new culture becomes less problematic and less of an enigma. For many people experiencing culture shock, the recovery stage is a slow process, involving periodic crises, setbacks, and readjustments.

As this process continues, the individual enters the fourth phase, the *recovery* or *adaption stage*. In this stage, people continue to grow in their ability to see both the positive and the negative of the new culture, which is accordingly reflected in their behavior and outlook toward that culture. They function effectively in the new culture, and their emotions are more controlled. Individuals are successful in resolving problems and in coping with the new culture.

Furnham and Bochner (1986) suggest that precisely the mundane, everyday encounters in a new culture cause the most stress for newcomers. Well-established habits, conventions, and patterns of social behavior no longer apply, and newcomers are faced with dissonance in their expectations for and in the actual outcomes of such encounters. Adjustment for newcomers entails learning to function under a different set of cultural codes.

A popular conception of the stages of culture shock is the "U-curve" of the cycle of culture shock and adjustment (Lysgaard, 1955). The initial phase, the honeymoon stage, is represented at the left high point of the U. As newcomers experience stage 2 or culture shock, they find themselves at the bottom of the U. As they go through the adjustment and recovery phases, they work back up to the top right point and finish more or less where they began, appreciative of the new culture, which is now not so new to them.

U-curve

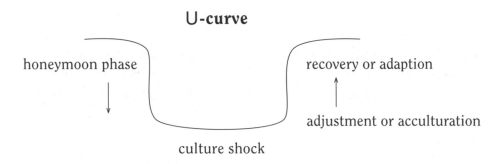

honeymoon phase

recovery or adaption

adjustment or acculturation

culture shock

The conception of the stages of culture shock as reflected by the U-curve has great intuitive appeal, yet questions have been raised as to the scientific validity of this concept. In their study, Ward and Kennedy (1996), for instance, found that the newcomers were happiest and most satisfied in the middle of their experience and less so both in the beginning and at the end. (See Black & Mendenhall, 1991, for a review of studies from the late 1950s through the 1980s on the U-curve adjustment hypothesis.)

Adler (1972, cited in Bennett, 1998:25) views culture shock as a five-stage process. First is the euphoria of the *contact stage,* where cultural difference is initially encountered. Second is the confusion of the *disintegration stage,* where a loss of self-esteem occurs. Anger occurs in the *reintegration stage;* here, the new culture is rejected, and the old one is reaffirmed. This stage is followed by the relaxed self-assuredness of the *autonomy stage,* where cross-cultural situations are handled relatively easily. The fifth and final stage is the *independence stage,* a stage of creativity where choice and accountability join a deep respect for one's culture and the culture of others. **(See Activity B—Knowing What's Coming).**

Causes of Culture Shock

Members of a given culture have certain shared expectations of appropriate social behavior, the motivations of others, and accepted outcomes of communicative interactions. Such expectations are largely the result of the enculturation process that normal individuals are exposed to as a functioning member of a set culture. Individuals are socialized to accept relatively narrow ranges of behavior as appropriate; members of a culture learn to do things in a certain way and to regard the behaviors surrounding these activities as proper. Contact with another culture leads to "shock" as individuals are confronted with different values, beliefs, attitudes, worldviews, and customs. These individuals face disparate assumptions about the role of language (both verbal and nonverbal); the nature, importance, and power of social relationships; and the construction and maintenance of identity. In many ways, culture shock is the result of stress, disorientation, and the need for new behavioral, cognitive, and affective responses for coping in a new culture. In addition, when individuals struggle with learning a new language, they find themselves at a loss. There are the constant mental and emotional strains of consciously having to think about how to express yourself in the target language and of not being able to convey the message you want to impart in the way you want. There is also the humiliation of not being able to express oneself in a way that agrees with an individual's intellectual level, social role, and status. Classroom learning suffers when students are experiencing any of these feelings of culture shock. Therefore, it is important for teachers to be able to recognize and understand the symptoms and manifestations of culture shock in order to help their students work through this stage. **(See Activity C—Wearing Someone Else's Shoes)**

Manners, courtship, family and societal relationships, and social interactions are rule-governed, intricate webs of behavior, most of which exist below the average person's level of conscious awareness. When people of one culture interact with those of other cultures, their expectations regarding the situations and their outcomes are often not met, resulting in cross-cultural misunderstandings and problems. Such problems include emotional upset and a sense of displacement, or not belonging. When individuals enter a different culture, most of the cues of social behavior that are familiar to them are no longer present; moreover, everyday cues with which they are familiar take on different interpretations and new meanings. These cues include the many ways in which individuals have been enculturated to function successfully in their culture. The cultural lenses of individuals filter their experiences and influence their interpretations of the social and environmental situations they face. Two individuals reared in two different cultures may interpret and react to such a situation differently because of their different cultural lenses, that is, because of differences in conceptions of the ramifications of that situation, as well as differences in perceptions about what is normal and appropriate behavior and under which conditions. The social and environmental situations affected by an individual's cultural lens include the basic interactions of everyday life, such as how and whom to greet, when to utter thanks, when and how to accept and refuse invitations, how to take conversational turns, and where and how to obtain essential information and basic necessities—to name a few. **(See Activity D—Colliding Cultures)**

How speech functions within a culture and in people's lives varies across speech communities (Gumperz & Hymes, 1972; Hymes, 1962). Communication patterns are largely determined by the culture to which people belong. Cultural premises and appropriate communication behavior (rules of speaking) are closely related to the way members of a given culture interpret the world, view social relationships, and identify group and individual behavior. When individuals from different cultures interact, they are operating under different behavioral norms and expectations. When people's expectations are violated, they often react negatively to the interlocutor. Simply because rhetorical language use may differ among the speakers, politeness may be understood as rudeness, or holding one's own may be regarded as pushiness. Different styles of discourse can also lead to culture shock. Gee (1996) describes a case report (Minnis, 1994) of a Hispanic American woman who entered law school and faced culture shock. A large part of her difficulties stemmed from conflicts between the discourse styles and expectations she encountered in law school, on the one hand, and those of her language community, on the other. Such discourse conflicts in which familiar rules and norms of communicative interactions are no longer recognized, accepted, or customary can threaten people's concepts of self-identity.

In addition, in a new culture, familiar cues guiding social interaction are often no longer operable. This leads people to make faulty attributions and to assign inaccurate interpretations to others' behaviors. Rather than attributing behavior to cultural differences, people explain behavior with reference to differences in personality type. Strangers to a culture do not react to the members of the culture as independent entities. Instead, strangers react on the basis of how they perceive the members of the new culture in the interaction. The majority of such social behavior is culturally influenced and remains below the level of consciousness; thus, culture shock occurs when an individuals' expectations of social behavior either conflict or fail to coincide with those of the other culture. Americans experiencing the bargaining at an Arab bazaar in Morocco or Kuwait may find Arabs contentious, aggressive, demanding, and deceitful. Rather than identifying bargaining behavior as appropriate cultural behavior within the Arab context, Americans are more likely to identify Arabs as people who embody what are considered negative personality characteristics from the American cultural standpoint. Neither Canadians nor Americans are accustomed to bargaining, except perhaps at a car dealership; in Canada and the United States, unlike in Arab cultures, bargaining is not viewed as an activity participants engage in as an accepted and expected social convention or custom.

Cultural Distance

The greater the cultural distance between two cultures is, the greater are the chance for and the intensity of culture shock. Cultural differences may be viewed in terms of objective and subjective cultures (Triandis, 1972). Differences in *objective culture* refer to such readily observable things as different eating habits, manner of dress, types of housing, and modes of transportation. Differences in *subjective culture* refer to more abstract concepts such as differing belief systems, values, norms of behavior, attitudes, and social roles. Triandis (1975) suggests two major dimensions relating to culture shock: external and internal elements of conflict. *External dimensions* refer to such areas as socioeconomic differences, exploitation of one group over another, and access to available resources (e.g., educational and vocational opportunities). *Internal dimensions* include self-identity, social support networks, and collectivism versus individualism. Furnham and Bochner (1986) suggest an additional dimension, namely, members' values and the degree to which members of different cultures may differ in their moral convictions and practices.

When individuals enter a new culture, culture shock results from experiencing differences in the objective and subjective elements and in the external and internal dimensions of this new culture. The more disparate two cultures are, the more individuals will encounter difficulties in cross-cultural communication, due to the greater differences in the elements and dimensions that govern personal behavior, interpersonal relationships, and communicative interactions. **(See Activity E—Semantic Associations)**

Cognitive fatigue

A major aspect of culture shock is *cognitive fatigue,* or too much information for the brain to process at once (Guthrie, 1975). Newcomers to a different culture must exert conscious efforts to interpret their new social and physical context—new language meanings, new nonverbal behavior, new contexts of meaning, new norms of social discourse, and new social roles and expectations. When people shift from the automatic mode of their own culture to the conscious mode required in their new culture, they often experience information overload. The conscious effort and concentration necessary to understand all the new information of the different culture is tiring and often results in mental and emotional fatigue. At the end of a day confronting myriads of cultural patterns, the newcomer is mentally, and often physically, exhausted (Seelye, 1997).

Aspects of Culture Shock

Culture shock has emotional, psychological, and cognitive impact on an individual's psyche. In addition to psychological responses, culture shock can also cause physiological and psychosomatic reactions. Culture shock arises out of the difficulties of adjustment to a new and different culture. Not only have familiar cues regarding social behavior changed for newcomers to a culture, but members of the new culture also do not hold the newcomers' values. Previously established expectations and predictions no longer hold true. Things the newcomers regard as good, desirable, beautiful, and valuable are not respected or valued as highly by members of the other culture (Pedersen, 1995). Difficulties adjusting to a new culture may arise out of something as simple as preferred meal times and table manners, a smile signifying disappointment rather than pleasure, or an early or late arrival that embarrasses or impresses. Or they may involve something more complex, such as women in the workplace, types of religious observance, or the question of whether a payment for services rendered is considered a bonus or a bribe.

Culture shock is not a sudden occurrence or the result of a specific event or even a series of events. It is the result of encountering a culture that has different ways of organizing the world (different values, norms, social behaviors, and customs), some or many of which threaten the newcomer's basic sense of self-identity. Culture shock is a cumulative process, which builds up slowly from a series of events or episodes. These episodes are difficult to identify, as they generally threaten areas of self-identity that individuals are unconscious of because these areas are intrinsic to the individuals as members of their particular culture. Furthermore, exposure to a new culture impacts individuals on different levels and in different intensities. North Americans in Korea, for example, are particularly confronted with these adjustment difficulties (Kohls, 1979, cited in Landis & Bhagat, 1996:68):

- "Person" status of foreigners
- General staring and rudeness in public
- Passive resistance as a communication strategy
- Extreme poverty and beggars
- Koreans' reactions to the influence of the United States in their country
- Theft, bribery, and dishonesty
- Cleanliness and sanitation
- Health problems
- Strange smells
- Adjusting to the food
- Learning to share
- Lack of privacy

Because Korean culture differs significantly in these twelve areas from what North Americans are accustomed to, difficulties in all or any combination of these spheres will most strongly affect North Americans' sense of culture shock. For example, because Korea is a collectivistic, high-context culture with a strong sense of face, speakers prefer more indirect communication strategies than do speakers of English. The concept of *nunch'i* embodies the Korean ideal of appropriate communicative interaction; speakers' abilities to interpret subtle verbal and nonverbal cues promote and maintain successful communication. Outsiders unfamiliar with *nunch'i* have difficulty interpreting and understanding the concept and so are likely to have unsatisfactory communicative interactions.

As another example, North Americans from Canada or the United States are members of heterogeneous immigrant societies whose citizens are generally egalitarian and tolerant of differences among people. Korea, for historical and geographical reasons, is a homogeneous culture, and anyone different is automatically an outsider, a "nonperson." This attitude is difficult for anyone to absorb and is certainly cause for culture shock. North Americans are also used to private space; outside of, perhaps, such large cities as Toronto or New York City, people expect a relatively large amount of personal space and privacy. A person's living quarters and possessions belong to that individual; no one else shares these unless specifically asked to do so. Even between married couples, there are "his" and "her" drawers, closets, and other areas of personal space, which are not invaded by the other partner. In Korea, a small, densely populated country, there is not the same concept of personal space and privacy; consequently, invasion of privacy and personal space are concepts at odds with Korean cultural perspectives. In sum, these examples illustrate some spheres where cross-cultural differences can lead to culture shock. **(See Activity F—Critical Incidents)**

Emotional level

On the emotional level, people suffering culture shock are likely to experience a gamut of negative feelings: anger, anxiety, depression, loneliness, homesickness, frustration, worry, irritation, helplessness, and hostility. Individuals may experience any, all, or some sort of combination of these feelings. Individuals may find themselves progressing toward the next stage and then again in the grip of and overwhelmed by some or any of these negative feelings. Mood swings are common. They can be triggered by something as minor as whether or not to form a line when waiting to get on a bus or by something more serious, such as the appropriate way to negotiate a contract. The anxiety and depression of an individual experiencing culture shock can result in both physical and psychosomatic illnesses. The emotional roller coaster can cause individuals to suffer from sleep disorders; others may feel a strong sense of loss and come to believe that everything was better for them at home. In extreme cases, culture shock can lead to more serious illnesses such as stomach ulcers, colitis, or eating disorders.

Uncertainty and anxiety are common in culture shock. Uncertainty is a cognitive response to unfamiliar situations. When individuals confront situations in which they are unable to predict other people's behavior, attitudes, feelings, beliefs, and values, they feel uncertain. People also feel uncertain when they are not able to explain the behavior of others. In a new culture, speakers may find uncertainty too high for comfort and may face varying degrees of culture shock. When people are faced with strange situations, it is normal for them to feel anxious. They do not know what is going to happen, how to react to what does happen, and when to react at all. They no longer have the appropriate automatic responses for social interactions. They are no longer sure of how to behave; there is now a large element of uncertainty in their daily lives. Because their new environment is unfamiliar, they no longer feel in control.

Closely related to uncertainty is anxiety. Anxiety is an emotional response to unfamiliar situations. People feel tense, worried, and/or apprehensive about what may or may not take place in these unfamiliar situations. Life begins to be a series of crises. Feelings of anxiety are often rooted in individuals' fear of damage or loss of self-identity and in their fear of being negatively evaluated by members of the new culture. As people confront greater uncertainty in their interactions with others, they become more anxious. A little bit of anxiety can be good, in that it increases energy and alertness and even causes an adrenaline rush. However, when people begin to suffer from more extreme anxiety, it has negative consequences for their behavior. Their psychological health is imbalanced; they lack a "high level host communication—cognitive, affective, and operational" (Gudykunst & Kim, 1997:351). In familiar environments, such as in their own culture, individuals will possess these three psychological processes simultaneously, in a well-coordinated and balanced manner. In an unfamiliar environment, such as in a different culture, individuals will often lack any one or more of these processes. This results in inner imbalance, turmoil, and anxiety. They begin to worry greatly over minutiae and irrelevant aspects of life and lose their concentration and ability to rationally approach problems and situations. Minor matters take up a great deal of their time and effort, and (to use a popular saying) people "can't see the forest for the trees." Petty incidents become major problems, and cultural differences become irritating and annoying. There is often an obsession with the cleanliness of the surroundings, with the type of food and food preparation, with the purity of the water, and with the hygiene habits of the culture members.

In more extreme cases, anxiety can lead to depression, which can have a seriously negative effect on individuals' energy levels. Decreased energy levels lead to erratic sleeping and eating patterns, which in turn tend to increase depression. Increased depression also leads to social withdrawal and isolation. As anxiety increases, individuals feel less and less able to interact successfully with others. According to Gudykunst and Hammer (1988), reducing uncertainty and controlling or reducing anxiety are essential in overcoming culture shock and moving into the adaptation stage. **(See Activity G—Evaluating Anxiety)**

Rational level

On the rational level, people who face culture shock come to recognize that familiar cues and signals no longer govern their interactions and social behavior. The nuances and shades of meaning that members of a culture understand, share instinctively, and use to facilitate everyday social interactions are no longer valid. Everyday life is no longer something automatically lived. Simple daily interactions become a puzzle. It is an effort to understand what is transpiring, how it is transpiring, and when something is transpiring. How does one greet people of different social status and gender? How do participants construct meaning? What construes a definitive answer? How is one's social role defined within the context of this new culture? What are the roles of teachers and students in the classroom setting?

There are cultural differences in almost all everyday activities, whether these involve, for example, greetings and leave-takings, the art of small talk, office protocol, classroom routines, or shopping habits and store hours. As people attempt to make sense of the new culture surrounding them, they will naturally rely on the categorizations, norms, and perspectives of their own culture. At times, this causes people to resort to negative stereotyping and strong ethnocentricity. Stereotypes, for instance, create expectations regarding how members of the other culture should behave. Unconsciously, individuals assume that their expectations are correct, and they interpret others' behavior accordingly. Consequently, individuals often feel they are being cheated or taken advantage of, and they become suspicious and distrustful of the intentions and motivations of members of the new culture. For example, students from other cultures entering the American or Canadian classroom may ascribe negative connotations to classroom behavior that is different from that which they view as the norm and develop resentment and anger toward their teachers.

Identity level

According to Turner (1987), identities can be divided into three broad categories: human, social, and personal. People's *human identities* are those things we share in common with other human beings; recognizing them involves recognizing what makes us all members of the human race. *Social identities* may be derived from individuals' societal roles (e.g., caregiver, teacher, entertainer), from such demographic categories as nationality or gender, or from membership in organizations, such as social or athletic clubs or political parties (Gudykunst & Kim, 1997). *Personal identities* are those characteristics that individuals believe they possess that differentiate them from others. These characteristics are an individual's personality traits and make an individual a unique person. People's *social identities* are those things they share, or assume they share, with members of their in-groups.

Because individuals experience changes in social roles and interpersonal relationships when they live in a new culture, they undergo *role shock* (Brynes, 1966). The amount of difference (both subjective and objective) between the two cultures leads to a loss or a change in social roles and hence in self-identity. The roles that comprise a person's identity are changed or even lost in a new culture. Our inborn physiological makeup is such that anxiety results when we are confronted with unfamiliar environmental cues. Without the support system of one's own culture to rely on, stress-producing unpredictability, helplessness, and a threat of self-esteem are more than likely to occur (Barna, 1998). New roles and social expectations create stress and anxiety for individuals, which in turn threaten their self-identity. A person's technical skills may no longer be valued, an elderly person may no longer receive the same respect and reverence, or a person may find his or her needs subsumed for the good of others. **(See Activity H—What's Normal?)**

Similar to Brynes's concept of role shock is Winkelman's (1994) concept of *personal shock*. A person's self-esteem, feelings of well-being, and satisfaction with life are created within and maintained by one's cultural system. When this support system is no longer available, individuals experience dissonance in their psychological makeup, which leads them to suffer emotional and physical problems in varying degrees. Zaharna

(1989:510) contends that although communication is generally regarded as a process of information exchange, it is actually an "act of creating and validating self-images." Therefore, newcomers to a culture will undergo *self-shock* as part of culture shock, because their identities, which are products of social interaction within their home culture, are no longer clearly predictable and identifiable. The culture is different, and the expected parameters of social roles and social associations are no longer valid, so newcomers are faced with uncertain and ambiguous communication events as well as inconsistent self-images. The result is self-shock.

Part of the process of culture shock is the process involving change and challenges to an individual's identities. People's social skills and self-identities are formed within a cultural setting. When this setting is changed, people have difficulty reconciling their social skills and sense of self with the new environment, as they are faced with the need to rethink their basic assumptions about the world and themselves. Similarly, the concept of identities and in-groups varies across cultures. In Japan, hotel guests of chains are viewed in a different light than hotel guests in Western cultures. Japanese hotel guests are often given a uniform or other identifying article of clothing, and they may be reassigned hotel rooms or even moved to another hotel without being consulted or given an option in advance. Such behavior is reflective of individuals being considered as part of the hotel in-group as long as they are guests of that particular hotel or hotel chain. From the Western perspective, being a hotel guest is an essentially anonymous process, one that does not confer any sort of group membership. Thus, in Western countries, offers of hotel uniforms or the random reassignment of hotel rooms would be viewed as a personal affront or an inconsiderate action—the antithesis of the Japanese view that such behavior reflects a hotel guest's social identity as part of the hotel in-group.

When the cultural context that accepts, permits, and influences individuals' behavior is no longer the same, this behavior is judged according to the new cultural values, beliefs, and norms. People's understanding of who and what they are is constantly being challenged and evaluated within a different social framework and is based on different cultural criteria. Behavior that was previously accepted may now be judged inappropriate or inadequate. Arriving late for scheduled appointments, eating with fingers instead of utensils, or removing one's shoes when entering someone's home are now viewed quite differently.

Members of collectivistic cultures are accustomed to interpreting their identity extrinsically, that is, in terms of how they fit into or form part of an intricate web of relationships. Members of individualistic cultures define their identity intrinsically, that is, in terms of who they are as individuals in their own rights. People raised in a collectivistic culture often encounter difficulties when they find themselves in an individualistic culture that expects and encourages individual expression, individual responsibility, and individual contributions. In an individualistic culture, harmony is of far less importance than what each individual can contribute to a situation, and competitiveness, whether in the classroom or in the workplace, is the norm. Those raised in individualistic cultures are just as likely to encounter difficulties when they enter a collectivistic culture that places great emphasis on group harmony, group consensus, and group obligations. Who they are as a person is no longer as important as who they are as a representative of a given group. In either case, adjustment to the new culture encompasses identity challenges and changes. Culture shock is a normal part of the process of such identity challenges.

Social relationships and networks also differ across cultures; newcomers are not integrated into the social web of a new culture the way they are in their own culture. Social relationships and networks play a critical role in determining individuals' sense of well-being, self-identity, and overall coping abilities in adapting to a new culture (Henderson, 1984; Henderson et al., 1978). Support from others has positive effects on people's perceptions of self, on their ability to handle stress and change, and on their general mental health. When people live in a new cultural environment, they can no longer rely on the previously established social relationships or networks of their own culture. Newcomers to a different culture no longer have the same sense of belonging, nor do they have the clearly defined roles and support systems that they had within their own culture. When people's self-identity is threatened, they often react by attributing negative stereotypes to members of the other culture and/or by becoming hostile or aggressive toward them (Gudykunst, 1998). **(See Activity I—Who Am I?)**

Although many of the symptoms of culture shock are psychological, culture shock is essentially a lack of the skills and knowledge necessary to function effectively and successfully in a new culture. An individual's motivation to adapt is possibly the single most important factor in determining how quickly newcomers pass through the stages of culture shock, (Guirdham, 1999).

A Learning Process

It is also important to understand that culture shock in and of itself is not necessarily a completely negative experience; culture shock has both negative and positive consequences. Furthermore, culture shock is not a permanent state but a transitional emotional phase, the intensity of which varies according to the individual. Bennett (1977) views culture shock as a component of *transition shock*. Transition shock is the result of a defensive response to the chaos that individuals feel when their worldview and their sense of identity are threatened; they are constantly confronted with the questions of who they are, what their role is, and what validity their beliefs have. Individuals can learn to cope with the symptoms by developing methods to channel all sorts of shock into personal development. In other words, rather than be defensive, people should convert their defensiveness into a positive cross-cultural learning experience.

Thus, culture shock, at least in its milder forms, is a learning opportunity. It is part of the normal adjustment process to another culture and can be an important step for self-development and personal growth (Adler, 1975, 1986; Kohls, 2001). According to Ting-Toomey (1999:246), positive effects of culture shock can lead to higher self-esteem, greater tolerance for ambiguity, and more cognitive openness and flexibility. Experiencing culture shock allows individuals to gain a new understanding of what elements contribute to their sense of self and their own psychological makeup. Experiencing culture shock also forces individuals to face their own ethnocentrism, while helping them gain new attitudes and perspectives on the nature of culture and its role in shaping its members and self-identity. Since cultures differ in their values, attitudes, and worldviews, culture shock is a natural occurrence of cross-cultural interaction.

Culture shock is also the process that provides individuals with opportunities to examine the degree to which they are influenced by their own culture and to understand the cultural "soul" of members of other cultures. Culture shock forces individuals to confront the social, psychological, moral, and philosophical differences between their own culture and another culture, and in so doing, it allows them to realize how values, attitudes, and worldviews are a result of the cultural influences shared by the members of a particular culture.

Teaching and Learning Connections

While culture shock cannot be prevented, teachers can play an important role in mitigating the effects of culture shock and in helping students move through the different stages. To deal effectively with culture shock requires recognizing, understanding, and accepting the feelings, sensations, reactions, and attitudes associated with culture shock. Once an awareness of the phenomenon is confirmed, steps can be taken to minimize and overcome culture shock. After all, culture shock is not a brief or trivial experience but a longer process that can have deep and prolonged effects if not dealt with effectively. Cultural awareness training can help teachers both understand where problems are likely to occur and offer ways to aid students to cope with culture shock.

Being knowledgeable about possible areas of cross-cultural differences can reduce culture shock. The language classroom can be an important means for helping individuals recognize the role of culture in their lives and for helping them develop cultural awareness so that they might recognize, better manage, and perhaps even mitigate culture shock. Since the newcomer bears the responsibility of becoming familiar with the customs, traditions, and contextual rules of the host culture, international students should be made aware of these customs, traditions, and rules and should be prepared to deal with them accordingly. Teachers and teacher trainers can help in this process by being cognizant of and sensitive to the role culture plays in the adjustment of new students to the classroom.

The classroom is an ideal place for giving students ample opportunities to simulate the culture shock experience, through varied role-play activities and simulations, consideration of critical incidents, and so on. Such activities can serve to activate some of the hidden dimensions in intercultural communication, and they can produce a feeling of comfort with and acceptance of the cultural enigmas and dilemmas that students would normally face in the real world. Thus, the language teacher has the responsibility of bringing to class a variety of effective methods, materials, and techniques to help reduce student anxiety and to generate in students a greater sense of cultural awareness and understanding.

Questions for Study and Discussion

1. In your own words, how would you define culture shock. Has your definition changed since you began reading this book and taking part in any of the activities? If yes, explain how.

2. According to the authors of this book, what are some causes of culture shock? Do you agree or disagree? Reflect on your own experience with culture shock. What causes could you add?

3. What are the three levels that culture shock impacts? Discuss each. Provide original examples, if possible. Which of the three levels do you consider to be most impacted by culture shock? Why?

4. Describe each of the four stages of learning to live in a new culture. How can you relate these to your own experiences or to those of someone you know?

5. Do you agree with Oberg's model of culture shock? Explain why or why not.

6. The authors of this book suggest that culture shock can be "a learning process." Reflect on this concept, explain what you think they mean by this, and describe how you believe you might make culture shock a learning experience in your classroom.

7. Not everyone experiences the same degree of culture shock. What are some of the variables that affect the severity of culture shock? Which variable do you consider the most significant? Reflect on yourself and consider your personality, your social networks, and other factors associated with differing degrees of culture shock.

III. Practice: What Activities Show Us

A. Defining Culture Shock (10–15 minutes)

When interacting with individuals from other cultures, whose backgrounds, ideas, and worldviews are different from ours and unfamiliar to us, we tend to feel various degrees of anxiety and a loss of control. Remedying this situation means moving out of culture shock.

Purpose: To develop an awareness of the meaning of culture shock

Procedure:

1. Read the following definition of culture shock (from "The Transitional Experience: An Alternative View of Culture Shock," by P. Adler, 1975, *Journal of Humanistic Psychology, 15*[4], p. 3).

   Culture shock is primarily a set of emotional reactions to the loss of perceptual reinforcements from one's own culture, to new cultural stimuli which have little or no meaning, and to the misunderstanding of new and diverse experiences.

2. Discuss this definition.

   Sample Questions:

   • Why is there an emphasis on emotion in defining culture shock?

   • In your opinion, is this an adequate definition? Why or why not?

3. Work individually. Write your own definition of culture shock.

4. Work in groups of 3–4.

5. Have each group agree on one definition of culture shock.

6. As a full group, share the small-group definitions.

7. Discuss the different definitions.

Sample Questions:

- What differences were there in your individual definitions?

- What were the similarities?

- What were the common elements among all of the definitions?

- Which problems did your group encounter in trying to agree on one definition?

- Why do you think these problems surfaced?

8. Be prepared to explain culture shock to someone unfamiliar with the concept.

B. Knowing What's Coming
(20–30 minutes, depending on class size)

There *are* things one can do to prepare for culture shock. The most important one is knowing that it is coming. Not expecting something causes you to react even stronger when you have to face it. Realizing that these experiences are not new, since one has had to adjust to new people in life before, is crucial. Thus, the nature of what one is doing is familiar even if the scale of it is overwhelming. Taking care of oneself and not being too hard on oneself helps. Keep the big picture in mind, for only through positive and/or negative experiences can one learn and grow.

Purpose: To develop an awareness of what to do to prepare for culture shock

Procedure:

1. With the full group, discuss one or two culture shock experiences you have encountered. These may include experiences within your own country.

Sample Questions:

- How could you have prepared yourself for these culture shock experiences?

- What can you do to prepare yourself for other culture shock experiences?

2. Work in groups of 3–4. Formulate some guidelines, suggestions, or principles for dealing with culture shock.

3. Discuss these guidelines/suggestions/principles with the whole group.

Sample Questions:

- What were the similarities/differences in these guidelines/ suggestions/ principles?

- What are some of the strengths of the guidelines/ suggestions/principles?

- What difficulties might students have in trying to apply these guidelines/suggestions/principles?

- On what guidelines/suggestions/principles can the group agree?

 A

To adapt for the language classroom,

Procedure:

1. Discuss culture shock as a full group.

2. Ask students to write about one culture shock experience they have encountered.

3. Share these experiences in groups of 3–4.

4. Discuss some of the experiences as a full group.

Sample Questions:

- How could you have prepared yourself for these culture shock experiences?

- What can you do to prepare yourself for other culture shock experiences?

- What guidelines or suggestions can you give for dealing with culture shock?

C. Wearing Someone Else's Shoes (25–30 minutes)

To better understand other cultural groups, one's perception of reality can be increased if one can step into someone else's shoes or see how others view something in a way very different from one's own. One's cultural spectacles blur one's vision when looking at other cultural groups.

Purpose: To achieve a deeper understanding of the national characteristics of cultural groups

Procedure:

1. Work in groups of 4–5. Instruct each group that it must set up an imaginary multinational company and fill the following positions.

   president   chief cashier

   managing director   public relations officer

   skilled labor   unskilled labor such as mechanic, janitorial services, and so on.

   Each position in this multinational company should be filled with *imaginary* individuals from different cultural groups and of different gender, such as French male, Mexican female, Nigerian male, or Indonesian female, and so on.

2. As a full group, discuss each group's choice of cultural group and gender for each of the positions. Make sure each group gives its reasons why a particular culture was selected for a particular position (e.g., cultural characteristics used as reasons may include punctual, hardworking, honest, serious, talkative, sly, emotional, reliable, money-conscious, forceful, wise, shy, caring, flexible, polite).

Have one participant record the reasons stated. The full group must then reach a consensus as to which members of which cultural group and gender should serve in the various positions.

Sample Questions:

- Why do we have an inherent tendency to generalize?

- How did you decide on your choices?

- Was there any particular cultural group or gender that was chosen more consistently for better positions? For worse jobs?

D. Colliding Cultures (20–25 minutes)

Routines are repetitive actions one no longer needs to think about when performing them. These include the minutiae of daily life, ranging from brushing your teeth to cooking to driving. When one no longer engages in familiar daily routines, one needs to reestablish these to adjust favorably to a new environment.

Purpose: To illustrate that being aware of one's behavior can minimize the culture shock one experiences in a new location

Procedure:

1. List three routines carried on in your own country and three carried on in a country you have visited. (If students do not have overseas experience, you may wish to ask them to reflect upon routines that they may have experienced or heard about in different regions of the country, cross-generationally, or observed in movies or other media.)

2. List those routines from your earlier list that differ from those in the United States. Examples follow.

   - Having a sandwich, rice, or soup for breakfast

   - Not having to say "excuse me" to one's companions when leaving to go to the restroom in a public place, such as a restaurant

   - Going to someone's home without calling first

- Greeting people by bowing or kissing on both cheeks

- Showing respect by addressing women with ma'am

3. Share some of the different routines with the full group.

4. Make a list of the cultures represented in the full group and discuss differences in routines.

Sample Questions:

- Why do some of the routines differ across cultures?

- Where there are no differences, why do you suppose that is so?

- Why is it important to be aware of your behavior in a new location?

 I, A

To adapt for the language classroom,

Follow-up:

- With a partner, prepare a role play demonstrating one or two routines from your own country (or a country with which you are familiar) that differ from those in the United States.

E. Semantic Associations (15–20 minutes)

Different words hold different connotations for people, even people who are members of the same dominant culture. As people move across cultural and language borders, differences in semantic interpretation increase significantly. Indeed, in the field of translation, entire books and journals are devoted to the issue of connotation, denotation, and meaning between and across languages.

Purpose: To illustrate how the same words can evoke different images and reactions among speakers

Procedure:

1. On the blackboard, list 8–10 nouns, such as the following: *conflict, community, friendship, religion, government,*

silence, job, family, terrorism, rabbi, free trade, senior citizen.

2. Ask participants to copy each word.

   • As they copy each word, they should also put down next to it the first word or phrase that comes to mind.

   • Emphasize that this is a word-association exercise. You are looking not for dictionary definitions but for participants' personal reactions to each word. Mention also that there are no right or wrong responses.

3. Work in groups of 3–4. Discuss the responses.

4. Be prepared to share the responses in a full group discussion.

   Sample Questions:

   • Why did you respond as you did to each word?

   • How did various students' responses differ?

   • What do you think might be the reasons for these differences (e.g., age, gender, life experiences, cultural/ethnic background)?

   • What do you think is the purpose of this exercise?

Follow-up:

   • Suggest that participants try this activity with people they know from different backgrounds and compare responses.

 I, A

To adapt for the language classroom,

Follow-up:

   • Have students try this activity with people from different backgrounds. Ask them to write a short essay comparing the responses they received.

F. Critical Incidents (15–20 minutes)

The following critical incidents are exercises focusing on culture shock. The situations described in each incident present cultural quandries. There is no single solution to each incident. The intent of the exercise is to stimulate insightful discussion by raising issues involving cultural dilemmas and to boost both self-awareness and awareness of others as individuals and as products of culture.

Purpose: To expand an awareness of differences in underlying cultural values and beliefs

Procedure:

1. Prepare different sets of two to four critical incidents. How many sets you prepare will depend on the total number of participants (e.g., for a group of 12 participants, prepare four sets).

2. Work in groups of 3–4.

3. Distribute the sets of critical incidents, and ask the participants to brainstorm possible solutions.

4. As a full group, discuss the critical incidents, their possible solutions, and the cultural values underlying the areas of cultural conflict.

5. Write your own critical incident. Share this with a partner or the full group.

Critical Incident 1

You have a student who recently arrived from East Asia. Although his English is quite good, he speaks hesitantly and with a noticeable accent. Your class requires a great deal of student discussion and active participation, but you have trouble getting this student to join in. In fact, he will only speak if you directly call on him. Other students don't feel comfortable working with him in small groups, because they feel he doesn't contribute. As the year goes on, you notice that this student is becoming increasingly quiet and withdrawn. He is also beginning to miss class.

Critical Incident 2

Paul, an American, asked his friend David, a Taiwanese student, whether he should invest all of his money in the stock market. David said he would think about it and get back to him. Paul was annoyed, because he expected an immediate answer.

Critical Incident 3

An international student wanted to express his apologies to his teacher for not having handed in a major assignment on time. He presented the teacher with a $50 gift certificate to a local store. The teacher informed this student that such bribes were unacceptable and would not change his grade. The student left the teacher's office feeling dismayed and insulted.

Critical Incident 4

Kathy, an American exchange student in Ghana, had slowly been getting used to the differences between the two countries. After awhile, she made friends with a number of local people her own age, which helped ease her feelings of being an outsider. One Monday morning, one of her male friends came home from visiting his village and gave her a chicken. She was a little surprised by the gift but accepted it, not wanting to hurt his feelings. On Friday night, he appeared at her door without notice, expecting her to go out with him. She was tired, felt homesick, and didn't want to go anywhere. He left, but he came again on Saturday. She again rebuffed him, not really wanting to "date" him, but on Sunday, he was there again. Over the next few days, she noticed that her new friends weren't as friendly toward her and seemed to be avoiding her.

Critical Incident 5

Eun and Sung, two Korean women, were walking down Church Street in Boston holding hands and talking together. As they continued walking down the street, people stared at them. Eun and Sung felt quite uncomfortable.

Critical Incident 6

An American exchange professor is feeling frustrated and annoyed. Whenever he asks a Kenyan for directions, something he does frequently because he is unfamiliar with the town in which he is teaching, he is given information along the lines of "Go a little way to the left" or "It's just down the road, past the police station." Unfortunately, his idea of "a little way" or "just down the road" seems to differ considerably (by several miles!) from the Kenyan idea.

Critical Incident 7

Walter, an exchange student from Germany, just deplaned from his trip from Frankfurt to New York City. He gathered his luggage and then hailed a taxi to take him to the International House at Columbia University, where he would be living this year. On the trip across town, on 125th Street, he saw garbage piled on curbsides, streets with litter, and graffiti all around him. He was appalled at how dirty Americans are.

Critical Incident 8

On market day, a Canadian exchange student living with a host family accompanied her host mother to the marketplace. Before they could finish their food shopping, the Canadian girl had to leave because she became nauseated by the sight of dead chickens dangling by their feet, whole heads of beef swinging on hooks, and swarming flies everywhere.

Discussion

Critical Incident 1

In many cultures, students are expected *not* to speak up and participate. The teacher is regarded as the expert and the one to impart important knowledge to the students. The combination of different classroom expectations and relatively weak speaking skills is causing the student in this incident to feel classroom culture shock. He may be missing classes to avoid having to speak up and getting involved in class in a way that makes him feel uncomfortable and embarrassed.

Critical Incident 2

Americans are more independent than are Chinese and love to solve problems by themselves. Chinese always do things carefully, solve problems thoughtfully, and are afraid to make mistakes. Because of this, Chinese often take time to express themselves, and Americans often do things impulsively.

Critical Incident 3

When does a gift become a bribe? The situations in which teachers may accept or expect gifts from students vary across cultures. What may be seen in one culture as an acceptable gift to express gratitude or an apology may be viewed in another culture as a form of inappropriate influence. Members of different cultures are generally unaware of the cultural appropriateness of particular actions and do not realize how these actions differ cross-culturally. When their culturally appropriate behavior contrasts with that of another culture, they may find themselves in a position of inadvertently offending or insulting members of the other culture. By the same token, when a person's actions are rebuffed because of differences in culturally appropriate behavior, that person may feel slighted or affronted.

Critical Incident 4

By accepting the gift, Kathy had inadvertently signaled her acceptance of the man as her steady boyfriend/fiancé. Refusing to go out with him three days in a row was insulting and offensive. The "cold shoulder" she was receiving from her other friends was their way of showing solidarity with him and reprimanding her for her behavior. Not understanding the social rules, both sides misinterpreted each other's behavior, and in Kathy's case, the misunderstanding quite possibly increased her feeling of culture shock.

Critical Incident 5
In Korea, it is not unusual for same-sex friends to hold hands. However, it is disturbing for members of the opposite sex to publicly touch each other. These norms are the opposite of mainstream North American norms.

Critical Incident 6
The need for precision is reflective of M-time cultures (see chap. 2). In these cultures, not only is time carefully scheduled and allotted, but distance, too, is vigilantly measured and apportioned. In Western European cultures, for instance, kilometer markers appear along all roads to indicate distance. In the United States, landmarks are often indicated by their position along mile markers. In the Florida Keys, for instance, commercial establishments identify their location with respect to the mile markers on U.S. Route 1, which traverses the islands. In other cultures, the precise distance to a place is of less importance than the location of that place. If the destination is down the road a ways, it is enough to know that it will be where the speaker tells you it will be; one need not know exactly how far away it is.

Critical Incident 7
When members of one culture have a negative first impression of those of another culture, problems often arise. In this incident, the expectation is one of cleanliness and the evidence is of apparent filth. In such a case, anxiety sets in until the notion drawn from the evidence is dispelled. Such a feeling of culture shock can be discouraging and can have a negative effect on an individual's stay in a new environment.

Critical Incident 8
Canadians and Americans are accustomed to having their poultry plucked and their meat cut up, shrink-wrapped, packaged, and often deboned. Food is displayed in refrigerated cases and sold in climate-controlled stores. Even in butcher shops, sides of beef will have the head removed, and the hanging sides are generally in giant refrigerators, out of customers' view. Fish is usually sold and served in fillets and is rarely served with the head, skin, fins, and tail still attached. North Americans, aside from farmers and ranchers, are generally not used to and feel uncomfortable with seeing dead carcasses.

A

To adapt for the language classroom,

Writing Critical Incidents

- See chapter 2, Activity F, for suggestions.

G. Evaluating Anxiety (10–15 minutes for initial activity; additional time for follow-up)

Anxiety and tension are common in cross-cultural experiences, where there are many uncertainties as well as personal involvement and risk. Anxious feelings that pervade the dialogue between nationals and foreigners can result in repeated collisions between members of contrasting cultures. On the part of a newcomer to a culture, this leads to helplessness and a feeling of being trapped.

Purpose: To help students gain insights into personal anxiety levels

Procedure:

1. Complete the following questionnaire.

    a. Next to each statement, indicate the degree to which you typically respond, according to the following scale:

    5 = always false

    4 = usually false

    3 = sometimes false and sometimes true

    2 = usually true

    1 = always true

    b. When you finish, find your score by adding all your numbers together. The highest possible score is 45, the lowest score is 9, and the middle score is 27. The higher your score is, the greater your anxiety level is.

	I am comfortable in new situations.
	I handle unstructured environments well.
	I don't become frustrated when things do not go the way I expect them to.
	I don't mind when my environment is changed without my knowledge.
	I am good at handling unanticipated problems.
	I can relax in unfamiliar situations.
	I feel comfortable working on problems even when I do not know all the possible ramifications.
	I feel at ease in situations without clear norms to guide my behavior.
	I adjust easily to new environments.
	I am not nervous when I am in situations where I'm not sure what to do.

Adapted from *Bridging Differences: Effective Intergroup Communication* (3rd ed., p. 230), by W. Gudykunst, 1998, Thousand Oaks, CA: Sage.

2. As a full group, discuss the implications of participants' scores and the relationship between anxiety and culture shock.

Sample Questions:

- How accurate do you think this type of evaluation is? Based on your personal experiences, do you see a relationship between anxiety and culture shock?

- Why do people with higher levels of anxiety tend to undergo stronger culture shock?

- How does tolerance for ambiguity and anxiety tie in to culture shock?

- What suggestions can you offer to reduce anxiety and stress in culture shock situations?

Follow-up:

1. Administer the preceding questionnaire to people who have lived or who are currently living in a country other than their own.

2. Ask the respondents about their culture shock experiences. See what correlation participants can make between the scores and the respondents' experiences.

H. What's Normal? (20–25 minutes)

Different paths in core beliefs emerge according to the culture one tries to impose on them. Simply looking at a person does not reveal an individual's cultural values. It is not one's manner of dress but how one says or does something that offers a deeper insight into what makes that person tick.

Purpose: To explore assumptions held about other cultures

Procedure:

1. Set up this exercise around a series of photographs with a common theme, such as

- People seated around a dinner table and eating in different cultures (e.g., in the United States, Japan, and Africa)

- People waiting to get on a bus in different cultures (e.g., standing in line vs. crowding around the door)

- Interior office views (e.g., closed office doors vs. open ones; rows of office desks vs. individual cubicles)

2. Work in groups of 3–4. Each group should choose one participant to record the group's observations of its set of photographs. The observations for each photograph should include a basic description of the photograph (e.g., people waiting to get on a bus in country X), what the people are doing (e.g., crowding haphazardly around the door/lining up in a row), and observations on how their behavior differs from how people in another culture would behave.

3. Each group should present its findings to the full group.

I. Who Am I? (15–20 minutes)

We are all members of groups. One group is a person's national or cultural identity, such as Canadian, German, Mexican, or Chinese. Another group may be our religious affiliation, such as Lutheran or Catholic Christian, Orthodox or Reform Jewish, Buddhist, or Sunni or Shiite Moslem. Still another may be our memberships within the family (e.g., mother, daughter, sister-in-law). Group membership may entail being part of a relatively small group, such as a country club, the local Parent-Teacher Association (PTA), a bowling league, or a chess club. It can also entail being part of a larger group, such as the student body of a university, the Sierra Club, or Amnesty International. All people are members of many different groups, all of which contribute to a person's sense of identity.

Purpose: To demonstrate how group membership contributes to a person's self-identity and sense of relationship with others

Procedure:

1. Have participants stand up in a long row. If the group is very large, have half of them stand up and the other half observe.

2. Inform them that you will call out various groups; as you call out these different groups, they should

- take one step *back* if they are members of this group;

- take one step to the *right* if either of their parents are members of this group;

- take one step to the *left* if they were members of this group in the past.

3. Call out different possible groups one at a time. Allow participants enough time to move into their new positions. Some suggested groups follow.

Democrat/Republican	liberal/conservative
man/woman	Girl Scout/Boy Scout
girl/boy	community volunteer
smoker/nonsmoker	band/orchestra member
athlete/fitness club member	theater/drama club member
education/social work/etc. major	
beer drinker/wine drinker/teetotaler	

4. Stop after you have called out 8–10 groups.

5. Ask participants to observe where they are standing now in relation to the others.

Sample Questions:

- How do your group memberships relate to those of others in the class?

- What do these group memberships tell you about yourself?

- Which of these memberships are more important to you?

- Do you feel that any groups you belong to that are not mentioned supersede any or all of those mentioned? Why?

- How can you relate what you have learned about yourself in this activity to the experience of culture shock?

IV. Further Readings

Articles

Adler, P. (1986). Culture shock and the cross-cultural learning experience. In L. Luce & E. Smith (Eds.), *Toward internationalism* (2nd ed., pp. 24–35). Cambridge, MA: Newbury House. (Reprinted from *Readings in intercultural communication,* (Vol. 2, pp. 6–21, by D. Hoopes, Ed., 1972, Pittsburgh: Regional Council for International Education.)

> The author of this article considers various concepts and definitions of culture shock. He examines the notion of culture shock as part of the cross-cultural learning experience in that it leads to greater cultural awareness and personal growth. This well-written article offers clear arguments and is generally regarded as a key introductory reading on the topic of culture shock.

Kim, Y. (1989). Intercultural adaptation. In M. Asante & W. Gudykunst (Eds.), *Handbook of international and intercultural communication* (pp. 275–294). Newbury Park, CA: Sage.

> This article offers a good basic introduction to the notion of culture shock. The author explains common terms and describes general concepts important in the study and understanding of this notion. She discusses numerous studies on adaptation among immigrants and sojourners (short-term residents) to a foreign culture from a range of fields including social psychology, cultural anthropology, and communication.

Zaharna, R. (1989). Self-shock: The double-binding challenge of identity. *International Journal of Intercultural Relations, 13,* 501–525.

> Two important concepts in cross-cultural communication—culture shock and self-shock—are explored in this article. While the primary emphasis is on self-shock, there is also a basic review of literature on culture shock. The article provides insights into what sojourners face emotionally, and it suggests why so many of them later suffer from reentry shock upon returning home.

Books

Davis, M. (1990). *Mexican voices, American dreams.* New York: Henry Holt and Company.

> In this book, different Mexican immigrants recount their experiences: how and why they came to the United States, their successes, and their failures. Interesting also are the sections where employers in various parts of the United States talk about hiring and working with Mexicans. The book offers a vivid description of both the tensions and the rewards of being bicultural and binational.

Hansel, B. (1993). *The exchange student survival kit.* Yarmouth, ME: Intercultural Press.

> This book was written in an attempt to help exchange students, both Americans going abroad and foreign students coming to the United States, to gain a better

understanding of the process of entering a new culture. The discussion is geared toward helping students avoid many of the common cross-cultural misunderstandings and problems that often occur as people adjust to a new culture. It is a valuable resource for teachers who wish to understand more clearly what their students may be facing, and it prepares teachers to offer students concrete suggestions for surviving culture shock.

Kohls, R. (2001). *Survival kit for overseas living* (4th ed.). Yarmouth, ME: Intercultural Press.

This book offers readers sound information on the process of cross-cultural adaptation and on culture shock, as well as suggestions for adapting to a different culture. The author provides suggestions on avoiding stereotyping, learning to understand the host culture, and thinking and looking at the world in different ways. The book also contains many useful strategies for managing culture shock, developing intercultural communication skills, and coping with reverse culture shock when returning to one's home country.

Storti, C. (2001). *The art of crossing cultures* (2nd ed.). Yarmouth, ME: Intercultural Press.

This book offers tips and strategies on what it takes to experience a new culture head-on and to succeed in the process. It includes writings from some of the best-known writers, poets, and observers of the human condition. The author focuses on culture shock and presents varied examples of cross-cultural misunderstandings.

Tenhula, J. (1991). *Voices from Southeast Asia: The refugee experience in the United States.* New York: Holmes and Meier Publishers.

This moving and informative work personalizes the events, problems, happiness, and rewards experienced by this immigrant group in adjusting to American culture. The author presents brief interviews with and poems and narratives by different refugees. The book also includes valuable background information on Southeast Asia and a useful list of additional readings.

Chapter 4
Nonverbal Communication

I. Anecdote: "Who me?"

A professor at a small northeastern college recounts her experience with unfamiliar nonverbal behavior and her confusion in interpreting the signal.

The language classes at my university are largely filled with Asian students. It has often been rather difficult to get these students involved in class activities, since they tend to be passive (rather than active) participants in the language learning experience. I have unsuccessfully tried many different techniques to solicit responses. At one point, I changed my approach and directed my questions at particular students.

One day when I was following this approach, I looked directly at Kumiko, a student from Japan, and said, "Kumiko, please give the class an oral summary of the reading on Albert Einstein that you were assigned for homework."

Kumiko made eye contact with me, gave a sheepish smile, and pointed to her nose.

Immediately I became self-conscious and asked, "Is there something on my nose?"

There was no response.

Looking at Kumiko, I asked her again.

She pointed to her nose again.

I had no clue what she meant, but I was thinking that there must be something wrong with my nose. Was it smudged with makeup? Was she making fun of the size of my nose? Was there something hanging from it? Or was I unaware of a bad smell in the classroom?

When I shared this classroom experience with a Japanese colleague later, she told me that pointing to the nose is the Japanese equivalent for the American gesture of pointing to the chest when one wants to ask, "Who me?"

Discussion of Key Issues

Nonverbal communication includes diverse elements. One of these elements is that of human gestures, which have often been greatly underestimated with respect to their influence on communicating speakers' meaning. Verbal discourse is considered the primary source of human communication, while gestures have traditionally been regarded as playing an auxiliary role or as trivial or insignificant. However, consider how mechanical and cold socialization would become if gestures were missing in our daily communication.

Gestures are personal, cultural, and biological. Tracing their geographical origin and the history of these actions helps us to understand them as a pattern of human behavior, specifically as a pattern of nonverbal communication. Gestures, however, are only one small part of what we understand under the term *nonverbal behavior*. All normal human beings engage in some type of nonverbal communication; what changes across cultures is the type of nonverbal behavior, the intended message the nonverbal behavior conveys, and the frequency and use of nonverbal behavior. Much of how we interpret what is being said and of the messages we impart are based on the subconscious transmission of nonverbal cues. Indeed, our body may give off signals that actually contradict what our mouths are saying. How many of us have been in situations where our interlocutors' body language indicated their dislike of us even though their words did not?

Chapter 4 investigates various aspects of nonverbal communication and cross-cultural differences and how differences, as well as similarities, can result in cross-cultural communication difficulties. In addition, we will consider how learning to interpret nonverbal cues can help us gain insights into different cultural meanings.

Questions for Thought

- How would you describe nonverbal communication?

- How does it manifest itself in our daily interactions?

- What are some nonverbal behaviors typical of different cultural groups?

II. Theory: What Research Tells Us

Definition of Nonverbal Behavior

In general terms, nonverbal behavior has been defined as communication without words (Birdwhistell, 1970; Hall, 1959). Such an elementary definition does not, however, account for the complexities of nonverbal communicative behavior. Not all nonverbal behavior or body language is communicative—that is, intended to convey shared meanings. For nonverbal behavior to be communicative, it must be part of a shared code of understanding among speakers. Such nonverbal behavior is as much a part of a rule-governed system as is verbal communication. It does not occur randomly, and various aspects and forms of nonverbal communication carry specific meanings for those sharing the same cultural rules.

A more complete definition of nonverbal behavior is offered by Leathers (1997:11).

> The use of interacting sets of visual, vocal, and invisible communication systems and subsystems by communicators with the systematic encoding and decoding of nonverbal symbols and signs for the purpose(s) of exchanging consensual meanings in specific communicative contexts.

From this point of view, nonverbal communication is made up of three principal interacting systems—the visual, the auditory, and the invisible.

Of the three, Leathers argues that the visual communication system is the most important.

Functions of Nonverbal Behavior

All cultures use nonverbal communication for a variety of functions; however, cultural differences in rules of display shape how and when these nonverbal behaviors are used for different functions. According to Ekman and Friesen (1969) and Patterson (1990), the most important functions of nonverbal behavior that are common across cultures include

- Expressing emotions
- Reinforcing, complementing, or accenting verbal messages
- Acting as a substitute for verbal communication
- Contradicting verbal messages
- Regulating and managing communicative situations
- Conveying messages in ritualized forms

Communication involves much more than the spoken word; a great deal of meaning is communicated nonverbally through our body language. Speakers use nonverbal cues to reinforce or emphasize oral communication. The types of cues, the frequency of their use, and the communicative situations under which they occur vary among cultures. Although nonverbal communication can take place without verbal communication (e.g., shaking one's head sideways to signal "no"), oral communication always involves some sort of nonverbal behavior, such as the speaker's tone of voice or sentence inflections. Most nonverbal behavior does not occur in isolation; it interacts and complements verbal behavior. Research in nonverbal communication suggests that understanding nonverbal behavior is key to understanding human communication (e.g., Feldman & Rime, 1991; Henley, 1977; Miller, 1988; Wolfgang, 1984).

Speakers regulate or control communicative situations through posture, gaze, extralinguistic cues, and other nonverbal behaviors. Body language can be used to determine when to begin a conversation, who is going to gain control of the conversation at any given point and for how long, and when to end the interaction. For example, an American's cue for turn taking in a conversational exchange with another American involves direct eye contact of the speaker with the listener for a second or so, followed by a glance away as the conversation continues. A few moments later, eye contact is established again, and so the cycle continues. If this contact does not occur, confusion sets in. In comparison, members of Asian cultures avoid eye contact and expect periods of silence between speaker turns. This expectation often makes it difficult for them to get a conversational turn in most American communicative situations. Members of still other cultures, such as the African American, Middle Eastern, and Mediterranean cultures, just begin talking with the hope of being let into the conversation, which Asians and European Americans view as interrupting. **(See Activity A—Talk! Talk! Talk!)**

Ritualized forms of nonverbal behavior are important aspects of communication. Whether or not to shake the other speaker's hand, how low to bow, or with whom to exchange kisses of greeting are examples of ritualized forms that vary greatly among cultures. Because these forms of nonverbal communication tend to be highly ritualized, they lend themselves more easily to description and delineation of function than do most other forms. **(See Activity B—What, for Me?)**

Nonverbal behavior provides much of the information that speakers process and manipulate in their social interactions. Speakers rely more on nonverbal cues than on verbal ones in determining and interpreting communicative situations (Davitz, 1969). In fact, more than 65 percent of the social meaning of a typical two-person exchange is carried by nonverbal cues (Birdwhistell, 1974). According to Hall (1959:2), "[w]hat people do is frequently more important than what they say." Speakers often rely on their nonverbal behavior to convey information regarding the actual meaning of their verbal messages. When interaction among speakers of different cultures is unsuccessful, the reason often includes different expectations for and interpretations of nonverbal behavior. Problems emerge when one interprets others' behavior based on one's own frame of reference.

Learning appropriate nonverbal communication is an integral part of the socialization process of the members of any given culture. The precise role nonverbal communication plays varies from culture to culture. In low-context cultures, such as North American and northern European ones, the verbal message is of central importance, and nonverbal behavior generally serves to complement and supplement verbal interactions. Members of high-context cultures, such as the Korean or Chinese cultures, believe that most meaning can and should be understood in the context in which speakers find themselves. A large part of meaning is conveyed, negotiated, and understood without resorting to actual words. Indeed, in Korean culture, the art of nonverbal communication is such an integral part of the language and culture that there is an actual term, *nunch'i,* that translates as communication with the body and eyes.

As a component of culture, nonverbal communication has much in common with language—both are coding systems that speakers learn and pass on as part of the cultural experience. There are three main reasons why miscommunication and confusion often arise with respect to nonverbal behavior in cross-cultural interactions (Ting-Toomey, 1999). First, the same nonverbal cue can signify different meanings in different cultures. In the United States, for instance, holding the index finger and thumb together in a circle means okay. This same cue in Brazil is used to insult someone. In Spain, to call someone over nonverbally, the fingers are curled toward the palm as the hand is flexed away from the speaker. To North Americans, this same gesture signals "good-bye."

Second, in most communicative interactions, more than one nonverbal cue is sent; generally, there are multiple nonverbal cues, which increases the possibility of uncertainties in interpretation. Because most nonverbal communication is culturally based, it often symbolizes what a culture has transmitted to its members. As different cultures speak different languages (or variations thereof), so different cultures avail themselves of different nonverbal behaviors.

Third, there are significant variations in nonverbal behaviors among the members of any given culture, based on such factors as age, gender, personality, intimacy, socioeconomic situation, and context. Touching patterns, for instance, almost always vary according to whether the gender of the speakers in a dyad is the same or different. In most Mediterranean cultures, it is acceptable for same-sex friends to hold hands, walk arm-in-arm, and generally touch each other more than is acceptable in many other cultures. Indeed, in such cultures as the United States or Canada, touching among same-sex friends is often regarded as inappropriate, particularly if the friends are heterosexual males.

A large part of nonverbal communication is unconscious and can be "unlearned" only with serious effort. Whenever speakers of one culture interact with speakers of a different culture, it is essential that speakers acquire new mental frameworks regarding how people feel in certain situations, what their behavior signifies, and how to respond to their behavior in the most appropriate manner. If the nonverbal behavior of one speaker is incongruent with another speaker's frame of reference, misinterpretations and miscommunication often occur. When a speaker does not know how to assess the intent and motivation of another speaker's nonverbal behavior, difficulties arise in the interpretation of the intended message. Moreover, nonverbal messages are misinterpreted more often than verbal messages, because so much of nonverbal behavior is below speakers' conscious awareness. **(See Activity C—Critical Incidents)**

Emotions

Certain nonverbal behaviors associated with basic human emotions (anger, fear, happiness, sadness, disgust, and surprise) are universal among all human beings, regardless of culture (Ekman, 1972, 1973; Ekman et al., 1987; Ekman & Keltner, 1997; Matsumoto et al., 1989). What differs cross-culturally is which emotions may be expressed under which conditions. Just as there are rules governing oral communication, so there are rules for communicating emotions. Cultural constraints determine when it is appropriate to show or communicate a speaker's thoughts, feelings, or emotions, as well as the intensity of these emotions. Culturally determined rules of display regulate both the display of emotions and what attitudes or emotions members of a particular culture are permitted and/or expected to express in a given situation.

Asian cultures limit their members in their permitted public display of emotion. Japanese culture, for instance, has very strict rules against expressing such negative emotions as anger and sadness. When Japanese speakers adhere to these rules while interacting with Westerners, the Westerners are often taken aback when Japanese laugh or smile in situations where Westerners expect anger or sadness. Although Japanese speakers are no happier over sad events than are Westerners, a public smile allows them to adhere to their cultural rule of avoiding inflicting personal sorrow on other people. In other words, this public smile does not indicate happiness but is meant to make amends for burdening someone else with one's own grief.

Latin and Mediterranean cultures, in contrast, are emotionally expressive cultures that support and encourage public manifestations of emotion. For example, Mediterranean people tend to use their eyes in varied ways for effect. Lewis (1999:137) notes that these include glaring (to show anger), glistening eyes (to show sincerity), winking with the eyes (common in France and Spain to imply conspiracy), and eyelash flutter (done by women to reinforce persuasion). Both male and female adult members of Latin and Arab societies also tend to cry more frequently in public situations, something generally unheard of by members of Finnish, Korean, and Japanese cultures.

Emotions are primarily expressed through nonverbal means. Facial expressions of anger, happiness, and dismay reflect the emotional state of the speaker. However, which emotion a given facial expression is intended to convey varies cross-culturally. As part of the enculturation process, children learn the rules of their culture that govern how emotions and feelings may be conveyed or even concealed. A smile on the face of a British, Scandinavian, or German business colleague means that progress is being made. However, the same smile on a Japanese businessman indicates anger or embarrassment. According to Lewis (1999), an unsmiling Arab implies desperation.

The circumstances under which emotional expressions are permitted differ from culture to culture. Just as children learn which facial expressions are used to convey which emotions, so, too, they learn the cultural rules that govern when and to what degree these emotions may be expressed. In Arab cultures, for instance, public displays of great emotion are common and expected. Spaniards tend to argue and quarrel in the presence of their business colleagues. In Britain, such public displays of emotion and altercation are generally less condoned, and the British, particularly British men, have traditionally been exhorted to display "a stiff upper lip." Japanese and Chinese cultural traditions permit even fewer public displays of emotion, such that speakers of other cultures often refer to Japanese and Chinese speakers as "inscrutable." In Russia, outsiders often wince at the constant arguments that they perceive the Russians to engage in, when, in fact, much of what sounds like argumentation to outsiders is lively discussion from the Russian perspective. The tone and loudness levels simply differ from what speakers of other languages are used to.

There is consistency in the recognition of facial expressions across cultures. A grimace, frown, or smile is so labeled among all humans (Ekman 1972, 1973). However, the culturally appropriate rules governing the use of facial expressions differ cross-culturally. Any given expression may have very different meanings from one culture to the next. A smile is recognized universally as an expression of friendliness; however, the appropriate expression of friendliness will differ cross-culturally. In one culture, a woman's smile to a male cashier indicates friendliness; in another culture, such a smile is interpreted as sexual enticement.

Differences in nonverbal behavior are often subtle, yet these differences can greatly hinder effective cross-cultural communication. As part of their enculturation process, individuals learn when and how it is appropriate to display any given emotion. They learn to interpret appropriately displays of emotion and the circumstances in which these occur. Culture influences and directs those experiences and is, therefore, a major contributor to how speakers send, receive, and respond to nonverbal symbols.

When speakers of one culture encounter people from other cultures, they often fail to understand them not only because of differences in language but also because of important differences in nonverbal communication. Difficulties in cross-cultural communication are common and often serious when a speaker is unfamiliar with the nonverbal communication patterns of the other culture. Socially competent speakers find themselves unable to interpret correctly the intentions of speakers of another culture, and by the same token, they find that their own signals are being interpreted inaccurately or inappropriately. Speakers cannot avoid reacting (often subconsciously) to their culturally influenced interpretation of other speakers' nonverbal cues. The issue in cross-cultural communication is that the decoding skills that speakers have spent a lifetime developing are no longer effective or sufficient to deal with these cross-cultural encounters.

There are subtle differences that affect speakers' abilities to understand people from other cultures. Nonverbal messages are typically ambiguous and may have various meanings, many of which are not obvious—even to the speaker. Nonverbal behaviors are continuous; they change regularly; and certain nonverbal behaviors, such as facial expressions, are often quite brief (Cacioppo & Petty, 1983). Nonverbal behavior is a product of the social context of a social interaction, and care must be taken in learning to accurately interpret the meaning of nonverbal messages. All of the various differences among cultures in such areas as the importance of age, gender, and status must be factored into interpretations of nonverbal behavior.

Different Types of Nonverbal Behavior

Most authorities agree that the realm of nonverbal communication comprises gestures, facial expressions, eye contact and gaze, posture and movement, patterns of touch (haptics), dress, silence, space (proxemics), and time (chronemics). *Paralanguage*—the sounds, movements, and gestures that relate to the flow of language—is also considered a critical component of nonverbal communication. Paralinguistic features refer specifically to auditory components of language, such as loudness, pitch, or tone. While these elements of nonverbal communication are universal, culture-specific rules govern their appropriate use in social and cultural contexts. In Arab cultures, for instance, loudness conveys sincerity and the strength of one's convictions, whereas in Asian cultures, loudness is equated with anger, dissent, and loss of control of one's emotions. Ting-Toomey (1999) suggests that the cultural values of different cultures influence the scope and permitted intensity of nonverbal behavior. Looking at the values of individualism versus collectivism, for instance, individualistic cultures tend to allow greater latitude for nonverbal behavior in terms of degree, spontaneity, and type. Collectivistic cultures tend to constrain and prescribe their nonverbal behavior more carefully, because of an emphasis on harmony in social relationships and in-group reactions.

Proxemics

Proxemics, or the use of space, refers to an area to which access is allowed or denied to other people or objects. Individuals' conception and use of personal space vary among cultures (Gudykunst & Kim, 1984; Hall 1959, 1983). Personal space can be conceived of as an imaginary bubble surrounding an individual. It is the distance speakers prefer to keep from one another in communicative situations. The "bubble" increases and decreases depending on the context and on such variables as speakers' gender, age, and social status. Cultures can be differentiated in terms of the intimacy of personal space preferred by the members of that culture. Hall (1966, 1976, 1983) argues that people manage intimacy by controlling their sensory exposure through the use of interpersonal space and distance. How this intimacy is perceived and maintained is culturally based. Different expectations of the use of personal space frequently lead to breakdowns in communicative interactions among speakers of different cultures. Arab speakers, for instance, position themselves much closer to each other than northern Europeans or North Americans find comfortable. Because the notion of personal space differs, speakers who feel comfortable with greater distance between them will try to move away from speakers who feel the need for closer interaction. In fact, police interrogators in the United States often use crowding of suspects' personal space as an intimidation tool. Such invasion of personal space leads to an increased sense of dominance and threat.

Those cultures in which people tend to stand close to each other and to engage in frequent touching are referred to as *high-contact cultures*. These include the Arabs, Latin Americans, Greeks, and Turks, among others. In a high-contact culture such as Egypt or other Arab cultures, people prefer to stand close to one another. When an Arab is in a communicative situation with an American, the American often feels crowded because his or her personal space is being infringed on, while the Arab feels frustrated because he or she is being kept at an uncomfortable distance from the other speaker. Those cultures in which people tend to stand away from one another and to avoid frequent touching are referred to as *low-contact cultures*. These include northern Europeans, Canadians, and Americans. In the United States, a moderate contact culture, people prefer to stand about "an arm's length" apart from one another. More extreme examples of low-contact cultures include most Asian cultures, where emphasis is placed on discrete nonverbal behavior, such as minimal eye contact between superiors and inferiors, minimal touching except between close same-sex friends, and active maintenance of space between speakers. **(See Activity D—Getting Together)**

Hall (1966) posits that differences in interpretations of personal space stem from cultures having different perceptions of the boundaries of the self. For North Americans and northern Europeans, that boundary is contained within their skin. This privacy zone includes their clothes and a small space around the body. In the Arab culture, however, the self is at a central core within the body shell. This view leads to a different proxemic pattern, where Arabs tolerate crowding and frequent same-sex touching. Elevator and public transportation behavior also differs. When

North Americans enter an elevator and someone else is already in it, they will move to the opposite end. Similarly, on uncrowded buses or subways, North Americans generally look for a seat away from other riders or at least choose to sit with a seat between them and another rider. Arabs, in contrast, will seek to stand or sit close to others, whether in an elevator or on public transportation. Asians, although low-contact cultures, also crowd together in public areas. Japanese subways are notorious for packing in people tightly, with people even assigned the job of pushing more people in before the doors close. Koreans and Chinese will also crowd in very closely in public transportation and think nothing of pushing everyone in the way to get on or off a bus or train.

The underlying reason for such crowding in Asian cultures, however, differs from that of the Arabs. The difference lies in the differing conceptions of self; members of Arab cultures seek out frequent and extensive contact (physical and social) with others, while Asian cultures tend to be densely populated societies that have no physical alternatives. Asians thus manage to maintain their personal space or bubble by avoiding eye contact or verbal exchanges with strangers, no matter how close they are sitting or standing to others.

The sense and use of space also vary among cultures. In offices, Germans generally keep their doors closed, whereas North Americans keep theirs open. For Germans, keeping doors open is both a violation of privacy and a distraction; how can one work distracted by the constant comings and goings of others? To North Americans, closed doors signal important meetings that are not to be interrupted. Continually closed doors, however, convey the idea of distance, reserve, and standoffishness. Japanese offices typically have no doors, and everything is open, accessible, and audible to everyone else. Employees in companies have desks arranged in tight rows with no partitions between them; only senior executives have private offices. **(See Activity E—Closing the Distance)**

When eating in restaurants, North Americans are accustomed to having a table to themselves and without disturbances from outsiders. In essence, diners' tables become their own personal space for as long as they occupy that space. In Italy, however, it is accepted for vendors and even beggars to enter a restaurant to sell their wares or to beg for money from the patrons. Such behavior is not viewed as an intrusion, since a table in a restaurant does not become the diners' "personal space," where they should be left to themselves and not disturbed except by the waiter. Related to this is the fact that North American restaurant patrons expect (and do receive) their own table; they do not share their table with other diners as the restaurant becomes full. In other countries, strangers may automatically take their place at any unoccupied seat. Personal space is maintained by such means as avoiding eye contact with members of the other party. Interestingly, in some areas of the United States, certain types of restaurants, such as those found in the Amish areas of Pennsylvania, offer "family-style seating," a euphemism for seating patrons with strangers. Part of the attraction of such restaurants is the unique experience of sharing one's personal space with strangers in a restaurant.

The use of space within the home also differs among cultures. In North America, the kitchen area is commonly used for eating, both for family members and with friends. In many cultures, the kitchen area is reserved solely for food preparation, while in other cultures, the kitchen is used for family members only. In many parts of Brazil, a signal that one has become accepted as a close friend, or an in-group member, is often an invitation to share a family meal in the kitchen. In North America, bedrooms are generally off-limits except to close family members, but in Honduras, the master bedroom is also where family members and close friends gather to watch television. **(See Activity F—My House)**

Kinesics

Kinesics refers to the body movements involved in communication, especially as these movements accompany speech. People communicate messages by the way they walk, stand, and sit. Body movements can convey emotions, indicate status of speakers relative to each other, and mark speakers' degree of intimacy. Actual postural behavior and the meanings body movements carry vary from culture to culture. More than 700,000 physical signs or movements are used to communicate, but how these are interpreted depends on the culture in which they occur. Sapir (1958) refers to nonverbal behavior as an unwritten, elaborate, and secret code. If one is unable to read the kinesic signs encountered in another culture, misunderstandings may easily occur. Smiling and laughing are vital kinesic signs in intercultural communication. These practices vary from one cultural group to another, especially as far as meaning.

Another noticeable kinesic behavior, bowing, is mostly found in Asian cultures, such as Korea and Japan. Westerners tend to shake hands as a form of greeting, while Asians have been accustomed to bowing. Though they no longer accompany a bow with clasped hands in front of the chest, Koreans or Japanese commonly greet others with a short bow, the depth of which depends on how much respect an individual chooses to show. Cultural changes are affecting this cultural practice in different Asian countries; different cultural groups appear to have their own degree of bowing. In Western countries, changes in hand-shaking practices are evident. In many Western cultures, hand shaking between men and women is a common greeting during initial formal introductions in professional settings. Formerly, such hand shaking occurred primarily between men. While such hand shaking between peers in formal contexts, regardless of gender, has become more common, differences remain in the occurrence and frequency of handshakes between higher- and lower-status participants. One American visiting professor in Chile found that shaking the hands of her students brought forth peals of laughter. For the Chileans, the dissidence between status and nonverbal behavior was farcical.

Another aspect of kinesic behavior is posture. On the American corporate scene, the display of a relaxed stance at work as displayed by African Americans has often been equated with casualness and a lack of enthusiasm for one's work, whereas a rigid posture with focused intent while at work has been viewed as a more desirable trait. It is quite evident that being sensitized to the kinesic system is a necessary cultural goal if one does not want to formulate a wrong interpretation of a kinesic signal and subsequently be misunderstood. In North America, posture and eye contact are good indicators of what speakers are actually thinking, thoughts that may be in direct contradiction to what they are saying with words. As one example, while a speaker's spoken words indicate calmness and peace of mind, his or her clenched fingers reveal that person's actual inner anxiety. Extensive studies in the United States have shown that jurors perceive those persons on the witness stand who maintain clear and firm eye contact as more trustworthy and honest than those who do not (e.g., Anthony & Vinson, 1987; Bennett & Hirschhorn, 1993; Vinson, 1982). In the United States, people expect those telling the truth to look them in the eye and those lying or trying to hide something to look away (Kleinke, 1986; Burgoon, Coker, & Coker, 1986).

Eye contact

American teachers expect their students to show that they are listening to them by maintaining eye contact with the teacher. When students fail to maintain such eye contact, teachers are likely to interpret this non-verbal behavior negatively. If students come from a culture that depends on students showing respect by not engaging in eye contact with teachers (their superiors), misunderstandings will occur.

Another important difference in nonverbal communication across cultures occurs in eye behavior. Research has shown that eye movements perform a variety of different and important communicative functions (e.g., Kleinke, 1986; Leathers, 1997; Webbink, 1986). The principal communicative functions of eye behavior include

- Indicating the attention and/or interest of the speakers

- Persuading listeners of the speaker's virtues, such as credibility, honesty, and respectfulness

- Establishing, maintaining, and ending degrees of intimacy among speakers

- Controlling or regulating the sequencing in the participation of the speakers in a communicative situation

- Displaying or revealing emotions

- Establishing and maintaining the power and status of the speakers

- Conveying impressions of self to the other speaker

While eye behavior performs such functions in virtually all cultures, the actual manifestations of eye contact or gaze vary. Cross-cultural differences are apparent in with whom one may have eye contact, the duration of the eye contact, and in which situations participants engage in eye contact. Members of low-contact cultures, such as China, Japan, and other Asian cultures, tend to avoid eye contact in communicative interactions. Americans and northern European cultures are moderate-contact cultures that engage in more eye contact than members of low-contact cultures but in less contact than members of such high-contact cultures as those of Latin America or the Mediterranean (Hall, 1966; Watson & Graves, 1966).

Conversations are also regulated and managed by eye contact. In the European American middle-class subculture in the United States, for example, eye contact is important and expected when communicating with someone. It is a sign of truthfulness and respectfulness in the classroom. Yet children in the lower-class African American subculture are taught not to make eye contact with people they respect; therefore, they will not look the teacher in the eyes. So, too, in some American Indian tribes, youngsters were taught that it is a sign of disrespect to have eye contact with an elder. In Arab countries, in Spain, and in Greece, close eye contact among men is maintained to the point of staring, implying dominance and reinforcing one's message. Such eye behavior between a woman and a man, however, has sexual overtones. Peruvians, Bolivians, and Chileans find it insulting not to have eye contact while talking, while Asians avoid direct eye contact as a sign of respect and deference. Germans maintain a steady gaze when communicating, whereas Americans tend to look at the left eye and then the right eye and then at something other than the speaker's face. In Russia, members of both sexes engage in steady direct eye contact, or staring. Therefore, Americans accustomed to catching a waitress's or clerk's attention by making eye contact will often be unsuccessful in Russia until they utter the word *devooshka* (girl) with a rising question intonation. In Taiwan, eye contact between peers in conversational settings is also important; however, it is also appropriate to rotate from actual eye contact to looking at people's sides, over their shoulders, or at their clothing, then back to actual eye contact. While such behavior on the part of Taiwanese is intended to make participants feel comfortable, it conveys a very different sense in North America.

Gestures

Gestures are an integral part of communication. Speakers use gestures daily, almost instinctively, whether to beckon someone, punctuate spoken discourse, or offer ritualized greetings. In the Italian culture, frequent and emphatic hand gestures are routine in everyday conversation, and they both reinforce and at times substitute for speech. Gestures that have acquired specific meanings are referred to as *emblematic gestures*. These include such gestures as the thumbs-up sign, the head shake, the two-fingered V sign, and signals used to beckon someone. The actual significance of any emblematic gesture may vary greatly from culture to culture. What may be a polite or friendly gesture in one culture may be an impolite and obscene gesture in another. While speakers in one culture may learn to use only a verbal command to indicate "halt" or "cease," speakers of another culture may learn that it is acceptable to hold an arm up in the air with the palm facing another person to indicate "stop."

The same or similar nonverbal forms of communication often serve different functions in different cultures. Misinterpretation and miscommunication occur when nonverbal communication behaviors are exhibited and used under different circumstances and to convey different meanings. For example, a thumbs-up gesture in the United States has a positive meaning, while that same gesture in Iran is extremely obscene. The hitchhiking signal used by Americans is taboo in New Zealand and Australia. In some cultures, such as those of the United States and Canada, a head nod up and down will indicate agreement, while this same movement in Greek culture will indicate disagreement. Similarly, the hand held up palm forward and fingers bending inward and outward will signify "good-bye" to an American and "come here" to a Spaniard.

Emblems are often used to replace verbal messages, whether to indicate "come here" or "no." These are also the easiest of the nonverbal behaviors to identify and those most often described in books attempting to list specific nonverbal behaviors that foreigners should understand and/or avoid. These gestures, however, are only the tip of the iceberg. For truly successful cross-cultural communication, speakers need to understand the greater role of nonverbal messages.

Related to emblems are *illustrators*. This term refers to nonverbal hand gestures that are used to reinforce, illustrate, or accentuate verbal communication. Members of certain cultures use a wider range of illustrators than do others. Italian speakers, for instance, are noted for their use of extensive hand gestures and are often described as "talking with their hands." Generally, members of Latin and Mediterranean cultures make more frequent use of illustrators than do members of Asian cultures, where such use is less extensive and more restricted. Certain illustrators, like emblems, also convey different meanings across cultures. In Mexico and Ecuador, it is inappropriate to indicate a person's size using a hand gesture to indicate height. This type of gesture is used only for animals and is particularly insulting to speakers from rural areas. In North America, such a gesture can be used to indicate the height for anyone or anything.

Haptics

Cultures differ in how they make use of and interpret touch behavior, or *haptics*. Crucial variables influencing haptics include gender, age, and status of participants. The meaning of touch behavior varies from culture to culture, as well as within subcultures. Touching can be used to show solidarity, support, dominance, attention, and affection. The meaning a touch has depends on various factors, including, for example, the cultural meanings attached to haptic behavior, how one feels at the time, past experiences, and the relationship with the person involved.

Overall, members of high-contact cultures engage in more tactile behavior than do members of low-contact cultures. Latin Americans touch members of the same sex much more frequently than do Asians. To show confidence in the speaker, for instance, a speaker may grip the other speaker's upper arm. In North America, women tend to touch more so than men. When touching occurs between men and women who are not intimates, the man usually initiates the tactile behavior, which can carry aggressive and/or sexual overtones. In some African cultures, speakers will continue to hold each other's hand while talking. For the Japanese, in contrast, most touching behavior is unacceptable and avoided as unhygienic.

Haptic behavior also varies in terms of what can be touched and what part of the body can be used to touch. In Thailand, it is insulting to touch someone's head, as the head is considered the seat or repository of the soul. For Moslems and in some African cultures, the use of the left hand to pass or touch something is extremely rude, as the left hand is considered unclean. It is also highly offensive to offer the left hand as a greeting or to use the left hand to give or receive something. In Korea, it is a show of politeness to hand someone something with both hands rather than with just one hand.

Chronemics

The usage and importance of time varies significantly among cultures. Cultures differ in how they structure, construe, and perceive time. Some cultures, such as Native American tribes and African cultures, emphasize present time and have no future constructs in their languages. Some cultures (e.g., the Chinese) place great emphasis on the past together with the present and the future. They regard time not as linear or as a forward-moving continuum but, rather, as operating along a more circular course. Time and sense of history also play different roles in different cultures. The cultures of the United States and Canada, for example, are very new in terms of history. Members of such cultures prefer to focus on the present and tend to regard events that happened 100 years ago as old. In cultures that have existed for much longer periods of time, people think nothing of discussing events from a century ago and feel a stronger bond with the past. In the early 1970s, Secretary of State Henry Kissinger, meeting with then Premier of China Zhou Enlai, reportedly asked him what he thought of the French Revolution that took place in 1788. The Chinese premier's response was, "Time will tell."

As we discussed in chapter 3, Hall (1983) has distinguished between two cultural patterns of time: monochronic (M-time) and polychronic (P-time). For members of M-time cultures, time is of the essence, is not to be wasted, and is to be scheduled and compartmentalized appropriately for maximum efficiency. Schedules and day planners are the norm, and the making and keeping of appointments are essential. Timekeeping devices of all sorts are ubiquitous, and clock time governs all activities. Cultures also differ in how importantly they judge the entire notion of "time." The United States, for instance, is a culture that places a great emphasis on time—with the common theme that "time is money" and the admonishment not to waste time.

Members of P-time cultures take a very different view of time. Time is more flexible. Appointments can be broken, several things can be scheduled simultaneously, and time cannot or should not be compartmentalized and fixed but is amorphous and must and will change frequently in response to myriad influences. In P-time cultures, time is not necessarily unimportant, but it is construed in different terms. Among Arabs, the future will be "as God wills" *(inshallah),* not something man determines, even if the future in question involves meetings arranged for tomorrow. Similarly, Spanish has the saying "El hombre propone y Dios dispone," which translates into English as "Man plans and God decides." Levine, West, and Reis (1979) found that lateness in Brazil, a P-time culture, meant something different than in the United States. They claim that rather than Brazilians being less punctual, they have a more flexible notion of exact time. Their concept of "two o'clock" not only entails that precise clock time when the big hand is on the twelve and the small hand on the two but encompasses a longer interval both before and after that exact point in time.

Different conceptions of the role and meaning of time can lead to cross-cultural misunderstandings, insofar as members of M-time may attribute negative personality traits to members of P-time. For instance, rather than seeing "lateness" as the product of a prevailing cultural norm including a difference in what time interval constitutes "late," M-time speakers may interpret lateness as being a cultural character flaw. Simi larly, members of P-time cultures may interpret the emphasis on strict definitions of time by M-time culture members as overly rigid. In addition, both socioeconomic and cultural differences in the availability of time keeping devices, such as clocks or wristwatches, can contribute to different constructions of the time interval surrounding the notion of "late." Hall (1983) and Levine et al. (1979) noted the lack of ubiquitous timekeeping devices at a Navajo Indian reservation and in the Brazilian populace in general. This contrasts to the situations in Germany, where public and church clocks chime every quarter of an hour, and in the United States, where clocks of all types are placed everywhere. **(See Activity G—Time Is Money)**

Silence

The role of *silence,* or the absence of talk, in communication also varies from culture to culture. In northern European and North American cultures, silence is viewed somewhat negatively. North American, German, French, southern European, and Arab speakers expect some sort of immediate response to a suggestion or a request. Initial silence is generally interpreted by them as a negative response. Asians and many Native American cultures view silence as an important and appropriate part of social interaction. Speakers from these cultures often use some moments of silence before offering a response to another speaker. Such initial silence conveys the listener's respect for the speaker; it indicates that the listener has heard the speaker's words and is giving them due thought. Silence is viewed as a time to learn, to think about, and to review what the speaker has said. In cultures that prize silence, responding too quickly after speakers have finished their turns is interpreted as having devoted inadequate attention and consideration to speakers' words and thoughts. Maintaining relatively long periods of silence may also lead to misunderstandings in the language classroom. When teachers and students hold different expectations regarding the length of response time to a question, for instance, teachers may regard students who are slow to speak as slow to learn, while students may regard teachers who expect more immediate responses as brusque. **(See Activity H—Cross-Cultural Trivia Quiz)**

Teaching and Learning Connections

Without a doubt, nonverbal awareness is a heightened sensitivity to the body language of other cultures in many variations, particularly since body language conveys up to 80 percent of one's message. There has been a great deal of research conducted in the area of nonverbal behavior. Extensive research has been done, for instance, on North American nonverbal behavior, including gender differences in nonverbal communication. Various studies have been conducted cross-culturally or within other specific cultures. Some studies have focused exclusively on one aspect of nonverbal behavior (e.g., gaze or interpersonal distance); others have focused on nonverbal behavior in specific settings (e.g., business). Most of this work is beyond the scope of this chapter (see "Further Readings"). **(See Activity I—Learning to Look)**

Knowing that what people say verbally may be complemented, supplemented, or even compromised by their generally intuitive use of nonverbal behavior is crucial for people attempting to communicate more effectively across cultures. Students should be sensitized to the varied possibilities of how to improve their awareness of the varied aspects and culturally influenced conventions governing nonverbal communication across cultures. There are a number of ways in which the negative effects of conflicting nonverbal communication habits can be lowered (Althen 1988:146). These include making others aware of the wide range of human activity falling under the category of nonverbal behavior, learning as much as possible about the nonverbal communication habits of others, avoiding exaggeration as to the effects of differences in nonverbal communication, and trying to avoid interpreting what others mean and evaluating their behavior based on one's own concepts of appropriate nonverbal behavior. Teachers can introduce varied classroom activities to engage their students in making inventories of these behavior types, thereby allowing students to discuss their own nonverbal behaviors and helping them to recognize these nonverbal behaviors and their meanings when used by others.

Questions for Study and Discussion

1. Define nonverbal behavior. Give original examples.

2. Describe the following aspects of nonverbal communication: proxemics, kinesics, gestures, haptics, chronemics, eye contact, silence. Discuss how these can differ cross-culturally. What examples can you provide from your own experience?

3. Discuss three functions of nonverbal behavior. Provide examples of each.

4. Compare high-contact cultures and low-contact cultures. What connections can you draw between these two cultural types and the use of nonverbal behavior in each?

5. Leathers defines what he believes are the principal interacting systems in nonverbal communication. Do you agree or disagree? Explain why.

6. How do differences in nonverbal behavior hinder cross-cultural communication? Give specific examples.

7. How do cultural values influence nonverbal behavior in individualistic cultures and in collectivistic cultures? Give actual examples.

III. Practice: What Activities Show Us

A. Talk! Talk! Talk! (15–20 minutes)

Individuals of various cultural backgrounds use different combinations of verbal and nonverbal cues to make each other understood. Some cultures are overwhelmingly verbal, while others are largely dependent on the nonverbal aspect of communication.

Purpose: To illustrate the role of nonverbal communication in face-to-face interactions

Procedure:

1. Bring in a kitchen timer or stopwatch.

2. Select a conversation topic of relevance and interest to the class, such as current foreign events, immigration laws, space exploration, school policies, or arranged marriages.

3. Work in groups of 3–4.

4. Set the timer, allowing participants 5 minutes to discuss the topic.

5. During their discussion, tell them to stand in a circle facing one another, keeping their hands in their pockets or their arms hanging straight at their sides. They are not to move or use their hands or arms at any time during the discussion.

6. As a full group, discuss the activity.

   Sample Questions:

   - How did it feel not to be able to move or use your hands and arms? Why?

   - How did this affect your ability to communicate?

   - What conclusions can you draw about yourself and nonverbal communication?

   - What are some implications for classroom teaching and language learning?

B. What, for Me? (15–20 minutes)

On which occasion to give someone a gift, what type of gift is appropriate, and how the gift should be presented and received are all factors that differ among cultures. By the same token, the symbolic role that gift giving plays also varies. In some cultures, the giving of gifts is an integral part of establishing and maintaining social relationships. In others, gift giving is a way of displaying personal wealth and status.

Purpose: To challenge students' cultural assumptions by the evidence presented in gift giving

Procedure:

1. Ask participants to reflect on gift giving customs in their culture.

2. Have them think about the wider implications of gift giving. In their reflections, participants should attempt to evaluate how gift giving fits into the larger cultural picture.

   Sample Questions:

   • How does gift giving reflect values that the culture deems important?

   • When (i.e., on what occasions or circumstances) are gifts exchanged? What kinds of ceremonies surround gift-giving occasions?

   • Among whom are gifts exchanged? Does this reveal anything about status, authority, or social roles?

   • What type of discourse surrounds gift giving events? Do participants engage in ritualized routines or elaborate thanks? (In Japan, for instance, when people give a gift, they often say, "Tsumaranai mono desu ga dozo" [This is a very poor gift, but please accept it], to emphasize their humbleness and modesty.)

3. Record the circumstances and reactions of the receiver on worksheet 2. In completing this worksheet, you may draw from personal experiences or situations you have observed in

Worksheet 2. Evaluating Gift-Giving Situations

Context	Reactions
A Japanese student offers his teacher a gift at the end of the school year and says, "This is a very poor gift, but please accept it."	The teacher is surprised by the gift and by the words of the student. He is not quite sure how to respond. He thanks the student and leaves the gift on the table. The student seems disappointed.

the media or in printed materials. Work individually or in pairs.

4. Working in small groups, pool and analyze data from the worksheets and report back to the full group.

5. As a full group, discuss these gift-giving events as a microcosm of larger patterns of obligation and control.

Sample Questions:

- Were you embarrassed when you received a gift?

- Were you hurt, insulted, or surprised by a recipient's actions and/or response to your gift?

- When you received a gift, did you keep it or return it?

- How did you feel as the gift giver?

C. Critical Incidents (15–20 minutes)

The following critical incidents are exercises focusing on nonverbal communication. The situations described in each incident present cultural predicaments. There is no single solution to each incident. The intent of the exercise is to stimulate insightful discussion by raising issues involving cultural dilemmas and to increase an understanding of the relationship between nonverbal behavior and culture.

Purpose: To expand an awareness of differences in nonverbal behavior

Procedure:

1. Prepare different sets of two to four critical incidents. How many sets will depend on the total number of participants (e.g., for a class of 12, prepare four sets).

2. Work in groups of 3–4.

3. Pass out the sets of critical incidents, and ask the participants to brainstorm possible solutions.

4. As a full group, discuss the critical incidents, the possible solutions, and the cultural values underlying the areas of cultural conflict.

5. Write your own critical incident. Share this with a partner or the full group.

Critical Incident 1

Mr. Singh and several associates check into a prestigious hotel in a major American city. After they have filled out the registration form and after the hotel desk clerks have verified the credit card information and length of stay, the clerks hand each person his key, being careful to smile and make eye contact with each guest. Mr. Singh and his associates are rather upset and wonder whether they have made the right decision in staying at this hotel. The clerks wonder about the abruptness, if not rudeness, of this group in never thanking or even greeting them.

Critical Incident 2

Laura, an exchange student from Mexico visiting a rural high school in the midwestern United States, has found herself the object of unwanted attention from male students in her school. The principal has also called her into the office and chided her for dressing "like a hooker" and wearing too much makeup. When she returns home crying, she finds her host parents siding with the principal. Laura is shocked and bewildered, because at home she has always been known as a "good girl."

Critical Incident 3

Brigitta, a native German high school teacher, invited her Spanish colleagues for cocktails at her home before their dinner reservation at 7:45 at a neighborhood restaurant. The time for cocktails was set for 7:00 P.M. When the time approached, her Spanish colleagues had not yet arrived. By 7:15, there was still no word from her colleagues. When they finally arrived at 8:30, Brigitta was furious. She was not accustomed to having friends arrive so late without an apology.

Critical Incident 4

An American army trainer had worked extensively with armed forces in Latin America. While there, he became accustomed to Latin American army personnel hugging him and showing other physical signs of friendship. Back in Washington, D.C., several years later, he attended an official military get-together honoring many of the Latin American military personnel he had worked with previously. Several of them asked him to accompany them on a sight-seeing tour of Washington the following day. He happily agreed.

The next day, he met them by the Washington Monument. After visiting the monument, the group began to walk down the mall toward the Capitol. Without a second thought, one of the Latin American military men reached for the American's hand and proceeded to stroll hand-in-hand with him. In shock, the American pulled away his hand and, without thinking, asked, "What do you think you're doing?" The Latin American became extremely offended and said, "I thought we were friends."

Critical Incident 5

Your class is a mix of Asian and Middle Eastern students. You are finding it difficult to conduct class discussions or do small-group work, because the Asian students remain silent while the Middle Eastern students dominate all discussions.

Critical Incident 6

A representative of several parents of Thai children has come to complain to the principal that the teachers are insulting the Thai children. One of the kindergarten teachers often pats the children's heads, and teachers in other grades frequently hand out papers or pass out books over the children's heads.

Critical Incident 7

Recently, a Canadian tourist went to Brazil. He found himself leery of taking taxis, because he had seen a taxi driver making a gesture that he couldn't understand and that he thought might mean something bad. Later, he learned that the driver had been making the gesture for "full."

Critical Incident 8

Masahide, a Japanese student, met his new roommate, Antonio, an Italian student, in the university dormitory. Whenever the two engaged in conversation, Antonio employed his hands, arms, shoulders, and head to make his point. Masahide was concerned, because he thought Antonio must be very upset and angry with him to be so emotional and demonstrative.

Discussion

Critical Incident 1
Eye contact means different things in different cultures. In some cultures, eye contact indicates that speakers are paying attention to one another; in others, eye contact signals aggression or sexual intent. In some cultures, avoiding eye contact is a sign of respect.

Critical Incident 2
Acceptable dress and the use of cosmetics are not the same everywhere. Whether topless bathing or the veiling of women, what one culture finds normal, another finds offensive.

Critical Incident 3
Time is often viewed differently across cultures. Germans are very time conscious and exact with time commitments, while Spaniards tend to be more casual and relaxed. Spanish people view arriving an hour or two within the agreed-on time as still being on time. When such a practice is unknown by the other party involved, conflicts arise.

Critical Incident 4

Who may be touched by whom and in which contexts varies cross-culturally. What may be perceived as normal touching behavior in one culture may be considered inappropriate or even insulting in another. It is important to become observant of the environment and the people around oneself in a new culture, to understand what is and is not appropriate nonverbal behavior.

Critical Incident 5

Asian and Middle Eastern cultures differ significantly in their use of silence, deference, and verbal strategies. In Asian cultures, members are taught to avoid confrontation, to defer to their superiors (including teachers), to avoid interruptions, and to use minimal body language—the opposite of Middle Eastern cultures. Given the great variation in appropriate and expected behavior, it is often very difficult for members of these opposing cultures to relate mutually in interactive learning situations.

Critical Incident 6

The head is considered sacred in Thailand, so it is inappropriate and indeed insulting to touch the head of a Thai person or to pass an object over a Thai person's head.

Critical Incident 7

Different gestures have culturally determined meanings; these are generally known as *emblems*. Although the same or similar gestures may be found in different cultures, the meanings often vary greatly. The North American index finger and thumb together signify "OK"; in Brazil, this is an extremely rude and offensive sexual gesture; in Japan, it means money. Emblematic gestures may also exist in one culture and not in another, as is illustrated by this particular critical incident.

Critical Incident 8

Certain cultures (e.g., Italians, Arabs, and South Americans) employ body language that is often different from that found in other cultures (e.g., Japanese or Finnish). Since body language plays a major role in communication, it is important that the parties involved understand its meaning unquestionably.

 I, A

To adapt for the language classroom,

Writing Critical Incidents

- See chapter 2, Activity F, for suggestions.

D. Getting Together (15–20 minutes)

When individuals are asked to alter their accustomed nonverbal behavior, some encounter difficulties in doing so, while others readily adapt to a new mode of communication. To appreciate a new way of nonverbal communication means to open oneself up to change.

Purpose: To increase understanding of the role of nonverbal behavior in communicative settings

Procedure:

1. Prepare a set of index cards for each group of participants, writing one of the following instructions on each card.

   - Tap your fingers on a hard surface when you want to make a point.

   - Frequently touch the person to whom you are speaking on the shoulder or upper arm.

   - Wink frequently at the other speakers in your group.

   - Nudge another speaker in your group when you want to speak.

   - Lean into the person to whom you are speaking.

2. Work in groups of 3–5.

3. Select a conversation topic of relevance and interest to the full group, such as current foreign events, team standings, crime, drugs, marriage, or teen dating.

4. Have the small groups discuss the topic for 4–5 minutes.

5. After this time period, distribute the index cards. Each participant receives an index card with instructions and is to read and follow the instructions without sharing them with the others.

6. Allow the groups to continue their discussions for another 4–5 minutes.

7. End the conversations and have the groups come together to discuss the activity.

Sample Questions:

- How did you feel about enacting the nonverbal behavior you were assigned?

- How did the behavior you were assigned affect your communication with others in your group?

- What changes in communication did you notice after you received your instructions?

- What effected these changes?

- With whom did you find it difficult to communicate? Why?

- What have you discovered about nonverbal communication and yourself?

 I, A

To adapt for the language classroom,

Sample Questions:

- How did you feel using the assigned nonverbal behavior?

- How did your assigned nonverbal behavior affect your ability to communicate?

- Did you find it difficult to communicate with any member of your group? Why or why not?

- What have you learned about nonverbal communication and yourself?

Adapted from a workshop presented for Youth for Understanding International Exchange, by J. Blohm, 1991.

E. Closing the Distance (10–15 minutes)

The concept of personal space varies from culture to culture. Whether one prefers to be close to or far away from another individual during a verbal encounter depends on one's cultural background and experiences.

Purpose: To demonstrate people's intuitive recognition of personal space

Procedure:

1. Choose four volunteers.

2. Ask two of the volunteers to step outside of the classroom and shut the door.

3. Instruct one of the two remaining volunteers as follows:

   * When participant X returns to the classroom, walk toward him or her.

4. Call one of the volunteers from outside of the classroom back in.

5. Both the volunteer from outside the class and the one from in the class should begin walking toward each other.

6. When they are directly in front of each other, stop them and have the full group discuss what happened.

   Sample Questions:

   * What happened the closer participant X and participant Y came to each other? (They usually begin to giggle, blush, look away from each other, and sometimes make wisecracks.)

   * Why did they do this?

   * How did you feel as you got closer to each other? Why?

7. Instruct the volunteer remaining in the classroom as follows:

   * When participant Z comes in, walk toward him or her, maintaining direct eye contact the entire time.

8. Call the other volunteer from outside of the classroom back in.

9. Both the volunteer from outside the class and the one from in the class should begin walking toward each other.

10. When they are directly in front of each other, stop them and have the full group discuss what happened.

Sample Questions:

- What happened the closer participant X and participant Y came to each other? (The one from outside the classroom generally breaks eye contact quickly and begins looking all around the classroom at the others.)

- Why did this happen?

- How did you feel while maintaining this eye contact? Why?

Follow-up:

- Conclude with a more general discussion of personal space.

Sample Questions:

- What have you learned about your personal space?

- Do you feel any differently about personal space with persons of the same sex than you do with persons of the opposite sex?

- How can you define your personal space?

- What role has culture played in your interpretation of personal space?

F. My House (10–15 minutes)

We are often not consciously aware of how much the use of space within our homes reflects our cultural upbringing. The spheres we regard as private and those we regard as public often differ between cultures. It is also of interest to reflect on how we as individuals create a sphere of personal space, even in crowded circumstances.

Purpose: To examine the relationship between the use of space in the home and in one's culture

Procedure:

1. Draw a rough diagram of your home on a separate sheet of paper.

2. Label each room or area.

3. Place an *X* in those areas reserved only for family members.

4. Place an *O* in those areas used for visitors and family members.

5. Discuss the areas selected.

Sample Questions:

- Do you have rooms for formal entertaining? If yes, when do you use these?

- If you live in a dormitory room or studio apartment with roommates, how have you created your own space? How does this compare to your classmates' use of space?

- Do you have a "guest bathroom"? If yes, in what ways does this bathroom differ from the family bathroom(s)? For example, are there special towels hanging in the guest bathroom?

- Do you close the bedroom doors when you have company? Why or why not? What influences your decision?

- Do you invite friends into your bedroom? Why or why not? What influences your decision?

 A

To adapt for the language classroom,

Follow-up:

- Write a reflective essay describing the connection between the rooms in your house, their use, and your culture.

G. Time Is Money (15–20 minutes)

Different cultures hold different views of the world, representing a kaleidoscopic outlook on the nature of reality. Time is one of these concepts, and it is seen differently by various cultures. For Americans, time is money. The Spanish and Italians lack adherence to punctuality. Asians view time as cyclic, or coming around again.

Purpose: To increase understanding of the concept of time in different cultures

Procedure:

1. Have participants share with the full group how the concept of time is viewed in their respective cultures.

2. Write their comments on the blackboard in two columns.

3. Ask them to indicate whether a comment on the board is positive or negative according to their experiences, by marking each with a plus sign (+) for positive or a minus sign (−) for negative.

4. Ask participants whether any patterns are developing (e.g., the mañana syndrome typical of Latino cultures, namely, the loose interpretation of what "on time" means; the deep sense of punctuality for Germans, Swiss, and Chinese; the lateness and warm apologies of Greeks).

5. Ask them to explain these patterns.

   Sample Questions:

   • Are the patterns geographical, cultural, or personal?

   • Are the patterns representative of a group or select individuals?

   • How does the concept of time affect personal relationships, business dealings, social life, and classroom etiquette?

   • Which groups fit into the M-time and P-time culture patterns? How did you determine this?

A

To adapt for the language classroom,

Procedure: Step 1

1. Discuss the concept of time and how the meaning and use of time differ cross-culturally. Then have participants share with the full group how the concept of time is viewed in their respective cultures.

   Sample Questions:

   • Omit last question.

H. Cross-Cultural Trivia Quiz (15–20 minutes)

Individuals of one culture are often unaware of the implications of certain nonverbal behaviors in other cultures. Such a lack of awareness may result in a display of nonverbal behavior found offensive by individuals of other cultures.

Purpose: To create an awareness of the appropriateness or inappropriateness of select nonverbal behaviors

Procedure:

1. Prepare copies of a cross-cultural trivia quiz. Use the quiz provided here (quiz 2) or make up your own.

2. Pass out the quiz and ask the participants to respond to each item with *true* or *false*.

3. After everyone has finished, discuss the responses.

   Sample Questions:

   • Did you choose *true* or *false?* Why?

   • In which instances would the nonverbal behaviors you found unacceptable be appropriate? Why?

   • In which cultures would the responses differ? Why?

Quiz 2. Cross-Cultural Trivia

True   False   1. Avoiding direct eye contact with the person with whom one is speaking is a sign of respect and deference.

True   False   2. Sitting so that the sole of one's shoe is pointed toward another person is considered insulting.

True   False   3. Frequent touching on the arm is viewed as a way to signal solidarity and rapport.

True   False   4. Giving someone the OK sign is the equivalent of what Americans term "giving someone the finger."

True   False   5. Touching a child's head is extremely offensive.

True   False   6. Nodding one's head in an up-and-down motion means "no."

True   False   7. Pointing with your foot or using it to perform such actions as moving a chair is considered poor behavior.

True   False   8. Public displays of affection such as hugging and kissing between members of the opposite sex are acceptable.

True   False   9. Hand-holding between same-sex friends is common.

True   False   10. It is important to stand an arm's length away from the person with whom you are speaking.

True   False   11. Waiting in orderly lines at cash registers and bus stops is the norm.

True   False   12. Honking your car horn is done frequently to signal a friendly greeting to a passing car or pedestrian.

Discussion of the Quiz

1. In many cultures, avoiding direct eye contact is a way of showing respect and deference. In North America, however, eye contact indicates truthfulness and is a way to show a person is paying attention to the speaker.

2. In some cultures, the soles of a person's feet are regarded as dirty, given that they are used to walk on. Showing someone the sole of one's shoe therefore signals an insult. For North Americans, "putting one's feet up" is a way of relaxing and indicating that the person feels at ease and comfortable in a particular situation. In other cultures, the sole of one's foot should never face another person, nor should a person's foot be used for pointing at or dragging an object.

3. In many cultures, frequent touching between members of the same sex carries no sexual overtones. It is an indicator of the speaker's attention, affinity, and camaraderie.

4. Gestures that are used to replace verbal communication and that have designated meanings to the members of a particular culture are called *emblems*. The meanings associated with emblems are arbitrary and vary from culture to culture. What may have a positive meaning in one culture may have just the opposite meaning in another.

5. In many East Asian cultures, such as Thailand, the head is viewed as the repository of a person's soul and should therefore not be randomly touched.

6. See number 4.

7. See number 2

8. In many cultures, including most Asian cultures, it is inappropriate for members of the opposite sex to touch each other or show affection to one another in public.

9. While many cultures have taboos against members of the opposite sex touching one another, they often accept same-sex touching as merely a sign of friendship without sexual overtones. In some cultures, such as Russia, where members of the opposite sex engage freely in public displays of affection, same-

sex hugging and even lip kissing are a perfectly acceptable means of greeting friends.

10. The amount of personal space that feels comfortable between speakers varies from culture to culture. In general, members of high-context cultures prefer less space, while speakers of low-context cultures prefer more. In Arabic, for instance, there is even a saying that encourages speakers to stand close enough to smell each other's breath. In general, speakers from North America, who prefer a greater distance, will continuously try to move away from an Arab speaker.

11. Waiting one's turn in line rather than pushing and shoving one's way to the front is generally the norm in North American and most northern European cultures (although not so in Belgium). One's personal space includes an immediate area around one's physical self that should not be violated by contact with strangers. In addition, densely populated countries simply do not have the room to allow each individual the amount of personal space expected by citizens of more spacious and less densely populated countries. Indeed, even in the United States, New York City, the city with the highest population density in North America, is somewhat of an anomaly in terms of personal space. Most New Yorkers have a much tighter and smaller definition of what constitutes personal space than do other North Americans.

12. Different cultures have different ways of greeting; what is offensive and even forbidden in one culture may have just the opposite meaning in another. In the Cayman Islands, for instance, people not only honk their car horns as a greeting but will often honk their horn when driving up to someone's house—even if that person is not expecting the other person to visit. Local people will go to their door or window to see who it is and then go out and invite the other person in.

 I, A

To adapt for the language classroom,

See chapter 2, Activity A, for suggestions.

I. Learning to Look (initial presentation: 10–15 minutes; discussion of observation 1: 15–20 minutes; discussion of observation 2: 20–25 minutes)

One of the most difficult things to do in life is to learn to observe or to record those everyday mundane things occurring around us. Precisely because these things are so mundane, so much a part of ourselves, we often never become aware of what we are doing and how we are behaving until something happens to violate that which we unconsciously assume to be the norm.

Purpose: To train our eyes to see what kinds of nonverbal language accompany conversational interactions and how nonverbal language may differ cross-culturally

Procedure:
This activity involves thorough preparation beforehand. It also requires several classes to complete the entire activity. However, the activity is well worth the time involved.

Initial presentation

1. Review worksheet 3, which lists the principal domains that can be included under the heading of nonverbal communication. Be sure you are clear about what each category on the worksheet refers to.

2. Review worksheet 4, which is an observation sheet.

3. Since completing worksheet 4 requires a lot of information, different individuals or groups should focus on different columns of the worksheet.

Observation 1

4. Have participants observe a meal at home, in a restaurant, or in a cafeteria.

5. Ask them to record on worksheet 4 the kinds of facial and body gestures used by the people in that setting.

6. Discuss participants' findings in class.

Worksheet 3. Principal Domains of Nonverbal Communication

Gaze	Touch
• eye contact	• hands
• length of eye contact	• arms
• other positioning of eyes	• head
Personal space	• other
• standing	• kiss
• sitting	• hug
• room arrangement	• handshake
• meeting/greeting	Kinesics
Facial expressions	• posture
• smiling	• bowing
• frowning	• positioning of
• angry demeanor	• feet
• raised eyebrows	• head
• noncommittal	• hands
Gestures	
• emblematic	
• illustrative	

This page is reproducible.

Worksheet 4. Observation Sheet

Use this worksheet to record information you observe.		
Participant Variables	Context: Physical/ Social Setting	Behaviors Observed

Sample Questions:

- What kinds of gestures did you observe between the following groups?

  same-/opposite-sex speakers   older/younger speakers

  strangers/intimates   higher-/lower-status speakers

  speakers from different cultures

- How did the gestures you observed relate to the conversation?

Observation 2

7. Select two or three scenes from movies on videotape or DVD that contain vivid samples of nonverbal communication. (It is very effective to use foreign language films with subtitles, so that students' attention is focused on the nonverbal, rather than the verbal, aspects.)

8. Before class, prepare video clips of the selected scenes.

9. Have participants complete another copy of worksheet 4 while watching the selections following step 5 under Observation 1.

10. Discuss the results of their observations.

Sample Questions:

- What kinds of facial and body gestures were used in the scenes?

- Which ones struck you particularly?

- Why was your attention drawn to certain nonverbal behavior?

- How do your observations compare with those of your classmates?

- What does this tell you about your (unconscious) non-verbal expectations?

- How has the nonverbal communication you observed enhanced or detracted from the communication process?

- If you observed a dubbed movie, did the facial and body gestures correspond to the conversations?

- Can you describe what, apart from the lips not synching, struck you as odd or inappropriate? Why?

 A

To adapt for the language classroom,

Follow-up:

- Write a summary of the kinds of nonverbal behavior accompanying conversational interaction. Include any cultural differences you observed that could lead to misunderstandings.

Alternative: Observation 1 or 2

1. Have different participants videotape various groups of people (e.g., people in a mall food court, in a park, at a sporting event, or in any other public place).

2. As a full group, observe the different videos, complete worksheet 4.

3. Discuss the group's observations.

IV. Further Readings

Articles

Ekman, P., Friesen, W., & Bear, J. (1984). The international language of gestures. *Psychology Today, 18*(5), 64–69.

> This article presents a brief review of some common gestures and the different meanings these have in different parts of the world. Illustrations are offered.

Hecht, M., Andersen, P., & Ribeau, S. (1989). The cultural dimensions of nonverbal communication. In M. Asante & W. Gudykunst (Eds.), *Handbook of international and intercultural communication* (pp. 163–185). Newbury Park, CA: Sage.

> The authors of this article provide a general basic review of the literature and a useful synthesis of the current directions of work on nonverbal communication and culture. In this context, the authors attempt to provide readers with an organizational framework for research on nonverbal communication in a cultural context.

Books

Andersen, P. (1999). *Nonverbal communication: Forms and function.* Mountain View, CA: Mayfield.

> This text provides an introduction to nonverbal communication and examines how nonverbal behaviors can communicate power, intimacy, anxiety, and other information. A specific chapter is dedicated to exploring cultural differences in nonverbal communication.

Hall, E. (1966). *The hidden dimension.* New York: Anchor Books.

> This is a classic book on people's attitudes about the use of social and personal space. Hall begins by taking a biological approach to space: he examines space requirements among animals and discusses our physical receptors of space (e.g., visual, tactile, olfactory). He next describes the human dynamics of space: intimate, personal, social, and public distance. He then compares various cultures on their perceptions and manipulation of space. The book concludes with a look at urban problems in the United States and at possible solutions with particular reference to the dynamics of space and culture.

Leathers, D. (1997). *Successful nonverbal communication: Principles and applications* (3rd ed.). Boston: Allyn and Bacon.

> This popular and practical book addresses how nonverbal behavior can be used to communicate successfully. Leathers discusses aspects of nonverbal behavior, provides exercises for developing successful nonverbal communication skills, includes analyses of various politicians and their nonverbal behavior, and has a worthwhile chapter on intercultural communication. The text is well written, interesting, and filled with examples and anecdotes, and each chapter concludes with references for further research.

Miller, P. (2000). *Nonverbal communication in the classroom.* Munster, IN: Patrick Miller Associates.

> This book offers a concise, in-depth introduction to the area of nonverbal communication and the classroom. The author covers such areas as eye behavior, body movements, and facial expressions and has included more than 50 illustrations. The book is an excellent starting point for anyone interested in learning more about nonverbal communication and teaching in the United States.

> "There is no reality except the one
> contained within us."
> Hermann Hesse

Chapter 5
Societal Roles

I. Anecdote: "It's a woman's job"

In a recent class discussion about gender roles/stereotypes, a 21-year-old Romanian student had a lot to say about an incident that had recently occurred to him.

"I don't know why I said what I did," Gheorghe said while he looked down and shook his head slightly. "Maybe it is just the way I'm used to being in my country. Anyway, my mouth worked before my brain," he said as he shifted in his chair and looked up at his classmates. "So here it goes. I was working in the cafeteria. I was the only man on that shift. Everything was fine, until the sweeping and mopping came up. I would never do that in my country, so I told one of my coworkers, a female, that I would not sweep or mop. She asked me why."

Gheorghe took a deep breath before he continued. He looked sheepishly toward his female classmates. "I said, 'It's a woman's job.' That was my big, big mistake. But that is the truth in my country. Within two minutes, all the staff learned what I had said."

He smiled as he tapped a pencil on his desk. He grinned at the class. "Now, every time I go in to work, my first job is to sweep and mop. I hope I didn't make another enemy with this story."

Discussion of Key Issues

What is accepted and expected behavior in one culture may very well be considered inappropriate or offensive in another. Likewise, specific roles and the concomitant expectations and behaviors associated with these roles often differ across cultures. Social role enactment may be determined by cultural practices, by law, and/or by the general norms of society. Religious beliefs can significantly impact how one views the workings of the world. People who come from a belief system that emphasizes fatalism and the essential powerlessness of the individual to alter events are much more prone to accept events as they occur and to de-emphasize individual attempts to alter the course of events. Likewise, certain religious systems stress the workings of the supernatural on an individual's health. As such, when confronted with illness, people who believe in such systems are as likely to turn to traditional folk healers as they are to Western-trained medical personnel.

Cultural cues about societal roles are not always obvious to those unfamiliar with a given society. Hindu women traditionally show that they are married by wearing a red powder on part of their hair and a red dot on the forehead. North American, Scandinavian, and French women traditionally wear a wedding band on the fourth finger of the left hand, while Spanish and Italian women wear a wedding band on the fourth finger of the right hand.

The accepted societal roles allotted to different members of various cultures vary greatly. In many cultures, older citizens are highly respected, even venerated. Especially for women, this is the time they attain a measure of respect and even freedom. Marriage, work, child rearing, aging, familial responsibilities, and intergenerational relationships are among some of the major areas of cross-cultural differences.

Chapter 5 considers social roles and expectations cross-culturally. Some of the topics covered include family roles, religious beliefs, medical practices, and women's roles.

Questions for Thought

- What are social roles?

- How are social roles affected by differing situational contexts?

- How do age and gender impact social roles?

II. Theory: What Research Tells Us

Defining Societal Roles

Culture resides in individuals; it is their identities, their beliefs, their roles, the relationships, and customs that make up the kaleidoscope of culture. Inherent in cultures is social structure, or the system of formal rules, social roles, and behavioral norms that constitutes an essential aspect of social organization. Within this larger social structure, social roles comprise one general class, which in turn is subdivided into many, less general subclasses. The specific subclasses of social roles and the specific composition of different kinds of social role vary considerably across cultures and may do so even within cultures.

Basically defined, a social role represents the cultural expectations of how people in a social position are expected to behave. All individuals enact a mixture of social roles within their culture. Some of the roles are *ascribed roles*. These are roles that derive from biological facts such as gender and/or age and from culturally determined factors such as birth. Only women, for instance, can be mothers; however, prohibiting pregnant women from working is determined by a cultural belief that pregnant women do not belong in the workplace. Other social roles are *achieved roles*. These are roles that a person attains through education, marriage, training, hard work, and so on. For instance, a person becomes a lawyer by going to law school and passing the bar examination, and a person becomes successful in business (like Bill Gates) by developing something society wants, needs, and uses. **(See Activity A—Who Is It?)**

Within every culture, people enact both ascribed and achieved social roles. Individuals perform a specified set of behaviors and occupy specific positions based on these roles, which are often culturally determined. Cultural norms govern the behaviors of a particular role. To some extent, these behaviors are exhibited by any person occupying that role, regardless of who he or she is or of his or her personal characteristics. In any culture, a teacher is someone who imparts knowledge and/or wisdom to others. How the teacher imparts this knowledge and how the role of teacher is regarded is often culture-specific. Teachers are viewed as strong authority figures in some cultures but as facilitators in others. Teaching methods vary from those that allow for and encourage active student participation to those emphasizing rote learning and memorization. Much of accepted teacher methodology is traceable to cultural preferences and beliefs regarding the social role of the teacher.

Role expectations refer to the demands of a role in a specific situation. For instance, a culture that demands modesty from women may require them to veil themselves in public or may expect them to keep their eyes lowered in conversation. Social roles, the cultural norms influencing these roles, and role expectations are arbitrary. Cross-cultural and historical differences reveal that what is considered "normal" or "accepted" is learned (Block, 1978; Boudreau, Sennott, & Wilson, 1986; O'Kelly, 1980). Culturally determined or ascribed roles often undergo change. The growing number of women at higher levels in the business world in North America is an example of this. Likewise, the definition of the role of "father" has changed in many countries to encourage fathers to play more nurturing roles in the upbringing of their children than has traditionally been the case. **(See Activity B—Male or Female?)**

Social roles are learned as a part of the enculturation process children are exposed to in becoming functioning members of their culture. These roles are learned through family, through institutions (e.g., school or church), and through peer groups. In some cultures, religion has been the determining factor in deciding which roles a person can perform; for example, in India, religious beliefs have led Muslims but not Hindus into professions connected with meat, such as the tanning of leather and shoemaking. The learning of social roles is both formal and informal. Some roles require formal and lengthy training such as educational degrees, apprenticeships, or on-the-job experience. Other role behavior is learned informally through interactions with and observations of others—family members, peer groups, and other members of one's culture. In Japan, women are encouraged to project a childlike image. Cartoon figures such as Hello Kitty and other cutesy characters decorate women's handbags, scarves, and jackets and even toasters.

To a great extent, people interact with each other on the basis of their social roles. Communicative interactions are directed by the role expectations associated with different social roles, the contexts of the interactions, and the definitions or interpretations the speakers ascribe to social roles. Since people's self-identity consists of a combination of social roles, different social situations will elicit different categories of a person's social roles (Boudreau, 1986). **(See Activity C—Mind Bender)**

Social identities

Interwoven with social roles is a person's social identity, which is determined in large part by the social roles he or she occupies. Personalities and behaviors are shaped by the identities individuals hold in different situations, as different social roles carry with them different sets of expected behaviors. Every individual plays many roles successively or simultaneously both within a culture and over the course of a lifetime. **(See Activity D—Being a Friend Means . . .)**

For each role people enact, they have differing conceptions of self-identity. For instance, a man who performs the roles of father, husband, son, neighbor, graduate student, and instructor will associate different traits and abilities with each role. As the circumstances of people's lives change, so do their roles and their social identities. For example, as individuals mature, they come to know and experience their identity through the roles they assume in work, marriage, and/or parenthood. These roles and social identities are significantly different from those they occupied as children or teenagers and will change again as people retire, are widowed, and/or become empty nesters.

We can categorize five basic groups of social roles (Hayes & Orrell, 1993).

* *Age and gender groups* (e.g., child, teenager, man, woman, retiree)

* *Household and family groups* (e.g., wife, aunt, son, grandmother)

* *Status groups* (e.g., manager vs. employee, senator vs. constituent, supervisor vs. worker, professor vs. student)

- *Occupational groups* (e.g., doctor, nurse, car mechanic, teacher, minister, secretary, politician, businessperson)

- *Shared interest groups* (e.g., Boy Scouts, Girl Scouts, country club, health club, Rotary Club, bowling league, bridge club, softball team)

These five groups illustrate how the essential types of social roles are found across cultures; what differs cross-culturally is the expectations and norms associated with the roles in each category. In addition, while we can categorize social roles into these five groups, these roles are by no means mutually exclusive. It is essential to remember that each social role is part of an interconnected web of social relationships within a society and that these roles and relationships are not static. As people's lives and situations change, their social roles and relationships change, too. **(See Activity E—Who Am I?)**

In addition to being associated with culturally determined behaviors, social roles are associated with sets of culturally determined expectations. In every culture, individuals will exhibit variations in role performance; to an extent, people are free to interpret or enact their roles as they see fit within the cultural, political, and social limits imposed on them. Overall, however, members of a culture will generally perform within the culture's expected parameters of behavior. Individual deviations outside the expected parameters are often accounted for within a culture by the identification of these deviations with unaccepted but culturally recognized sets of behaviors "outside" the norm. These different behaviors often form the expected parameters of cultural subgroups within the main cultural group.

For each of the many social roles people hold, they have a somewhat different self-concept of themselves. In a person's role as father, for instance, he may regard himself as provider, disciplinarian, and caregiver. In his role as son, he may regard himself as child, oldest sibling, and dependent from his parents' point of view. In the same man's role as manager, he may regard himself as authority and as responsible and powerful. As people think of themselves in different roles, different traits and abilities are emphasized. In addition, an individual's persona is determined in part by the cultural and social stereotypes of the roles he or she enacts.

While many types of social roles are found across cultures, the cultural expectations of the role behaviors differ widely. To illustrate, in North

America, repercussions for public servants accused and found guilty of corruption are serious; corruption among civil servants, while admittedly present, is considered morally wrong, unacceptable, and punishable. In other cultures, such as the Korean culture, corruption among civil servants is recognized as having unfortunate social consequences, yet it is not viewed as morally wrong (Szalay, 1981). The difference in the perception or interpretation of the concept of corruption lies in differing role expectations for civil servants. In North America, civil servants are expected to perform their roles impartially without receiving outside rewards or gifts. Civil servants in Korea, who have myriad obligations to the various members of their in-groups, expect gifts as part of getting their job done; role expectations are such that in-group obligations take precedence over any abstract duty to the society as a whole.

In North American and most European cultures, employees' efforts and hard work are important in the maintaining and advancement of one's position. Promotion is generally based on how effective and responsible an employee is. Overall, employees strive to "get ahead." In some cultures, however, working hard and getting ahead are secondary to maintaining good relationships with one's boss or superior. Personal relations are more important than the work itself; how strong these relations are will influence how quickly an individual is promoted and rewarded. In some cultures, an employee is regarded as an integral member of a company's group of workers. Relationships and teamwork are emphasized. Success is shared by all, and guilt is diffused when something goes wrong. At the same time, social roles and professional roles are not separate and distinct. Workers are expected to spend a great deal of time socializing with others from their workplace after work and even on weekends.

Different expectations of role behavior carry over into conceptions of politeness. Manners toward the members of one's in-group versus those outside this network often vary considerably. In Arab cultures, for instance, remarkably polite manners and extensive courtesies are shown to members of one's in-group, while Arabs often exhibit rude, offensive, or hostile behavior toward outsiders. What North Americans view as common courtesy toward strangers, for instance, the Arabs view as unnecessary and superfluous behavior toward members of out-groups.

Role conflict

When people move from one culture to another, they often find their identities in conflict as a result of *role conflict.* The social role or roles they occupy in one culture may differ and even be incompatible with the ones they occupy in the new culture. For example, immigrants who are doctors, teachers, or professionals of other types may have to assume the role of student to study English on their arrival in the United States. They can not practice their respected professions until adequate English language proficiency is demonstrated and until any U.S. exams in their respective fields are successfully completed. When positions in their fields of expertise are unavailable to them for one reason or another, they are forced to drive taxis, work as busboys or dishwashers, clean houses and offices, or perform other menial tasks to make a living.

New and different role expectations may also conflict with a person's norms or beliefs. It is often difficult for Western women to accept the restrictions that are placed on women's freedoms in many Moslem countries. In the fall of 2001, a controversy erupted over an order dating from the Gulf War that American servicewomen in Saudi Arabia cover themselves with long head scarves and black robes, or *abbayas,* when off base. After Lt. Col. Martha McSally, the highest-ranking female fighter pilot in the Air Force, filed a lawsuit that branded the dress code unconstitutional and charged that it improperly forced American women to conform to others' religious and social customs, the order was lifted in January 2002. The lifting of this ban in turn sparked sharp criticism from Saudi officials and clergy, who declared that all women in their country were subject to the same laws. The question arises, where does one draw the line between cultural insensitivity and respect for another's cultural norms and beliefs?

People's social identities depend on their social roles. When the status of any of these roles changes, it upsets the balance in the web of social roles surrounding each individual. Such an imbalance often leads to culture shock and/or self-esteem issues. For instance, take a well-respected reporter who decides to leave her home country and study intensive English in a program in the United States. Due to her low level of English proficiency, she finds herself placed in beginner language classes. Suddenly she finds herself no longer occupying her social-occupational role of "reporter," which entails a belief in herself as a strong and effective writer, a good communicator, and a competent manipulator of written words. In addition, there is a concomitant loss of status; now she is a student and not a professional. Because people assess themselves in comparison to others, when an individual's role or roles change, these comparisons must also change. Since maintaining self-esteem is essential to preserving social identity, change or conflict in social roles can lead to a decrease in self-esteem (Meyers, 1999). **(See Activity F—Critical Incidents)**

Social interaction

Communication plays an integral role in a culture's social system. How people communicate is in many ways dependent on the roles different speakers are enacting in communicative situations. Understanding a culture's system, whether intuitively or explicitly, allows members of that culture to make accurate predictions about people's roles and their expected behaviors. An integral part of language and social roles involves knowing the rules of discourse and social interaction.

When role conflicts occur between members of different cultures, the accuracy of an individual's prediction of another's behavior decreases because the expectations and assumptions about the behaviors of the other speaker are no longer shared. In some cultures, for instance, people who perform services for others are not thanked; in others, such thanking is a normal courtesy. An American bellhop, taxi driver, or cashier expects a thank-you when a service is concluded. An East Asian Indian would regard such thanks as superfluous, if not insulting, because one does not expect or give thanks for those performing their jobs (Apte, 1977).

Status

Cultures have hierarchical divisions of status in terms of social class or ethnicity. There are generally clear distinctions between individuals who are rich and individuals who are poor, as well as between those who are white and those who are not. Japan is an example of a culture characterized as a vertical society, or *tate shakai,* where there is a distinct ranking of someone above or below someone else. This is particularly evident in Japanese business dealings, where status dictates not only what is said and how it is said but also what tactics can be used. Lewis (1999) notes that within their own societal web, the Japanese know unequivocally the manner they should use to address a superior, an inferior, or an equal within their class hierarchy.

There are also societies with horizontal divisions of inclusion and exclusion, in terms of different tribes or classes of people. In Africa, for instance, Nigerian work groups must be comprised of members of the same tribe, for it would be extremely unfavorable to have a person from another tribe in a position of authority. In the Hindu caste system of India, people are born into specific castes to which they and their descendants are bound for life. Within a caste are subcastes, so that Hindu Indian society is both horizontal and vertical. People's caste determines what professions or trades they may engage in, whom they may marry, where they may live, and even which types of traditional clothing they may wear.

In many cultures, status is ascribed, although in societies where there is vertical movement among social classes, becoming a member of a certain profession can confer a high status. In Asian cultures, for instance, teaching is a highly respected and well-rewarded profession; in Latin American cultures, engineering is a high-status profession. Pursuing a religious vocation often confers high status in societies worldwide and can be a means of moving to a higher social class.

High/Low Power Distance

Power distance is the term used to refer to how widely an unequal distribution of power is accepted by the members of a culture. It pertains to the degree in which the less powerful members of a society accept their inequality in power and consider it the norm (Hofstede, 1980). In cultures with high acceptance of power distance (e.g., India, Brazil, Greece, Mexico, and the Philippines), people are not viewed as equals, and everyone has a clearly defined or allocated place in the social hierarchy. In cultures with low acceptance of power distance (e.g., Finland, Norway, New Zealand, and Israel), people believe inequality should be minimal, and a hierarchical division is viewed as one of convenience only. In these cultures, there is more fluidity within the social hierarchy, and it is relatively easy for individuals to move up the social hierarchy based on their individual efforts and achievements.

High/Low Uncertainty-Avoidance

Uncertainty-avoidance is defined as the degree to which a culture feels threatened by certain situations (Hofstede, 1980). Providing stability, structure, and security through formal rules and exhibiting a higher level of anxiety, stress, and aggressiveness are characteristic of cultures with high levels of uncertainty-avoidance (e.g., Germany, Greece, and Japan). Cultures with high levels of uncertainty-avoidance and low acceptance of power distance tend to be less rigid, more receptive to notions of the individual and of individual success or failure, and less bound to inflexible social roles and to expectations regarding social roles. Cultures with low levels of uncertainty-avoidance (e.g., Scandinavian countries, the United States, and the Netherlands) feature risk-takers, flexibility, tolerance, and relaxed people who prefer as few rules as possible. Cultures with low levels of uncertainty-avoidance and high acceptance of power distance tend to be conservative, with distinct ascribed social roles and strict expectations regarding the enactment of those roles.

Sex Roles and Gender

Each society has its own definition of what is female and what is male; in other words, each culture assigns certain characteristics, types of behavior, and social roles and expectations to women and men. In many instances, there is no genetic or biologically determined basis for these determinations; although "mother" and "father" are biological distinctions, "female work" and "male work" are not. Enculturation and socialization are gender-specific (Boudreau et al., 1986), as well as culturally determined. Role expectations are influenced by prevailing cultural norms; as part of the enculturation process of childhood, children learn to adopt the attributes of social roles and to meet the culture's or subculture's expectations of these social roles.

Gender is perhaps the greatest cultural divide. Equality of the sexes continues to be an unusual value in the world. Gender determines what men and women may consider as realistic role enactments. Children learn at an early age to distinguish how male and female roles differ. Their impressions serve as a lens as to how interaction with both sexes will be carried on in their culture. In Japan, China, Korea, and other countries that trace their influences to Confucianism, the father ranks first in everything that happens in society. In Arab societies, male children have traditionally been favored over female children because men contribute more to the family's influence in the community (Nydell, 1987).

Children of families who immigrate to North America are often affected by a conflict between the societal roles of the family's home culture and those of their new culture. Their family's home culture may value education highly, but if the parents need help at home either in the household or to care for younger siblings, it is generally the female children who will be unable to participate in after-school activities and extracurricular events or who will even be forced to drop out. In many cultures, education for male children is considered of greater importance because male heads of households are the family breadwinners and because sons are responsible for providing for elderly parents and other needy family members. Female children are expected to assume their prescribed roles of nurturers and caregivers, whether in their parents' household or their husband's. In addition, detention or after-school help with learning may create problems if the children are expected to help their families at home or at work at these times.

In many cultures, a child's gender will determine if the child is schooled, for how long the child will receive schooling, and what (if any) vocational and/or professional opportunities will be available to the child. Cultures ranking high on the measures of power distance and uncertainty-avoidance most clearly segregate the social roles and social behaviors along gender lines. In India and in Arab cultures, males are clearly the preferred sex in both cultural practices and legal realities.

Some researchers (Hofstede, 1980; Samovar & Porter, 1995) suggest that a masculine, or male-oriented, society is one that has clearly defined gender roles according to which men are to be assertive, ambitious, and competitive while women are to be nurturing (e.g., Greece, South Africa, Japan, Italy, and Mexico). There is a great desire for achievement in this type of society. In comparison, a feminine, or a female-oriented, society (e.g., that of Scandinavian countries) shows more fluidity and overlapping social roles for both sexes. Here, neither males nor females need to be competitive or ambitious. There is more of a drive toward interpersonal relationships with people in general, regardless of gender.

Self-Identity and Culture Shock

Because people interpret and evaluate themselves according to the social roles they occupy, people's self-identity is a function of how individuals interact with each other as enactors of the various social roles they hold. Likewise, how individuals interact with one another is guided or influenced by the expectations associated with the roles that the speakers enact during an interaction.

Changes in social roles and expectations and confrontation with different, often conflicting values and norms cause deep emotional responses, responses that are often unconscious but that are serious nonetheless. Since social identity is intricately linked to a person's social roles, change in the status of any of these roles upsets the web of social relationships and impacts on a person's notion of self-identity. **(See Activity G—Self-Discovery)**

Closely allied with culture shock is loss of self-identity (see chap. 3). Newcomers to a different culture are often confronting changes in their social roles and in their self-identity. A refugee, for instance, will be facing myriad changes in social roles and will be forced to operate out of different identity systems that both overlap and, at times, conflict. Consider the role difficulties facing the husband and father of a family from a traditional, agricultural society who, with his family, has sought refuge in an industrialized society. The husband and father must adapt to a new cultural expectation of no longer being the only—or perhaps even the major—breadwinner. His wife now needs to work outside the home to help support the family, and she may find a higher-paying position than he does. In addition, the man must adapt to new cultural expectations in his role of father. Rather than just be the provider, he is also expected to take a more active role in rearing his children, particularly if his wife is successful in finding employment and he is not.

Household and Family Roles

Kinship is the universal basic principle of organizing individuals into social groups, roles, and categories. Some form of organization based on parentage and marriage is present in every human society (Moerman, 1988; Schweizer & White, 1998). Both the notion of and the composition and structure of family differ substantially cross-culturally. Which relatives are considered members of a family unit, the social roles and expectations they enact, and their status within the family structure are determined by culture.

Individual responsibilities or role enactments within the family are in large part determined by hierarchical roles, which in turn are determined by the larger culture. Children in western European and North American cultures tend to enjoy a long period of childhood and adolescence, relatively free of responsibilities other than school and perhaps a few chores in the home. Children in traditional agricultural societies, in contrast, are often expected to become active contributors to the general welfare of the family. This may take the form of working alongside parents in fields, taking care of younger siblings, or tending to household chores. In rural areas of Kenya, Mexico, and India, children as young as three or four years of age perform such tasks as washing and tending animals (Segall, Dasen, Berry, & Poortinga, 1990). Older adults in western European and North American cultures often choose to spend their retirement years enjoying a multiplicity of activities. In fact, many older adults even choose to move away to more benign climates, whether Florida, the Canary Islands, or the south of Spain. In more traditional societies, older adults tend to live with their younger family members and continue to participate in the extended household. No longer capable of providing physical labor, they are utilized as counselors, advisers, caregivers, and repositories of knowledge.

In Western industrial cultures, the nuclear family household, albeit undergoing notable changes, remains the fundamental family unit; in many other cultures, an extended notion of family includes what members of Western industrial cultures perceive as more distant relations. In collectivistic cultures (e.g., Vietnamese, other Southeast Asian, and many African cultures), where the family, rather than the individual, is viewed as the basis of society, several different generations often reside together in one home. Extended families including grandparents, aunts, uncles, nephews, and cousins may all reside together. Married children live with their parents or include a place for their parents when they move to a new home. Since wives are expected to live with their husbands' families, the middle generations are usually members of the husbands' families.

In many cultures around the world, marriage is seen as a requisite stage of one's life rather than as a life choice for an individual to make. Marriage is a central social institution necessary both for procreation and for establishing, maintaining, and promoting social ties. In the African Manika culture, for example, marriage is more than a union between a man and a woman. A marriage becomes an alliance between two families, with specific rights and obligations due all members of each partner's family. Through marriage, kinship is maintained and augmented, and often the in-group—comprising the new family members—expands significantly. Marriage joins not just two people but two families, two larger kinship units. Disrespect toward a family member is likely to lead to marital discord, since such disrespect disturbs the balance in the larger unit (Bird & Shopen, 1987). Marriage is regarded similarly within Chinese culture. The whole family, particularly elders, has input into the marriage. It is important that one's spouse be someone who will maintain the family pride and who will make content and proud not only the extended family but even long-dead ancestors. As a result of family role expectations in Chinese culture, the wife generally spends more time with, and may actually be considered a more integral member of, her husband's family than her own. This practice is reflected in a Chinese saying that married daughters are "as water poured out."

Who is considered a member of one's family, even without consanguineous ties, differs across cultures. New in-group alliances can be created through religious ceremonies, such as confirmations and baptisms, where a godparent becomes a second parent to a child (Bandon, 1993; Brown, 1999; Howard, 1998). In some cultures, such as the Filipino or Dominican cultures, the role of the godparent confers extensive social and at times even legal responsibilities.

In adjusting to new ways of thinking, new patterns of social interaction, and new social roles and expectations, family units face new challenges. Different family members often adjust at different paces to a new culture, which affects roles and relationships within the family structure. Children generally learn the target language more quickly and easily than do other family members. Often, these parents find themselves in situations where they must depend on their children to interpret for them. Such dependence reverses the role and status of the parents and children and threatens the self-identity of the parents, while simultaneously causing stress among the family members.

Husbands and wives

Traditional cultures emphasize prescribed gender roles for husbands and wives. Husbands hold the role of providers, while wives hold the role of caretakers for the home and family. Even in those cultures where more and more women hold political office or other white-collar positions, there are still clear gender divisions and differing gender role expectations for men and women. Working women are still accountable for the majority of housework and childcare, in addition to their full-time work responsibilities (Hochshild & Machung, 2003). There is a clear division of labor between the sexes, and children grow up imitating their parents' roles and fulfilling parental and societal role expectations.

When members of such traditional cultures move to a new culture, they often face role changes or reversals. A common result of moving to a new culture is the loss of or a change in social position and power and in occupational role. A wife who follows her husband overseas for assignment loses her support system, her status within her in-groups, and, in many cases, her occupational role. Similarly, immigrants are often unable to work in their professions, whether due to lack of language proficiency, the inability to transfer credentials, or other factors. When unemployment or underemployment of men occurs, particularly in refugee situations, women are often forced into the workforce to help support their families.

The resulting changes in gender roles often cause strains on traditional marriage and family relationships (Ito, Chung, Kagawa-Singer, 1997). For example, female immigrants are often compelled to work in knitting mills or sweatshops or to take jobs cleaning homes or offices, just to make ends meet. When mothers must work, their children become latchkey children unsupervised from the time they come home from school until their parents come home from work. The man in such a situation is no longer the sole breadwinner for the family. He must accept the reality that there is a need for two incomes in the household and that his wife is helping to fill that need.

Mothers, fathers, and children

Social roles, expectations, and rules regarding socializing between young males and females vary greatly. Conflicts often arise when families move to another culture where the social roles, expectations, and rules are different (Dinh, Sarason, & Sarason, 1994). In many cultures, dating is frowned on or even forbidden. Children remain in the parental home until their marriage—which may or may not have been arranged for them. Their role in the family requires them to respect their parents (and other family elders) and defer to their decisions. Interaction among family members and other in-group associates is valued over the development of children's independent social lives. Dating, if done, takes place among members of one's own in-group and under the auspices of the older members of the family unit. In some cultures, dating, while permitted, is seen as a prelude to marriage and is taken very seriously as an opportunity to become acquainted with one's (potential) life partner. Social expectations are such that if a girl meets someone new—perhaps at college, perhaps through another friend—it is the young man's responsibility to introduce himself to the girl's parents and to ask their permission to date their daughter. In addition, he needs to inform them of his family background, hometown, education, and future prospects.

In many cultures, children, even grown children with careers, are expected to live with their parents before marriage. In North America, college students often think nothing of living far away from home to attend a particular university. In many other cultures, choosing a university often includes considering how doing so will allow students to maintain familial ties. This may entail remaining close to home or attending a university in an area where there are other family members to watch over the student and preserve the family connection.

When making any type of important decision, traditionally in Asian and Arab cultures even adult children consult with and ask permission of their parents. As their parents age, they are responsible for supporting them in their old age. This is especially true of sons (and their wives), who are often expected to care for elderly and ill parents.

Often, medical practitioners attempting to treat an older immigrant family member will directly address not the older person but a younger, more fluent family member. Similar situations arise with immigrant families during school parent-teacher conferences or in meetings with school officials. However, this failure to work within traditional hierarchies where age is granted all respect and decision-making powers both insults the entire family and results in confusion and misunderstandings. For many traditional cultures, the oldest person of the social or family group must, by virtue of age, assume the role of mediator, head authority, and spokesperson. Crucial decisions must be addressed to those with the power and status to make the decisions, regardless of English language proficiency (Fadiman, 1997). In Hmong society, for instance, even if the only fluent speaker is a child or teenager, the teacher, doctor, social worker, or other person should directly address the oldest person present and let that person then listen to the younger person's translation. Such actions prevent the undermining of culturally established correct behavior and social role expectations, allowing everyone to save face. **(See Activity H—Relationship Circles)**

Another important area of cultural difference is that of parental discipline. Many cultures consider corporal punishment for children's misbehavior as an appropriate practice, but it conflicts with prevailing attitudes in North America, where parents whose children come to school bearing evidence of physical disciplinary actions often find themselves faced with school authorities and/or social workers intent on intervention. Parents from cultures that accept corporal punishment need to be informed of American and Canadian cultural norms of appropriate disciplinary measures, whereas North American authorities need to realize that their intervention can threaten the parents' authority role in the household. Families accustomed to using corporal punishment may find it difficult to implement other means of exerting authority and maintaining control or may believe other means to be inadequate and insufficient for dealing with misbehavior. Such concerns need to be addressed by school officials and social workers when confronting the issue of corporal punishment.

Friends and friendship

In North American society, friendships are formed quite easily, whether with neighbors, colleagues, associates, classmates, or others. Some of this ease may be attributed to the history of immigration and the mobility of people within the United States and Canada. A more important factor, however, is the lack of culturally prescribed obligations and privileges associated with friendship. This stands in contrast with many other cultures, especially those that place high emphasis on in-group (vs. out-group) membership, where friendships are rarely casual and carry significant expectations and responsibilities. The larger extended family is often not strictly determined by biological relationships; intimate friends are similarly considered family members. In the Dominican Republic and the Philippines, standing as godparent at the baptism of a child can serve as a formal acceptance into that child's extended family, regardless of blood ties. In the African Maninka culture, being someone's friend entails being accepted by the entire family as an in-group member. An insult directed toward one's friend automatically extends itself to all members of one's family. Forgetting the name of a family member the friend has been introduced to is considered a serious insult, akin to forgetting the name of one's own aunt or uncle in North America (Bird & Shopen, 1987).

The value of loyalty to one's friends is very strong in Japan. A crucial element of Japanese self-identity is embedded in one's in-group membership. One of the most important Japanese in-groups consists of one's peers. Participating in in-group activities is a means of manifesting loyalty to one's in-group. Doing things with one's peer group is both demanded by societal expectations and desired by the individual to strengthen his or her in-group identification. If a group of peers get together for socializing, it is inappropriate to make excuses and announce that one has to leave ahead of the others. Everyone must leave together. In fact, even among teenagers, if a mother calls a student inquiring when he is going to come home, he will reply, "Soon." This implies not that he is about to leave for home but, rather, that he has heard the question and will leave when everyone else does.

Arab cultures also have a much deeper understanding of what encompasses the notion of friendship. For Arabs, friends are those people on whom one can rely to give help and grant favors as much as possible (Nydell, 1987). Friends are not merely people with whom one enjoys spending time but people one can call on when one needs something. A request from a friend can never be turned down; one must always indicate a willingness to help, even if one cannot. Yet, since it is not always possible for a friend to actually carry out what has been requested, it is not taken amiss if nothing comes of the request. The important factor is that one can ask for a favor and, because of the rights and obligations associated with friendship, will not be refused. Whether or not there is follow-through will depend on circumstances or *inshallah,* or "as God wills." There is no stigma attached either to asking for help or to the inability to grant a request.

Cross-cultural difficulties can arise when there are differences in expectations regarding the obligations and duties of a friend. What means in one culture merely the asking of a favor may in another culture be viewed as an imposition. For instance, in Mexico and Algeria, it is considered acceptable to ask a friend to help one find a job, give a recommendation, assist in college admission, or loan money. In North America, much depends on the individual relationship between the friends rather than on underlying cultural and social expectations. Generally, unless the person is truly a close, personal friend, such a request may be awkward. Even in cases involving close friends, many people would feel uncomfortable making or complying with such a request, as is reflected in the saying "Neither a lender nor a borrower be." Thus, misunderstandings may arise in cross-cultural situations where role expectations conflict.

Nydell (1987:20) recounts such an incident occurring between an Egyptian university student and an American professor. While settling in Egypt, the Egyptian had helped his professor extensively, even helping him to find a maid and purchase furniture. Later, this student expressed the desire to continue his studies in the United States and asked this same professor to use his influence to help him procure a graduate fellowship. The student felt spurned and insulted when the professor replied that the student simply did not have the necessary grades, so there was no point in even trying. According to Nydell, the more appropriate response would have been for the professor to sidestep the grade issue and to simply make helpful gestures such as helping the student find information on fellowships and helping him with the application process. Such behavior would have avoided a direct confrontation, maintained the harmony in the friendship, and met the necessary social and cultural expectations without compromising the professor's integrity.

Education and Social Roles

In collectivistic and high-context cultures, which have a strong sense of in-groups and out-groups, it is not possible to separate a problem, issue, or concern from an individual. What one family member does reflects on the rest of the family. A family member is not merely an individual in his or her own right but a part of an intricate, close-knit web of relationships. Education, for instance, is generally highly valued in Asian cultures. Traditional Asian families expect their children to do well in school and may feel ashamed and responsible if a child does poorly or needs special attention. When parents are confronted with children who are doing poorly in school, it can be a severely face-threatening situation. Role expectations are such that an individual is considered a representative of the whole group.

Role expectations differ among Asians and North Americans with respect to classroom behavior. In Asian cultures, school discourse is generally more formal, and social roles and their expectations are more rigid. Teachers are considered the repositories of knowledge in Asian countries; children rarely question or challenge a teacher, since that would be a disparagement of the teacher's role. The social distance between teachers and students is significant, and the boundaries are not to be crossed. Informality, familiarity, and sociability with one's teachers are unthinkable for Asian students. The social role expectation of a teacher in Asian cultures is not that of mentor or facilitator but, rather, carries within it the responsibility for conveying important knowledge to the younger generation. Thus, Asian students are often "passive observers," because the social role expectations of being a student include not challenging the teacher, always behaving modestly, and not interrupting in class.

American and Canadian teachers expect students to interact and participate actively in the classroom and to show creativity and initiative in the learning process. Asian parents, in contrast, expect and teach their children to be quiet and obedient and to refrain from questioning their elders, including teachers (Cheng, 1991, 1994). Many Asian students find the intimacy between teachers and students in the United States and Canada to be threatening to their notions of social order, because it violates their notion of social harmony. Their strict codes of classroom behavior and permissible discourse contrast to the more open and freer classroom patterns of U.S. classrooms.

Age Roles

There are cultural differences in how aging and the aged are valued. The characteristics that are ascribed to the different stages of life are important in different cultures. Some cultures are youth-valuing cultures, where vigor, idealism, and freshness are highly regarded. North Americans, for instance, prefer youth to old age. Young people dominate advertisements, movies, TV, and almost all aspects of North American culture. Youth is seen as synonymous with initiative, with creativity, and with inspiration. Because such a high value is placed on youth, American and Canadian men and women often go to great lengths to retain a youthful appearance, whether through cosmetics, hair treatments ranging from simple coloring to hair transplants, plastic surgery, or still other means.

Other cultures place a high value on age and experience, traditionally the dominant pattern of most cultures of the world. Arab and Asian cultures, especially, typify this value. In China, seniority in age determines power within and outside of the family. In Japanese, Vietnamese, and Native American culture, the senior members of the society are to be respected for their lifelong work, their knowledge, and their experience. They are accorded a place of honor everywhere.

Cultural value orientations toward age determine which social roles children enact, how they enact these roles, and when they enact these roles. In some cultures, children are considered very important. Their importance is made apparent by their early involvement in varied religious ceremonies and other respected activities. In a collectivistic society, children are taught to think in terms of "we" rather than "I," while in an individualistic society, the reverse is true. Asian languages are very conscious of status and age; children always refer to each other by their birth order (e.g., "elder sister," "younger brother"). Children learn self-reliance, responsibility, loyalty, and social skills through the family and are expected to show respect toward their elders. Children may demonstrate such respect by using special forms of address when speaking with their elders or, as in Arab cultures, by kissing the hand of older people to whom they are introduced.

Teaching and Learning Connections

Gay (2000:43) notes: "Culturally responsive teachers have unequivocal faith in the human dignity and intellectual capabilities of their students. They view learning as having intellectual, academic, personal, social, ethical, and political dimensions, all of which are developed in concert with one another." To function better in the classroom environment, it is crucial to understand those who share this environment with us. In the Chinese tradition, for example, the phrase *ba zhe shou jiao* [teaching by holding his hand] is representative of the idea that learning takes place through continual, careful shaping and molding. Americans, in contrast, hold self-reliance as a principal value, emphasizing that one has to learn how to think for oneself in order to solve problems on one's own. Such differences in perspective should be addressed in the language classroom, where students can be exposed to materials that give them a better understanding of different culture groups and their concepts of social roles and expectations.

Culturally responsive pedagogy defines the roles and responsibilities of teachers. Diamond and Moore (1995) have categorized teachers as cultural organizers, cultural mediators, and orchestrators of social contexts for learning. As cultural organizers, teachers must understand how culture operates in daily classroom dynamics and must create a learning environment that illuminates cultural and ethnic diversity. This can be accomplished in the language classroom through cultural sensitivity training and cross-cultural awareness activities. As cultural mediators, teachers must provide opportunities for students to participate in critical dialogue about conflicts among cultures and to analyze inconsistencies between mainstream cultural realities and those of different cultural systems. This can be achieved through such activities as simulations and role plays. As orchestrators of social contexts, teachers must recognize the significant influence that culture has on learning. They must shape teaching processes to harmonize with the sociocultural contexts and frames of reference, or the ways of interpreting the world, that are somewhat typical of ethnically diverse students. One means for achieving this is content-focused discussion.

Questions for Study and Discussion

1. Define social roles. How can we distinguish between ascribed and achieved roles? Which roles differ across cultures? Explain why.

2. Discuss the concept of social identities. Do you agree with the categorization of social roles into five basic groups? Explain why or why not. What examples can you provide to support your point of view?

3. Explain the relationship between the concept of high/low power distance and social roles. Provide examples.

4. What is the relationship between the notion of high/low uncertainty-avoidance and social roles? Provide examples.

5. How is self-identity enacted through social roles? How does this differ across cultures?

6. What factors influence change in social roles and role expectations? How can such change trigger conflict?

7. What positions are held by the old and by the young in different societies?

8. How are children viewed from a cross-cultural perspective?

III. Practice: What Activities Show Us

A. Who Is It? (20 minutes; additional preparation before class by the participants)

Social roles vary cross-culturally. Likewise, the expectations of role behaviors differ widely. When an individual moves into a different culture, a conflict may arise as a result of a loss of personal identity or an incompatibility with a new cultural role. As a result, an individual's culturally determined expectations may be challenged, questioned, disparaged, and/or belittled.

Purpose: To categorize distinguishing features of varied social roles

Procedure:

1. Have participants bring in pictures of cultural behaviors they find disturbing (e.g., women wearing veils over their faces; women as firefighters; a youngster holding a shotgun; a person kissing someone's ring; a person bowing in front of another)

2. Ask them to explain to the group why they selected their particular pictures.

3. Instruct them to devise lists of at least six social roles exhibited in their pictures. Ask them to prioritize these lists by making the bottom three roles those that they would have

the most difficulty adjusting to and the top three those that they would have the least difficulty adjusting to.

4. Display the lists on the blackboard for all to consider.

Sample Questions:

- What do the results tell you about a society and its social roles?

- Could you adapt to the behavior demonstrated should you be asked to do so? If so, would you do so easily or with difficulty?

- Why would you want or not want to adapt to the behavior demonstrated in the pictures?

5. Complete the task by having participants compare their answers to those of their classmates.

Alternative:

1. Teacher brings in a collection of pictures representing a diversity of dress, behavior, and actions.

2. Follow steps 3 and 4.

B. Male or Female? (20 minutes in class; additional work before class by participants)

Gender roles are largely defined by the society in which an individual lives. Though these roles were once rigidly ascribed by culture, they tend to be more fluid in today's world. Men and women are redefining themselves both culturally and socially throughout many parts of the world.

Purpose: To acquire a better understanding of male and female roles cross-culturally

Procedure:

1. Before class, ask students to read materials on different cultures, with particular emphasis on gender roles. Assign to each student a different country from a prepared list (e.g.,

Argentina, Australia, Canada, China, France, India, Iran, Japan, Kenya, Mexico, Poland), or allow students to select a country of their choice, making certain that each continent is represented in the class and/or that major religious and cultural groups are represented.

2. Divide the class into groups of 4–5.

3. Have participants present the findings of their research to their respective groups.

4. Ask participants to categorize their findings, on a scale of 1–5 (with 1 as the lowest and 5 as the highest), as to how women are rated in relation to men in the societies they studied. They should note the degree or range of difference in equality in gender roles.

5. Have each group share and discuss their results with the full group.

   • If similar findings are presented, discuss why.

   • If very different findings are presented, discuss why.

Sample Questions:

   • What regions of the world have placed women in low roles? What regions have placed them in high roles?

   • Which societies are patriarchal? Which are matriarchal?

   • How do gender roles manifest themselves in the following social roles?

   father/mother   husband/wife   child/young adult

 A

To adapt for the language classroom,

Procedure:

1. Discuss what gender roles are and how they differ cross-culturally.

2. Ask students to read and take notes on materials about different cultures, with particular emphasis on gender roles. Assign to each student a different country from a prepared list (e.g., Argentina, Australia, Canada, China, France, India, Iran, Japan, Kenya, Mexico, Poland), making certain that each continent is represented in the class and/or that major religious and cultural groups are represented. Some suggested Web sites for information follow.

http://www.members.tripod.com/~marklsl/Writings/japan.htm

http://www.lupinfo.com/country-guide-study/

http://www.oneworld.net/guides/gender/front.shtml

C. Mind Bender (10 minutes)

Cultural expectations of social roles often make it difficult to see and understand other ways of enacting those roles. Opening our eyes to other possibilities will help us look at situations from outside our own cultural lenses.

Purpose: To underscore the importance of how cultural expectations and social roles can limit our thinking

Procedure:

1. Read the following story to the class.

   A man and his son, both unconscious, were admitted to the local hospital ER (emergency room). The ER doctor on duty, who was the most qualified to deal with their injuries, looked at them and said that another doctor would have to treat them. Why was this?

2. Discuss possible answers to the question from the story. The answer appears at the end of this activity.

3. Discuss why it was difficult to come up with the answer.

   Sample Questions:

   • Why was it difficult for you to answer this question?

- What social role expectations influenced the answers you gave?

ANSWER: The ER doctor in the story is a woman and is the wife and mother of the patients. It is generally difficult for students to arrive at this answer, because people tend to assume that the doctor is male.

D. Being a Friend Means . . . (10–15 minutes)

Our social circles consist of different members from varied in-groups. To appreciate the range of these social contacts, it is important for individuals to comprehend the value of these social ties within one's culture as well as cross-culturally.

Purpose: To gain a deeper personal understanding of the responsibilities and/or obligations friendship entails

Procedure:

1. Prepare copies of the friendship quiz provided here (quiz 3) or make up your own.

2. Pass out one copy of the quiz to each participant.

3. Have participants quickly respond to each question, going with their initial reactions.

4. After participants have answered all the questions, have them go back over the items and think about why they answered as they did.

5. Review and discuss the quiz as a full group.

Sample Questions:

- Why did you answer as you did for each statement?

- What might make you change your decision in each case? For example, what different kinds of circumstances would influence you to reevaluate your answer?

- What factors played a role in your answers?

Yes   No   1. I would lend close friends large amounts of money.

Yes   No   2. I would help any of my close friends to get a job in my organization or company.

Yes   No   3. I would help my friend on a test by giving him or her the answers.

Yes   No   4. I would take care of my friends' children while my friends went away.

Yes   No   5. I would help a close friend do something illegal.

Yes   No   6. I would intervene in my friend's marital problems.

Yes   No   7. I would write a positive recommendation for any of my friends, regardless of their abilities.

Yes   No   8. I would help my close friends with their homework.

Yes   No   9. I would like to help a close friend.

Yes   No   10. The first person I would turn to if I needed help would be a close friend.

- To what extent do you think your responses were based on personal experience?

- To what extent do you think they were based on your cultural background?

- How would you define the term *friend?*

 A

To adapt for the language classroom,

Follow-up:

- Write an essay explaining your views on the roles and obligations of friends.

Alternative:

- Pass out two copies of the friendship quiz to each participant and have participants respond on one copy. After full group discussion of the quiz, have participants take a clean copy and give the quiz to someone outside of class from a different cultural or ethnic background. Compare the responses from the outside informants and discuss them with the full group.

Sample Questions:

- Did your answers differ?

- If yes, what factors might have contributed to your differences in opinion?

E. Who Am I? (10–15 minutes)

Social roles categorize people according to how they are expected to behave. Besides the biological roles we are born with, there are other roles that we assume on our own. Both types of roles help shape a person's self-identity.

Purpose: To see how our self-identity is tied to our different social roles and relationships

Procedure:

1. Have each participant write 15 statements beginning with "I am."

2. Share the statements in groups of 3–4 or with the full group.

3. Discuss what these statements indicate about each person.

Sample Questions:

- How many of your statements link you to socially defined groups?

- What are these groups?

- How are the roles you play in these groups different? How are they similar?

- How and why do these roles change over time?

- How would you describe the nature of your interactions with others? For example, are you independent? Are you responsible for other family members?

- What differences were indicated by these statements (e.g., in gender, in culture)?

- What similarities were indicated?

- If you had to choose one defining role, could you? Why or why not? If you could, which role would it be and why?

F. Critical Incidents (15–20 minutes)

The following critical incidents are exercises focusing on an area of cross-cultural conflict or miscommunication. The situation described in each incident presents a problem related to differences in cultural attitudes toward and enactments of social roles. There are no right or wrong answers in this exercise; the point of the exercise is to stimulate thought-provoking discussion based on the incidents. The goal of considering critical incidents is to increase awareness of and sensitivity to cultural differences and to heighten awareness of differences between personal and cultural beliefs.

Purpose: To expand awareness of differences in underlying cultural values and beliefs

Procedure:

1. Prepare different sets of two to four critical incidents. How many sets you prepare will depend on the total number of participants (e.g., for a group of 12 participants, prepare four sets).

2. Work in groups of 3–4.

3. Pass out the sets of critical incidents, and ask participants to brainstorm possible solutions.

4. As a full group, discuss the critical incidents, possible solutions, and the cultural values underlying the areas of cultural conflict.

5. Write your own critical incident. Share this with a partner or the full group.

Critical Incident 1

One of your students comes to your office to inform you that she will miss the next week of school because her cousin has died. You are taken aback but, wanting to be accommodating, suggest that she take along a homework packet that you will prepare for her, so that she doesn't get too far behind. When she leaves your office, she is visibly upset.

Critical Incident 2

The mother of one of your students approaches you. Her eldest son wants to rent an apartment near the university he is about to attend and needs a recommendation. The mother asks you to write this recommendation for her son, whom you have never met.

Critical Incident 3

Ms. Hulas recently accepted a teacher training position for an international aid organization. She is in charge of EFL curriculum implementation for middle schools in a major city of a third world country. Since receiving this position, she has held several workshops to train the teachers in the new curriculum. When she went to observe classes last week, she found that the teachers had implemented none of the curriculum changes.

Critical Incident 4

Mr. Jones and his family have just been transferred overseas to Asia from a city in the southeastern United States. Mrs. Jones, a teacher, has taken a leave of absence. In addition to her teaching, she has always prided herself on her skills at gourmet cooking, gardening, and various crafts. In her new home, she has been provided with a housekeeper, a maid, a nanny, and other servants, who have shown themselves quite perturbed when she has tried to do anything around the house or garden. Mrs. Jones is becoming quite frustrated, bored, and rather disgusted by life in her new environment.

Critical Incident 5

Prom night, one of the most anticipated events of the school year, is quickly approaching. You enter your classroom early and find one of your immigrant students quietly sobbing at her desk. When you go to comfort her and try to find out what the problem is, she tells you that her parents have forbidden her to accept a date to the prom with a boy she likes. Her parents' culture generally does not allow dating and certainly does not allow dating with someone outside of one's own cultural and social group. She is heartbroken and asks for your help.

Critical Incident 6

Peter is talking about his family with his new friend Hide, who is from Japan. Peter has been sharing his feelings about his sick, elderly parents. He mentions that they will most likely go to an assisted-living facility or nursing home, since they can no longer manage on their own. Hide is shocked by such a decision.

Critical Incident 7

Anna was approached by her friend and classmate Irina for answers to the take-home examination given in a biology class that both students were taking. Irina was absent many times, did not do most of the readings, and scored poorly on the midterm exam. Anna said no to her request. Irina was very angry.

Critical Incident 8

John Lennon, one of the former Beatles, stayed at home to raise his son Sean. He did the daily chores connected with a stay-at-home mom and was content in doing so. His wife, Yoko Ono, went out to work daily. When Walter shared this story with his friend Ahmad, the latter shook his head and squirmed in disbelief.

Discussion

Critical Incident 1
In North American culture, cousins are generally not that close, but in many cultures, extended family ties are much tighter. Funerals in some cultures are more involved and require more active participation, even from more "distant" relatives. Suggesting homework, while appropriate in many cultures, could be seen in this instance as a lack of sympathy for the student, who has just lost a family member.

Critical Incident 2

Different cultures have different notions of in-group membership and of subsequent social obligations and responsibilities. In some cultures, particularly collectivistic ones, members of the family are regarded as a unit. From the point of view of the mother in this incident, a teacher acquainted with some members of the family would be able to offer a recommendation for another, unknown member because the family represents that individual and vice versa.

Critical Incident 3

It is important to understand and work through chains of command in cultures with high levels of power distance and uncertainty-avoidance. In such cultures, not working through the hierarchy is unacceptable and will hinder or prevent program implementation. It is necessary for Ms. Hulas to work first with the teachers' superiors before she actually begins training the teachers.

Critical Incident 4

In certain cultures, individuals hold specific roles that are indigenous to their place in their societies. When a cultural outsider disrupts the normalcy of insiders' work routine and so-called lot in life, the insiders become suspicious and insulted, even when the outsider does so with no malice intended. As a result, members of each culture involved are negatively affected, as they question their social identities.

Critical Incident 5

In many cultures, dating is not acceptable. Even in some cultures where it is acceptable, dating must take place between members of the same in-group, and another family member often must accompany the couple. As this girl's teacher, it would be difficult for you to intervene in such a situation. You might be able to work with a go-between, preferably someone who is from the girl's culture and who has the appropriate status and respect.

Critical Incident 6

In many cultures, the elderly are given well-deserved honor, praise, and respect. Elderly parents automatically live with their children, as part of the extended family. The children accept taking care of their parents as part of their defined role in life and as an opportunity for giving back to their parents for all that their parents have given to them during their lifetime. The parents in these cultures would not consider moving into an assisted-living facility, nor would the children consider placing their sick elderly parents in a nursing home, regardless of the burden that not doing so might impose on other family members.

Critical Incident 7

The sharing of notes, tests, answers, and so on is considered a normal part of everyday school life in some cultures, such as Russia. It is not seen as cheating or being unfair in these cultures. However, in the United States, this type of behavior is unacceptable and often regarded as plagiarism.

Critical Incident 8

In Middle Eastern and many other societies, male and female roles are clearly defined. A woman has her duties and responsibilities in the home, caring for her husband and for her children. A man also has his set of responsibilities, providing for his family through work outside the home. Any deviation from their stated roles is looked on with disapproval and contempt and, in some cases, is even punishable by law.

 I, A

To adapt for the language classroom,

Writing Critical Incidents

- See chapter 2, Activity F, for suggestions.

G. Self-Discovery (8–10 minutes)

Differences rather than similarities are more apparent when we encounter individuals in our own culture and outside of our culture. Though the tendency is to focus on contrast, we also need to focus on similarities. To do so, we must begin with our own self-identity, to understand how we are perceived in relation to others.

Purpose: To demonstrate that people often have more in common with other people than they think

Worksheet 5. Discovering Similarities

Column 1 Me	Column 2 Partner 1	Column 3 Partner 2
1.		
2.		
3.		
4.		
5.		
6.		
7.		
8.		
9.		
10.		
11.		
12.		
13.		
14.		
15.		
16.		
17.		
18.		
19.		
20.		

This page is reproducible.

Procedure:

1. Prepare copies of worksheet 5.

2. Hand out one copy of the worksheet to the participants.

3. Ask them to turn to the person on their right and find out as many things as they can that they have in common with each other.

4. Have them list these items in columns 1 and 2.

5. After 2–3 minutes, ask participants to turn to the person on their left and repeat steps 3 and 4, listing similarities in columns 1 and 3. Stop after 2–3 minutes.

6. Discuss results as a full group.

   Sample Questions:

   • How many found more than 15 things in common?

   • What did you learn about yourself and your partners during this activity?

   • Can you name any unusual things you discovered about each other?

   • What can this activity tell us about social groups, societal relationships, and societal roles?

 A

To adapt for the language classroom,

   Sample Questions:

   • Omit the final question.

Adapted from *The Big Book of Team Building Games* (pp. 25–27), by J. Newstrom and E. Scannell, 1998, New York: McGraw-Hill.

H. Relationship Circles (20–25 minutes on day 1; 15–20 minutes on day 2)

In-group membership incorporates culturally determined social obligations and responsibilities. Expectations and norms associated with social roles, however, differ cross-culturally. Since these roles are in constant flux, individuals need to understand them within and across cultures.

Purpose: To expand awareness of one's own social relationships and of the social relationships of members of other cultures

Procedure:

1. Prepare enough copies of worksheet 6 so that you have two copies for each participant.

2. With the full group, generate a list of people with whom the participants have social relationships. A sample list follows.

parents	spouse	brother(s)
grandparents	sister(s)	uncle(s)
aunts	children	first cousins
second cousins	acquaintances	good friends
casual friends	coworkers/colleagues	classmates
boss	parents-in-law	sister(s)-in-law
brother(s)-in-law	neighbors	business associates

3. Pass out one copy of worksheet 6 to each participant. Ask participants to label one circle "Me," then to place each type or group of persons from the list into the different circles. Participants should draw lines connecting each circle closer or farther away from the circle labeled "Me," based on the following criteria.

   • How responsible are you for that person?

   • How many of your personal and/or intimate thoughts do you share with this person?

   • How much does this person mean to me? How close do I feel to this person?

Worksheet 6. Relationship Circles

This page is reproducible.

- How responsible does this person feel toward me?

- How much would I be willing to do and/or share with this person?

4. Ask participants to share and discuss their results in groups of 3–5. Have one member of each group record the discussion.

Sample Questions:

- What types of people did you put in each circle? Were your decisions based on familial ties, in-group membership ties, a combination of both of these ties, or other factors?

- What do the words *close* and *intimate* mean?

- What differences do you see between your relationship circles and the circles of the others in your group?

- What are these differences based on? Where do they come from?

5. Have the small-group recorders present what they have recorded to the full group.

6. Pass out a second copy of worksheet 6 to each participant. For homework, assign participants to ask an informant from another culture to complete the relationship circles using the list of people generated by the full group and using the same criteria. Participants should not show informants the circles that the participants completed.

7. After their informants have completed the circles, participants should compare their informants' results with their own.

8. Have participants bring their compared results to class and discuss them.

Sample Questions:

- What were some of the differences between your informant's and your own results?

- What cultural factors underlie the differences?

- What was the principal similarity?

- Why do you think this is so?

Alternative:

- Have participants chart their relationships by using concentric circles or linked boxes instead of separated circles.

Concentric relationship circles

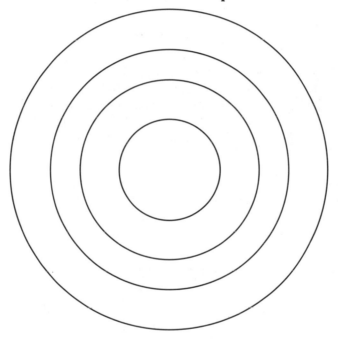

Linked relationship boxes

IV. Further Readings

Articles

Coltrane, S. (1988). Father-child relationships and the status of women: A cross-cultural study. *American Journal of Sociology, 5,* 1060–1095.

The author of this article reviews numerous theories of child rearing, male-female societal roles, and status and evaluates these with data from 90 nonindustrial societies. He finds that in societies where fathers assume a greater child-rearing role, women seem to be more involved in the public life of the community and to have greater status, at least relative to those societies where the father is removed from all or most child-rearing activities. This informative article has some statistical analysis but assumes little previous subject knowledge.

Hofstede, G. (1994). The cultural relativity of the quality of life concept. In G. Weaver (Ed.), *Culture, communication, and conflict: Readings in intercultural relations* (pp. 131–142). Needham Heights, MA: Ginn Press.

This article is a collection of research data on dominant work-related value patterns in 53 countries and regions. The data suggest how national cultural patterns affect the definitions of the quality of life in these particular areas of the world.

Hwang, K. (1987). Face and favor: The Chinese power game. *American Journal of Sociology, 92*(4), 944–974.

The author of this article offers insights into the cultural values underlying social behavior among Chinese. The author is himself Chinese and attempts in this article to apply Western social exchange theory to the realities of such collectivistic cultures as the Chinese. This is a good article for those interested in gaining a better understanding of cultural norms controlling Chinese interpersonal arrangements.

Mbabuike, M. (1991). Ethnicity and ethnoconsciousness in the New York metropolitan area: The case of the Ibos. In F. Salamone (Ed.), *Studies in third world societies* (Publication No. 36, pp. 83–91). Williamsburg, VA: College of William and Mary, Department of Anthropology.

This article describes how Ibos in the New York area have both maintained and adapted their native language, customs, and traditions, as well as certain sociocultural and political institutions, to life in New York. The article, while referring specifically to Ibos in New York, offers valuable insights into the adaptation and maintenance mechanisms of an essentially rural, developing culture confronted with coping in an urban environment in a developed nation.

Weinstein-Shr, G., & Henkin, N. (1991). Continuity and change: Intergenerational relations in Southeast Asian refugee families. *Marriage and Family Review, 16*(3–4), 351–367.

This article covers four major areas: the types of experiences Southeast Asian refugees tend to share in fleeing their homelands; the common problems they face in adapting to the United States; the resources available to them for successful survival; the changes the refugees face in social and familial roles and the impact on those changes on different generations. This is an informative, useful article for anyone wishing to understand more about Southeast Asian refugees.

Books

Augustin, E. (Ed.) (1993). *Palestinian women: Identity and experience.* London: Zed Books.

This book focuses on Palestinian women living in the occupied territories and on their experiences since the *intifada.* At the same time, this book offers worthwhile insights into Palestinian life and culture. The author chooses a somewhat unusual, but very effective, approach: She first presents factual background on a particular topic and then has various women of different social backgrounds describe their personal experiences related to that topic.

Brooks, G. (1995). *Nine parts of desire: The hidden world of Islamic women.* New York: Anchor Books.

This book offers readers an engrossing study of the convergence of Islam, pre-Islamic customs and traditions, politics, and the influence of Westernization in the lives of women in different Moslem countries. Plenty of factual information is interspersed with lively anecdotes.

Bumiller, E. (1990). *May you be the mother of a hundred sons: A journey among the women of India.* New York: Fawcett Columbine.

The author of this book explores the lives and roles of Indian women today through extensive interviews with women from a variety of socioeconomic backgrounds, ages, and regions of India. This is a fascinating book, written for the layperson. Chapter topics include arranged marriages, women working in and outside the home, population control, and the women's movement.

Calloway, B., & Crewey, L. (1994). *The heritage of Islam: Women, religion, and politics in West Africa.* Boulder, CO: Lynne Riemer Publishers.

This well-written book focuses on Islam and women in Senegal and northern Nigeria. The authors trace the different historical contexts, the different socialization processes, and the different degrees of Westernization and modernization of Senegal and northern Nigeria—two very different societies that share the same religion but have had disparate historical and social experiences.

Delgado-Gaitan, C., & Trueba, H. (1991). *Crossing cultural borders: Education for immigrant families in America.* New York: Palmer Press.

Through ethnographic study, the authors of this valuable and informative text attempt to examine minority styles of learning in the home and in school in an effort to understand better why there has been such a rate of failure among certain minorities. Although the authors focus on one particular group of Hispanic children, many important parallels are drawn to the experiences of other minority populations. Topics covered include the role of culture in learning, as well as social interaction and learning practices in the home environment as compared to the school environment.

El-Solh, C., & Mabro, J. (Eds.). (1994). *Muslim women's choices: Religious beliefs and social reality.* Providence, RI: Berg Publications.

Although an older publication, this contributed volume is a useful examination of Muslim women from a variety of societies and communities. The different contributors look at the interaction of different cultural influences and Islam. A wide range of topics is covered, ranging from the position of women in Azerbaijan to women's labor in the garment industry in Bangladesh. There is also a good bibliography, for those interested in further research.

Haddad, Y., & Lummis, A. (1987). *Islamic values in the United States.* New York: Oxford.

This book provides a very readable look at mainstream Muslims in the United States. The authors try to present an overview of Islam as practiced today among immigrant groups in the United States. This book is a valuable introduction to American Muslims and to the conflict and adaptation of Islamic values within the context of general American society. Topics include comparison and discussion of Islamic laws, American societal norms and civil law, and gender issues.

Luce, L. (Ed.). 1992. *The Spanish-speaking world.* Lincolnwood, IL: National Textbook Company.

This book, consisting of five sections, is a very interesting and informative overview of the Hispanic world. The first section introduces the reader to the concept of cross-cultural studies and includes readings that spotlight American cultural assumptions and Americans' perceptions of foreign cultures. The remaining sections examine different Spanish-speaking communities: Mexico and the Caribbean, Latin America, Spanish-speaking communities in the United States, and contemporary Spain. The various authors, whose disparate backgrounds highlight the diversity of people who fall under the label *Hispanic,* manage to furnish readers with helpful and informative material in a most enjoyable, readable manner.

Popenol, R. (1990). Cambodian marriage: Marriage and how it is changing among Cambodian refugees in Philadelphia. In P. Kilbride, J. Goodale, & E. Ameisen (Eds.), *Encounters with American ethnic cultures* (pp. 296–311). Tuscaloosa: University of Alabama Press.

The author of this book describes some of the key differences between Cambodian and American marriages and looks at some of the changes beginning to take place as young Cambodians grow up in American society. The central role that the family, particularly one's parents, plays in Cambodian marriages is discussed.

Sokolovsky, J. (Ed.). (1990). *The cultural context of aging.* New York: Bergin and Garvey.

The essays in this book explore two primary areas: (1) what does growing old mean in different cultures and (2) what functions or roles do older adults have in these different cultures. The book is organized around various topics, such as intergenerational ties and social change among older adults. This allows readers to turn to a particular topic and find pertinent information about diverse cultures under each heading. Societies covered include the Hausa of Nigeria, Native American groups, African Americans, and Swedes.

Zinn, M., & Eitzen, D. (1990). *Diversity in families* (2nd ed.). New York: Harper Collins.

A widely used college text, this book offers the general reader a good introduction to the American family—to the ideals, images, and myths surrounding the American idea of family and to the different types of American families that actually exist in the United States. The authors also consider in detail social and economic changes affecting the American family, including divorce, remarriage, violence, work, income, and the economy.

Chapter 6
Pragmatics and Communication

I. Anecdote: "It's academic"

One of our colleagues taught an intermediate-level ESL writing class that could have been called a miniature United Nations, because it contained international students from China, Colombia, India, Iran, Japan, Taiwan, Uzbekistan, and Vietnam. At the time she was teaching this class, she narrated the following story.

> My students are very excited about their writing class. They are eager to improve and want to do everything to make progress. For each chapter covered, we always watch a short video of 2–3 minutes to better understand the writing task to follow. Unfortunately, not everyone finds the video useful.
>
> My Colombian student said angrily, "It's a waste of time. We should do more grammar and more writing."
>
> Two other students concurred with a loud "Yeah, yeah!" So I proposed eliminating the video for the remainder of the semester. Suddenly, some of the students voiced loud disapproval.
>
> An Iranian student yelled out, "Just because he doesn't like it doesn't mean that the rest of us agree!"
>
> In a second loud voice, the Uzbek student shouted, "I like it and it is good! We should have it!"
>
> Another Iranian student screamed out, "Don't stop it!" I looked around at the other students.

Then, the student from Vietnam remarked in a low, but audible, voice: "The video is very useful. It helps us to learn by giving us examples of the kind of essay we are going to write later."

The students from China, India, and Taiwan did not say a word. They just sat there. So what did I do?

In an authoritative voice, I said: "This is a democracy, isn't it? We'll go with the majority and continue with the video presentation." There was a sigh of relief from the students, and the lesson went on.

We share the preceding narration not simply to remind you that classroom learning differs among language groups and cultures but to alert you to the differences in acceptable communication patterns from members of different cultures.

Discussion of Key Issues

The communicative intent or meaning that speakers intend to convey is culturally based, context specific, and influenced by a variety of variables that carry different weight in different cultures. Cross-cultural misunderstandings often arise because speakers do not share the same cultural presuppositions. Difficulties are often linked to speakers' beliefs or assumptions about such factors as the importance of group harmony and face; the emphasis on directness or indirectness in discourse; the weight attached to social status; and the use of nonverbal aspects of communication, such as body language and physical space.

To foster effective cross-cultural communication, speakers should become aware of cross-cultural differences in the appropriateness of different discourse styles, in rules of speaking, and in the relative importance assigned to different context variables. Such awareness enables speakers to become more cognizant of possible sources for cultural misunderstandings and helps them to understand better their own communicative behaviors and often subconscious reasons for discourse choices. Moreover, this awareness provides speakers the possibility of consciously adjusting their discourse to the cultural and situational context of the exchange.

Chapter 6 explores how speakers use language in social contexts and the relationship between language and culture. It examines the many communicative interactions speakers engage in, ranging from speech acts (e.g., greetings, apologizing, and complaining) to conversations and other types of discourse. We will discuss how culture influences both speakers' communicative choices and their understanding and interpretation of conversational styles and discourse modes, as well as the miscommunications that occur as a result of cross-cultural differences in these areas.

Questions for Thought

- What are some verbal discourse differences that can lead to cross-cultural misunderstandings?

- What is the connection between language and culture?

- Why can developing pragmatic awareness lessen cross-cultural misunderstandings?

II. Theory: What Research Tells Us

Language and Communication

Language is a defining characteristic of human beings. All humans use language in some form or another to communicate with others. Regardless of what culture and language children are born into, normal children will master most aspects of their language at a relatively early age. All languages share underlying universal features; however, they differ in how speakers' messages are realized. In other words, while all languages share aspects of universal grammar (UG; see, e.g., Chomsky, 1986; Cook, 1988; Crain & Thornton, 1998), languages differ syntactically, lexically, phonetically, and pragmatically. Language exists within the context of culture; expectations and understandings of language use are conditioned and influenced by the values, belief systems, and worldviews of the speakers' culture.

Since the primary goal of language is to communicate messages from one speaker to another, listeners need to understand the messages speakers are attempting to convey. Being able to understand one another entails more than understanding the core or literal meanings of utterances. Communicative interactions are dynamic processes in which speakers assess myriad variables (including setting, age, gender, and status of the speaker), respond to verbal and nonverbal cues, and adjust speech style and patterns accordingly. Successful communication entails sharing the same or similar interpretations of the intent and meaning of the messages and being able to negotiate successfully one's way through the communicative interaction.

Language is ambiguous by nature. Speakers do not communicate in isolation. Meaning is jointly constructed by speakers within the communicative setting wherein speakers negotiate the messages they wish to convey by manipulating the structures and discourse patterns of the language (Scollon & Scollon, 2001). Together, speakers shape the communicative interaction, the nature of which must take into account myriad factors. As speakers negotiate meaning, they need to be able to adapt their speech to the situation and to react appropriately to the messages conveyed by others; speakers need to display competent communicative behaviors. Speakers' participation in communicative interaction is a reflection of their social roles and social identities, the discourse patterns of their language, and the particular context in which the speakers find themselves at any given moment.

Communicative interactions take place within contexts that include setting, status, gender, and age of the participants. These variables are critical in determining how speakers will use language to convey intended messages. However, not all variables carry equal weight in all languages and cultures. The degree of impact these variables have on speakers' choice of discourse style and type of communicative exchange differs cross-culturally. In addition, the range of choices available to speakers reflects the importance that different variables hold in each language and culture. A culture's beliefs, values, and norms are reflected and reinforced by the discourse patterns of a language. Cultures strongly concerned with the maintenance of face are also the most likely to value indirect discourse styles. Likewise, speakers in cultures that are very concerned with social status and power distance will place strong emphasis on the appropriate use of honorifics, formal terms of address, and other linguistic means to reflect these factors. In cross-cultural encounters, speakers need to be able to recognize and understand how these variables are sensitive to different cultural interpretations and thus produce different realizations of discourse patterns between languages.

Speakers communicate effectively when they share the same expectations, beliefs, and interpretations of the social context and of the speakers' roles and identities. Cross-cultural variations in communicative behaviors stem from differences in how speakers of different cultures perceive and use language, both verbal and nonverbal. Misunderstandings are based on two major premises. First, people expect members of other cultures to behave according to shared norms and rules of behavior. Second, people do not realize that the same behaviors can have different interpretations in different cultures (Albert, 1983; Albert & Triandis, 1985). Pragmatics examines assumptions, communicative goals, and speech acts used to attain specific goals, namely, how linguistic structures are used by speakers in different interactional contexts. **(See Activity A—In the Limelight)**

Communicative intent

Communicative misunderstandings often result when speakers from different cultures engage in interactions in which the speakers follow the rules or norms of their own speech communities. When these rules and norms differ, misperceptions often result with regard to *communicative intent,* or the purpose of a message. These misunderstandings occur not only between speakers of different languages or from different cultures but also between intimates, between colleagues and coworkers, between strangers and intimates, and between males and females within the same culture (e.g., Giles & Coupland, 1991; Tannen, 1994; Tzanne, 1999; Wodak, 1996).

Interpretation of speakers' communicative intent is not predictable based on the core definition or referential meaning of a word or structure alone. The *context* in which the speakers produce the utterance is key to interpreting and understanding communicative intent, that is, the actual meaning that speakers wish to convey with their words, rather than the literal meaning of the words themselves. According to Gumperz (1971:285), "Effective communication requires that speakers and audiences agree both on the meaning of words and on the social import or values attached to choice of expression." To understand this requirement at the word level, consider the statement "That's an interesting picture." What does the word *interesting* mean here? Is this word referring to its core definition of "fascinating" or "engaging," or is it being used as a polite euphemism for the speaker's true feelings, for example, the picture is ugly, awful, disgusting, or ridiculous.

At the sentence level, consider the statement "It's cold in here." This statement can be construed as a statement of fact; the utterance would then be taken at its literal meaning. At another level, however, it can be viewed as an indirect request or directive, meaning, for example, "Please turn up the heat" or "Please close the window." The only way the listener can accurately understand the actual intended meaning of the statement *(illocutionary intent)* is by understanding the context in which the statement is uttered. Speakers draw inferences about meaning that are derived from speakers' knowledge about language and the world. These inferences are generally fixed and drawn quickly. In many instances, intended meanings are conveyed using phrases that have acquired a conventionalized, nonliteral ("indirect") meaning. The question "Can you open the window?" does not necessarily question the speaker's ability to perform such a physical action but, rather, carries the illocutionary or pragmatic effect of a request. Understanding the statement "It's cold in here" poses no problem for speakers who share the same knowledge about that language, the same rules of speaking, and the same understanding of the particular context in which the phrases are uttered. They understand intuitively the complex relationship between the function or intended function of an utterance, the form or structure by which it is expressed, and the situational variables affecting the intended meaning.

When speakers speak different languages and come from different backgrounds, they often do not share the same schemata for the negotiation of meaning in communication interactions. The meanings and the inferences they draw from an utterance may be wrong. Such misidentification or misunderstanding of a speaker's intent because of differences in conversational routines or formulaic expressions is common between speakers from different cultural and language backgrounds (Meeuwis & Sarangi, 1994; Tannen, 1984; Thomas, 1983; Ulichny, 1997; Wodak, 1996). Languages differ in the illocutionary intent of their messages and in the types and use of specific communicative behaviors, routines, and rituals utilized by their speakers. Consider the following situation.

> A Greek student in the United States told an American classmate and friend of his that she was welcome to visit him any time. She replied that she would love to come to Athens and see him during spring break. Later, when she booked a reservation at a hotel, George was hurt, and Erica was surprised by his curt behavior.

Both participants are clearly not happy by what has happened, and neither participant is sure as to why this is so. What we can probably conclude is that there was an apparent misperception about the intent of the invitation and the acceptance of that invitation. Erica, the American, thought she was going to enjoy a pleasant vacation sight-seeing with a Greek friend in Greece, whereas George assumed that Erica's acceptance of his invitation implied that she would stay with him.

Speech Acts

Speech acts have been defined as all the things speakers do with words when they speak, whether this be greeting, thanking, complaining, apologizing, or other (Austin, 1962). In other words, speech acts refer to the purpose of a speaker's utterances. Speakers who do not use pragmatically appropriate language run the risk of appearing uncooperative, ill mannered, rude, or a combination of all three. Such misinterpretation of communicative intent is heightened in cross-cultural situations. The speech acts themselves are etic; that is, all speakers in all languages engage in greetings and leave-takings, offer advice, utter directives, express apologies, and so on. However, the etic manifestations of speech acts are language specific and culture specific. In other words, when these speech acts are used and how they are expressed differ. There are important differences in how these speech acts are expressed (linguistic or language differences) and when they are expressed (pragmatic differences). Much of the difference between speech-act use is embedded in different cultural norms and assumptions governing communicative interactions. All languages have some linguistic means and sociocultural norms for greeting another person. It is rather obvious that languages use different phrases to greet; less obvious are the rules governing who greets whom first, what social variables (e.g., status) must be observed in the greeting, and even whom one greets. For instance, North Americans recognizing a neighbor they may only know by sight will still generally offer a greeting when encountering them outdoors, in the apartment hallway, or around town. By comparison, in many Asian cultures, greeting someone whom one really does not know well is not done. These cultures apply different social norms to members of an out-group than to the members of one's in-group. **(See Activity B—Meet and Greet)**

Required competences

To understand the meaning of a sentence and the speaker's intended meaning requires two kinds of knowledge. Understanding the literal meaning is contingent on knowledge of grammar, while understanding the intended message depends on knowledge of context. According to Bachman (1990), we may label these two types of language knowledge as organizational competence and pragmatic competence. *Organizational competence* refers to speakers' grammar knowledge, or their knowledge of linguistic units and how they systematically function together, at both the sentence level and the broader discourse level, according to the rules or patterns of a language. We can subdivide *pragmatic competence* into illocutionary competence and sociolinguistic competence. *Illocutionary competence* can be described as speakers' knowledge of communicative interaction and the ability to carry out or engage in successful communicative interaction; *sociolinguistic competence* characterizes speakers' ability to know what to say and how to say it in a given sociocultural context, or the "rules of speaking" (Fraser, 1990; Hymes, 1969, 1972).

We may also describe sociolinguistic competence as both appropriate and effective ability. *Appropriate ability* refers to speakers' capacity to engage in those communicative behaviors deemed as proper and suitable within the parameters and expectations of their particular culture. *Effective ability* describes speakers' capacity to employ those behaviors that allow them to achieve desired outcomes (Lustig & Koester, 2003). Shared interpretations of what constitutes competent communicative behaviors are an essential component of speakers' cultural knowledge.

Miscommunications or breakdowns occur when members of different cultures do not share the same organizational and pragmatic competencies. Of these two types of competencies, pragmatic competency is the more difficult to learn and observe, because it is so closely tied to the often subconscious cultural values, beliefs, and norms governing individuals' behavior and interaction patterns. For example, North Americans are often upset at the perceived rudeness of Koreans who fail to offer an "Excuse me" or "I'm sorry" in situations such as bumping into someone accidentally or touching a stranger unintentionally in public. Americans and Canadians, members of low-context cultures, expect a direct, overt apology embodied in the ritualistic "I'm sorry" or "Excuse me." At the same time the North Americans are attributing rudeness to the Koreans, the Koreans are taken aback at the perceived North American confrontational style in taking such overt notice of their physical contact. In such situations, Koreans, members of a high-context culture, rely on more subtle means to apologize, such as facial expressions, gestures, or even murmuring an "U-meo-na!" [Oops!] to themselves.

Pragmatic competence

Part of the enculturation process for children and adolescents is becoming pragmatically competent, that is, learning how to communicate effectively and appropriately. Pragmatic competence entails knowing how to encode, decode, and sequence discourse within a communicative interaction. Since communicative strategies vary according to the situational context and such factors as social power, social and psychological distance, and the degree of imposition involved in communicative interactions, children must learn to evaluate and to weigh these variables. In learning the language of their culture, children are also acquiring the ability to assess the interplay of contextual variables (e.g., formality and informality) and individual variables (e.g., gender, age, rank, and prestige), and they are learning how these variables affect their discourse choices.

Speakers must adapt or adjust their language according to the social context in which a communicative interaction is taking place. Speakers will choose different ways of communicating when they speak to young children, to peers, or to strangers. When a six-year-old child hits a playmate, the playmate may say, "Stop it! Don't do that!" Or the mother may say, "Matthias, you shouldn't do that." When a teenager hits a friend, the friend may reply, "Cut it out, Joe." When a stranger does the same thing, one could respond, "Kindly refrain from doing that." Both children and language learners must develop pragmatic competence to become effective and proficient communicators.

Topic appropriateness

Topic appropriateness is also an area where there are cultural differences and where misunderstandings often occur. In general, North Americans are uncomfortable discussing how much money they earn, nor do they react well to questions from strangers regarding their personal and/or family lives. Questions such as "Why don't you have any children?" for instance, are viewed as intrusive by Americans and Canadians yet are both appropriate and necessary in other cultures. As part of their greeting routine, Koreans immediately ask in which year a person was born, a rather offensive question according to North American ideas. Because Korea is a very hierarchical society, it is essential that speakers know each other's ages in order that they may choose the appropriate verbal and nonverbal discourse strategies. Even the difference of one calendar year requires the use of such a respectful honorific as *older sister* or *older brother* and the corresponding discourse strategies. Because Korea is a very collectivistic society, the honorific system reflects the idea that even though speakers may not be related through kinship ties, they are all "members of one family." Arabs tend to impart a great deal more personal information about themselves than do members of other cultures. Arab cultures are highly collectivistic cultures where personal status and self-identity are intimately linked to a person's overall social status and family background; thus, it is important for speakers to learn about each other's in-group network as soon as possible so that each person can be classified appropriately.

"What is your blood type?" is an unusual question from the Western point of view. From the Japanese and Korean perspective, such a question is quite normal, as people of these cultures believe that specific personality traits are related to blood type—a belief very similar to Western notions of astrology and signs of the zodiac. Most Westerners are surprised by such a question, both because they are unaware of the concept of a relationship between blood type and personality and because many of them do not even know their own blood type.

In addition to topic appropriateness, the importance of pragmatic competence is further realized in how topics are introduced into communicative exchanges. Scollon and Scollon (1981) found significant cultural differences in expectations about how conversations should be opened and in the consequences throughout the conversation as a result of the opening pattern. For example, Asian speakers have a tendency to provide a great deal of background information before stating their main point. This approach differs from that of Westerners, who expect the main point to be made initially so that the other speaker can react to it. **(See Activity C—Critical Incidents)**

Discourse styles

Speakers must also understand and follow the generally unwritten and subconscious rules for different modes of discourse, whether telling stories, discussing in a classroom, presenting a proposal, or conversing with friends. Often, speakers' preferred mode of discourse conflicts with the majority notion of appropriateness, both consciously and unconsciously. Esikovits's (1998) work on sex differences in Australian speech revealed that discourse styles used by adolescent girls and boys followed different rules of speaking. While the girls used speech similar to that of the larger society, the boys preferred to deviate from the accepted rules of speaking, to "affirm their own masculinity and toughness and their working class anti-establishment values" (p. 51).

Heath (1983, 1992) found that the white middle-class literacy expectations of American schoolteachers negatively affected the school performance of children from blue-collar and African American households. The type of language interaction and discourse styles found in the classroom differed radically from the use of language, both oral and written, found in the children's homes. Unaware of these (sub)cultural differences, the students were unable to participate successfully in the classroom, often leading to their eventual failure in the school system. Such pragmatic differences and resultant miscommunications are often exacerbated in cross-cultural situations (Delpit, 1995; Taylor & Whittaker, 2003). Wintergerst's (1994) research on ESL student-teacher interaction found that the types of questions teachers ask students affect student language output in the classroom. An awareness of different expectations regarding question types and functions, as well as modification of discourse patterns, can help teachers engage students more actively in discussion and can improve students' overall school performance (Mehan, Lintz, Okamoto, & Willis, 1995).

The norms governing pragmatics are strongly rooted in the larger cultural context in which they occur. Collectivistic cultures place great importance on saving face and avoiding confrontation. Speakers from such cultures employ politeness rituals and indirect communication strategies that foster a balance between the competing goals of desired outcome and maintenance of relationship harmony. For example, a Japanese businessman avoids issuing an order or a directive but only hints at one. The justifications or reasons for the implied directive are listed in varied subordinate clauses presented before the main clause. The illocutionary or communicative intent of the main clause is clear to the Japanese staff members. The English command "Complete the task by tomorrow morning" is represented roughly by the Japanese statement "Your boss hasn't been around today, but he could show up unexpectedly at any time." Although no directive is issued in the latter case, the Japanese staff members understand exactly the communicative intent of the message and act accordingly.

Conversational exchanges

The nature of the structure of conversational exchanges often leads to cases of miscommunication between native and nonnative speakers of a language. Speakers expect that certain utterances will lead into other specific communicative exchanges or turn-taking sequences. When an exchange sequence is broken because of cross-cultural or crosslinguistic differences in turn-taking sequences, miscommunication occurs (Schegloff, 1984, 1987, 1992). In other words, breakdowns in the expected organization or sequencing of communicative interactions cause misunderstandings and miscommunication. When invited to a person's home, Americans and Canadians will often offer compliments on the host's home and furnishings. In addition to being a sincere show of admiration and appreciation, such compliments evince rapport and friendliness between guest and host. In India or parts of the Middle East, however, a person's compliment on an object is often interpreted as an indirect request for that particular object. In some cultures, such as in Korea or Egypt, an offer of something to eat or drink should be refused the first time. The first invitation is offered out of politeness norms; it is courteous to always offer a visitor to one's house refreshments. Likewise, out of politeness, the visitor should refuse this initial offer and wait for a second or even third offer of refreshment before accepting. Then and only then has the host signaled that the invitation to partake is truly a sincere one and not a courtesy offer. Along similar lines, a "no" response to a request by a Russian will not necessarily be interpreted as a refusal. "No" must often be repeated several times in order for the Russian to accept the refusal as definite and not as something still open to negotiation.

In addition to differences in expectations regarding turn-taking sequences, different expectations with respect to pause length in turn-taking behavior between members of different cultures also result in misunderstandings regarding speaker's intent (Clyne, 1994). Examining informal dinner conversations between Americans and Spaniards, Berry (1994) found that differences in the amount of overlap between turns between Spanish and American speakers led each group to attribute negative characteristics to the other. The Spanish participants in the study indicated that they thought the Americans "didn't really listen and didn't like to talk," and the Americans perceived their Spanish counterparts as "aggressive" and unwilling to let "anyone else have the floor" (p. 189).

Another potential area of cross-cultural misunderstandings is the use of backchannel cues, utterances listeners make in the course of a conversational exchange to signal to the speaker that they are indeed paying attention. Boxer (1993) found important differences in the use of such backchannel cues as "uh huh" or "hmmm" between American English speakers and Japanese speakers of English. Additionally, backchannel cues can encompass utterances—such as "wow" or "that's nice"—that indicate the listener's reaction to or make general comments about the speaker's words and utterances. Japanese norms of interaction both allow for and expect much more frequent use of such backchannel cues than does English (White, 1989). Many times, Japanese will use backchannel cues at points in conversational exchanges where English speakers expect an actual conversational rejoinder. When Japanese speakers transfer their norms of use for these backchannel cues into English, American and Canadian speakers feel frustrated and uncomfortable because they expect more substantive turn-taking responses to their comments. **(See Activity D—Evaluate Your Voice)**

The larger social aspects that are negotiated and conveyed through language use can be quite difficult for nonnative speakers to learn. For instance, outsiders often characterize Americans as insincere, because the former perceive in the latter a tendency to offer "insincere" invitations. International students often complain that an American student will say something like "Let's get together sometime" and never follow up with a phone call or visit. Similarly, we have had experiences where our former students from other cultures have dropped by unexpectedly after we have casually said, "You'll have to come over some time."

The issue is not whether or not Americans are insincere but the pragmatic function of an invitation in different cultures. In American English, invitations are not necessarily invitations at all but conversational routines to express camaraderie or rapport with another speaker. Research has shown that there are actually two types of invitations: those that are truly invitations and those that are *pseudo-invitations* (e.g., Wolfson, 1981; Wolfson et al., 1983). Real or sincere invitations are something that must actually be negotiated among speakers; they are part of an elaborate negotiation process that allows speakers to withdraw from the interaction at any time without losing face or injuring the feelings of other participants. Pseudo-invitations, however, function as indicators of positive social interest without making a firm social commitment, which speakers may not wish to keep. Pseudo-invitations are characterized by vague or ambiguous lexical choices, such as *anytime, sometime, soon, one of these days,* and so on. These types of invitations often begin with *when* clauses, as in the following examples.

Let's get together *when* things settle down.

Let's plan on meeting *when* the project is finished.

Consider the following conversations.

Conversation 1

   A: We should really try to get together *sometime*.

   B: I know, I know. I'd really like to, but things are so crazy now.

   A: Maybe we'll have more time *when* the holidays are over.

   B: Yeah, once Christmas and New Year's are over, I'll have time to breathe again.

   A: Me too. Let's talk again *sometime* after the holidays and see what our calendars look like.

Conversation 2

   A: We should really try to get together *sometime*.

B: Yeah, that would be good. The next couple weeks are really crazy for me, but the last week in January would probably be OK.

A: Let me check my calendar (pulls out PDA, checks the week). I'm open on that Wednesday. How about you?

B: (Checking appointment book) Mmm, Wednesday would be OK if it's after 10:30.

A: OK. Let's do lunch. How about 1?

B: You got it. I'm putting you down right now for 1 on the 27th.

Note the speakers' use of indefinite lexical phrases and *when* clauses in conversation 1. Contrast this with conversation 2. Although Speaker A begins the communicative sequence with the word *sometime,* Speaker B begins the negotiation toward a true invitation by focusing on a specific time (the "last week in January"). Speaker B picks up on this by pulling out a PDA and focusing on a definite date and time. In conversation 1, a pseudo-invitation has been issued and acknowledged. Both speakers have established the desire to get together, without actually fixing a firm date and time; however, the issuance and acceptance of this pseudo-invitation has functioned to establish positive feelings between speakers. In conversation 2, a pseudo-invitation has been negotiated into an actual invitation.

Real invitations involve a negotiating process that allows speakers to either commit to an actual time, date, and/or place or withdraw gracefully if either party is in truth not interested in going beyond the pragmatic function of a pseudo-invitation. This type of conversational negotiation is below the level of awareness of most speakers; they are not consciously aware of the function (or even existence) of pseudo-invitations or of the negotiation process involved in securing an actual invitation. Because this communicative behavior is below the conscious awareness of most native speakers, it is difficult for them to identify it and hence for them to explain it to nonnative speakers. For nonnative speakers, this type of conversational routine leads to misinterpretation because it is outside their ken of experience or their schemata of discourse processes.

Communicative Styles or Registers

The rules governing social interactions are in large part an integral part of a speaker's cultural knowledge, although these rules generally lie below the level of conscious awareness. Since these rules are generally subtle, unwritten, and unconscious, even native speakers may have difficulties understanding them, as evidenced by the popularity of such mavens of social etiquette as Judith Martin, who publishes regularly as "Miss Manners" in a syndicated advice column. Until speakers find themselves in situations where the rules or norms of conversational interaction are broken, they are often unaware that such rules or norms even exist.

Speakers also do not express themselves identically in all social situations. The relationship between speakers and the context in which the communicative interaction is taking place determine which *communicative style* and *register* speakers will choose to use. In a communicative setting, speakers evaluate the degree of formality of context and the relationship between participants based on such variables as age, status, gender, and distance. Based on their evaluation of the context, speakers use different communicative styles, that is, different types of language and/or grammatical structures, including such elements as formality or informality, colloquialisms, dialectal differences (e.g., accent), and semantic choices.

Consider, for instance, the following greetings.

[1.] Yo, Joe!

[2.] Hi, Joe!

[3.] Hello, Joe.

[4.] Good afternoon, Joe.

Based on nothing more than these printed words, we can infer the following. Greeting 1 is most likely to be used between younger males of the same peer group, in informal settings such as walking across campus or running into one another at a coffee shop. Greeting 2 will be used in almost any informal situation between two people who know each other, regardless of gender. Greeting 3 can be regarded as somewhat more formal, but it would not necessarily be so, depending on the speaker's intonation and the social context. If, for instance, the speaker drew out the *hello,* as in "Helloooo, Joe," the greeting immediately becomes less formal and more sociable. Greeting 4 is the most likely to be employed as a more formal greeting among speakers who know each other on a first-name basis. Knowing which greeting is appropriate in which social context is part of the cultural knowledge of speakers. When nonnative speakers are unaware of the pragmatic ramifications of an utterance, they will fail to communicate successfully their intended meaning. An overly casual greeting can set the tone for a brusque, rather than pleasant, exchange.

Inappropriate communicative style is not limited to communicative interactions between native and nonnative speakers. In cultures experiencing rapid change and where language does not reflect explicit social hierarchies through the use of formal/informal pronouns and the use of extensive honorifics or other devices, confusion is widespread with respect to choosing the appropriate style or register. In such cultures, it is not unusual to read and hear comments like those in the following excerpt from a syndicated U.S. newspaper advice column.

Dear Miss Manners:

I sometimes need to telephone a "support staff" for assistance on the operation of my computer and other technologically advanced pieces of equipment in my home. The person taking my call invariably requires, before serving me, that I give my first name, which is then used in an apparent attempt to create a sense of intimacy between us. Although put off by such a request from an individual utterly unknown to me, as well as often two generations younger than I, I feel pressured to acquiesce for fear that I will be denied the information which only that company can provide me. I would appreciate advice on handling this situation.

Let us imagine that the young person who helps you has been doing so for years, carefully addressing you as Mister and Sir. Implausible, Miss Manners knows, but bear with her for the sake of argument.

One day, overcome by the bond that has grown, you might say impulsively, "I'd be very pleased if you would call me Horace." Your tone of voice would show that you meant it as a compliment.

Okay, now use that tone to say, "I would be very pleased if you would call me Mr. Sleeks." (Martin, 2002)

Language is part of social situations; it is a socially situated behavior subject to an interplay of sociopsychological factors (e.g., Eckert &

Rickford, 2002; Giles & St. Clair, 1980). A speaker's language is never "fixed" or "constant." Rather, it is perpetually in a state of flux, changing according to the setting; the relationships of the speakers; the speaker's purpose, mood, and attitude; and any number of other variables. In response to these and other variables, speakers change their style of speech. How speakers express themselves with peers in an informal setting such as a restaurant or classroom will differ from how they express themselves in a job interview for an important career opportunity. Moving between any of these styles is not necessarily a conscious effort.

Miscommunications can arise when speakers differ in their interpretation of which style is appropriate. In communicative interactions involving native and nonnative speakers, a lack of information about or a lack of understanding of the parameters of successful interactions is common. Nonnative speakers may, for instance, be unaware of nuances or subtleties conveyed by certain language forms; in addition, pragmatic transfer, the transfer of sociolinguistically appropriate forms from the native language to the new language, may also occur. DeCapua (1989, 1998), in her research on complaints, found that Germans speaking in English often used the modal verb *must* in situations where Americans would expect the use of the softer *should*. Both *must* and *should* translate directly into the German *müssen* and *sollen;* however, the pragmatic uses of the terms differ in the two languages. The miscommunication of intent was a result of a negative pragmatic transfer of the appropriate use of *müssen*. Consequently, native speakers of American English often evaluated the German speakers negatively. The American speakers based their judgments of German rudeness not on speakers' actual character but on their (mis)use of English.

Part of the enculturation and socialization process of children and adolescents within any language community is helping them understand the differences in use and appropriateness of different communicative styles. Subconscious pragmatic rules need to be brought to the level of conscious perception (Scollon, 1999). This kind of knowledge needs to be brought into teacher training classrooms to enable students to develop a greater awareness of where communication difficulties are likely to arise when working with particular cultural groups. Even speakers sharing the same language but coming from different cultures encounter similar difficulties. In the southern United States, speakers use *ma'am* or *sir,* as a sign of respect. In England, such use is unusual; *sir,* for instance, is used only with royals or senior aristocracy, in the military, and at public formal occasions. Thus, an American from the south answering a British police-man with "Yes, sir" would find himself regarded not as polite but, rather, as ironic or sarcastic. Among the police, the use of *guv* or *guv'ner,* rather than *sir,* would be the rule in all but the most formal circumstances.

Several Japanese students have recounted that upon coming to the United States, they were initially reluctant to order at McDonald's, be-cause they thought the workers were always angry. The Japanese students thought that maybe because they themselves were Asian or maybe be-cause their English wasn't that strong, the workers were angry about hav-ing to wait on them. Later, as they spent more time here, they realized that the discourse patterns of the McDonald's employees, which are char-acterized by rapid rotelike questions and minimal personal interaction, are the norm for fast-food restaurants, where the emphasis is on service that is fast and, from the North American standpoint, friendly. For these Japanese students, the terseness and brevity of the communicative ex-change, as well as the type of questions asked by the workers, indicated a lack of politeness, respect, and/or willingness to help the customer.

Stylistic variations are often very subtle and are often the most dif-ficult for nonnative speakers of the target language to learn. For example, nonnative speakers may use colloquial expressions in more formal situa-tions, male speakers may use syntactic forms or make semantic choices viewed as "feminine," or speakers may employ syntactic structures that are unsuitable for a particular situation. It is often jarring for American college professors to be greeted by international students with "What's up?" Although an atmosphere of (relative) informality is the norm in American university classrooms, the degree varies and may not be read-ily apparent to the nonnative speaker unaware of the nuances. A greeting that is appropriate among friends, peers, and even certain people of higher status is not necessarily appropriate in other situations. A colleague has pointed out, for instance, that when she teaches writing courses in the ESL institute, her students address her by her first name, but when she teaches freshman composition, she is addressed with her title—a some-what confusing situation for students who have made the transition from one program to the other.

Conversational or interactional routines

Miscommunication and misunderstandings also arise in the area of con-versational or interactional routines. *Conversational routines* are phrases and rejoinders that carry specific pragmatic meaning for a discourse function that has either subsumed or replaced the literal referential meaning and that allows for one of a limited set of responses (Aijmer, 1996; Hymes, 1962; Leech, 1983). All languages make use of numerous routines or formulaic speech patterns, especially for such speech acts as greetings, thanks, leave-takings, apologies, and so on. In American English, a common greeting is "Hi, how're you?" A speaker's use of "How are you?" is usually not to inquire about a person's state of health or being but as a phrase that is part of the greeting routine. The expected response is something along the lines of "Fine, and you?" A response detailing the state of one's health is generally not appropriate. In other languages, part of the greeting may include conversational routines such as "Have you eaten?" or "Where are you going?" Nonnative speakers often feel frustrated when they are unfamiliar with the pragmatic functions of conversational routines, because their focus on literal referential meaning can cause them to misunderstand the meaning or intent of the message. **(See Activity E— Telephone Endings)**

Communication styles in high- and low-context cultures

Chapter 2 discussed Hall's (1976) distinction between high-context and low-context communication. High-context cultures are those cultures that rely on implicit and shared meanings to communicate. Speakers from such cultures tend to use indirect speech strategies, subtle nonverbal cues, and setting to impart the intended message. Low-context cultures, in contrast, rely on explicit codes—such as direct verbal strategies and overt nonverbal cues—to convey the intended message. Various cross-cultural studies have found that people's communication styles are influenced by their cultural background (e.g., Blum-Kulka & House, 1989; Clyne, 1994; DeCapua, 1998; Meier, 1996). Speakers use discourse strategies that assume shared knowledge of the norms and rules of communicative interaction, shared sets of attitudes and values, and shared interpretations of context, setting, and speaker variables.

In individualistic cultures, speakers tend to choose more direct discourse styles to convey their intent to their hearers. There is less emphasis on or concern for the "we," or how the speaker is a representative of a group or larger network. The stress in an individualistic culture is on the "I," or how the speaker comes across as an individual in his or her own right; thus, speakers tend to elect speech strategies that clearly convey the intended message (Ting-Toomey & Kirogi, 1998).

Overall, members of collectivistic cultures generally prefer indirect means of discourse as a way of maintaining face and avoiding face-threatening acts. Rather than directly make requests of, engage in conflict with, or offer a refusal to one's hearer, members of collectivistic cultures tend to use speech strategies that indirectly signal their intent (e.g., Ting-Toomey, 1985, 1999). According to Hofstede (1991), most collectivistic cultures avoid saying no because doing so is too direct and confrontational and thus threatens the face of both speaker and hearer. Speakers from collectivistic cultures prefer indirect responses, such as "Maybe," "We'll get back to you," or " I'll see," which they will use whether or not they agree or acquiesce. When the teacher asks, "Do you understand?" Asian students in the classroom often say yes, even when they do not understand. This yes response does not entail understanding on the hearer's part but only suggests that the hearer has heard the speaker. To say no would show disrespect for the teacher by implying that the teacher did not or could not present the material clearly. In a collectivistic culture, it is important to maintain harmony by acknowledging and preserving status and rank, while simultaneously shifting the possibility for blame, shame, or any sort of dishonor away from a speaker.

An American teacher in Japan recounts that when she first went to teach in Japan, she would smoke in the English teachers' staff room. Since there was an ashtray in the room, she thought smoking was acceptable, when in fact the ashtray was only there for special or important guests. Smoking by teachers in the staff room was actually frowned on. She finally learned of the other teachers' disapproval of her smoking when a Japanese teacher from another department who had lived several years in the United States came and explained to her that smoking was not permitted in staff rooms. She was very embarrassed and asked why no one had told her so previously. The teacher said that the teachers had indicated their disapproval but that she had not noticed—they had opened the windows, regardless of the outside temperature; left the room when she lit up; or made various indirect comments. This Japanese teacher realized there was a communication problem between the Japanese English teachers and the American, because he had lived in the United States and knew that more explicit communication was required in order to get the message across to her.

In Arab cultures, hearers will offer an affirmative response to a request as a discourse strategy to signal rapport and simultaneously maintain face. When an Arabic speaker says yes in response to a request, it does not necessarily mean that the speaker's request will be honored. Rather, such a yes implies that the speaker's request has been heard and that the hearer has all intentions to act on it accordingly. However, the result is actually viewed separately from the request. If something is not acted on, no blame rests on the individual; rather, it is *inshallah,* or "as God wills." Consequently, Arab speakers are not necessarily upset if there is no follow-through to a request because by saying yes the hearer acknowledged it and stated his or her intentions to act on it, though circumstances came between the hearer's intentions and ability to act. Through this discourse strategy, the speakers have maintained their face even though they cannot feasibly comply with or fulfill the request.

People from different cultural and language backgrounds may see conversational roles or the context of a conversation differently (see Huang, 1996; Keenan, 1976; Spencer-Oatey, 1993; Tannen, 1986) and may therefore get different messages from the same utterance in the exact same context. For example, Asians tend to have a preference for an inductive pattern for topic introduction, while Westerners show a preference for the deductive pattern. Facework (see chap. 2), which entails a period of speakers' getting warmed up to each other, is apparent in the Chinese inductive pattern in Taiwan. The speaker introduces the topic, but the actual topic discussion will be delayed until speakers have engaged in facework. Delayed topic introduction by Asians has frequently resulted in cross-cultural miscommunication, since Westerners and Asians are often unaware of the cultural and traditional practices regarding the initiation and continuation of their respective discourse patterns. **(See Activity F—Learning to Look)**

Teaching and Learning Connections

Second language learners' understanding of a second culture is affected by their culturally shaped worldviews. In our daily lives, we use language unconsciously; we predict and explain other people's behavior based on our shared language and cultural knowledge. When we step out of our cultural world, we find that there are other ways of communicating—ways that go beyond just learning the lexicon and syntax of a language. We must learn to look beyond our own cultural lenses to become more open to seeing unfamiliar or unexpected behavior from a different perspective. When confronted and confounded by what is different, we need to consider what the contributing factors might be. Does failing to thank someone in a service encounter signal rudeness or the lack of a corresponding norm in the other culture? While saying thank-you is the accepted conversational routine in most Western cultures in service situations such as checkout lines at stores, the same is not true in some East Asian cultures. There, a thank-you in such contexts signals a reprimand, as people who are doing their jobs appropriately do not need or expect thanks.

Even when different languages share the rules and norms for speech-act production, the actual realization of the speech act may differ. Cohen, Olshtain, and Rosenstein (1986) found that Hebrew learners of English were unaware of certain distinctions that native speakers of American English made between forms for expressing apology. In several situations in their study, the learners spoke only the word *sorry,* a translation from the commonly used Hebrew *slixa,* where native speakers of American English expected more involved apologies. Thus, participants in cross-cultural encounters must learn how to become discriminating observers of behaviors in order to better predict probable pragmatically appropriate language use, while learning what types of pitfalls and negative situations result from inappropriate language use and interactional norms and how to avoid them. The importance of becoming aware of differences in the norms of communicative interaction cannot be stressed enough. As Thomas (1983) has pointed out, when speakers are confronted with violations of expected norms (pragmatic failure), they attribute negative personality or behavioral characteristics to the person violating these norms, rather than considering the violations a matter of the learner's second language proficiency.

Pragmatics is concerned with how speakers use language and construct meaning within social contexts. Pragmatic competence entails knowledge of speech acts and speech function, as well as knowledge of dialect, register, and other cultural factors in language use. Second language learners should become aware of the various options available to them as a result of the pragmatic system of the target language. Learning how to do things appropriately with words involves learning how to use a combination of linguistic resources in a contextually appropriate way. The potential problem in teaching the pragmatic system of any language is both the sheer number of speech acts and language functions and the paucity of research in this area to date. A more productive approach is for language teachers to help their students become aware that pragmatic functions exist in a language and to help them learn to become better observers and interpreters of language in social context.

Because culture is part of most contexts, communication is rarely culture free. Language learners need to be aware of differing cultural frameworks, that is, their own and those of others. If they are not, they will use their own cultural assumptions to interpret the messages of the target language, where the intended meaning may be based on quite different assumptions about culture. In some cultures, students simply call out the answer to a question in the classroom without waiting for the teacher to recognize them first. In others, students only respond when being called on, and in still others, students raise their hands and wait for teachers to acknowledge them. Different classroom behaviors can cause confusion in multicultural classrooms when students' and teachers' expectations of classroom etiquette differ or even conflict. Some students may find it difficult to ever respond, others may dominate the classroom, and teachers may feel frustrated or threatened. **(See Activity G—On the Spot)**

In work on international teaching assistants (ITAs), gender issues, and cultural interpretations of appropriateness, Boxer and Tyler found that there were cultural differences with respect to teacher-student relationships (Boxer & Tyler, 1996; Tyler & Boxer, 1996). While the majority of the American undergraduates in their studies did not think it appropriate for an ITA to stop by a student's apartment unannounced, many ITAs found the scenario acceptable. Some of the ITAs noted that this type of behavior would be neutral and normal in their home cultures (Boxer, 2002:191). Thus, developing students' skills in intercultural communication is an appropriate part of language teaching.

A variety of studies conducted by Gumperz and various colleagues (e.g., Gumperz, 1977, 1978, Gumperz & Tannen, 1979; Gumperz, Gurinder, & Kaltman, 1982) found that Indian and Pakistani immigrants often experienced communication difficulties with native speakers of British English. These communication difficulties often resulted in negative character judgments on the part of the British. British speakers' perceptions of Indian and Pakistani speakers as rude were based primarily on differences in which lexical, syntactical, and intonational choices were considered appropriate to convey communicative intent. What the Pakistani and Indian speakers intended to convey was not what their British hearers interpreted as having been said. One reason for this was a tendency by the Pakistanis to say no throughout their conversations. For the Pakistanis, saying no functioned as a pause filler in their native language; however, in English, saying no has no such pragmatic function but conveys instead a negative and antagonistic attitude.

Developing pragmatic awareness

As Kramsch (1993:8) points out, culture awareness training should be seen both as enabling language proficiency and as being the result of reflection on language proficiency. Such a perspective on culture and the language classroom allows teachers to view the classroom as a promoter—and at times even a source—of cross-cultural investigative fieldwork. Judd (1999:154) categorizes the techniques for developing pragmatic awareness in second language learners into three broad categories: cognitive awareness, receptive skill development, and productive use. An awareness of the differences that occur between speech acts in the native language and those same acts in the target language constitutes *cognitive awareness* activities. Such awareness may be achieved through presenting and discussing research findings on speech acts and having learners procure information through observations, questionnaires, and interviews. Merely presenting linguistic formulas without sufficient background or discussion of context is inadequate. Language learners need to be given detailed information on such participant and contextual variables as status, gender, intimacy, location, and degree of formality.

Receptive skill development moves beyond simple cognitive awareness and enables learners to recognize and understand speech acts through actual practice, using teacher-designed materials, published textbooks, media (e.g., video or cassette recordings), or naturally occurring data. To successfully complete a receptive skill activity, learners should be able to identify the speech act occurring and the sociological environment in which it takes place. Beyond receptive skill development is the development of *productive use,* which encourages learners to use appropriate communication strategies. Cloze-type activities, role plays, and simulations may be used to help learners produce specific pragmatic features.

Since it is difficult, if not impossible, to identify the range of all potential meanings and interactional moves, participants in cross-cultural communicative interactions need to develop skills that allow them to become discriminating observers of behaviors. Moreover, it is difficult to actually teach pragmatic competence. Not only is there a paucity of research to support such teaching, but the research that exists tends to be insufficient, tends to be drawn from elicited or laboratory-style data, and covers few speech acts in a limited number of languages (for further discussion of these issues, see, e.g., Kasper, 1999; Kasper & Dahl, 1991; Meier, 2003; Rose, 1994; Wolfson, Marmor, & Jones, 1989). Better cross-cultural observation skills allow speakers to better predict probable pragmatically appropriate language use and interactional moves used in another culture. At the same time, language learners need to develop the skills that will help them be aware of the potential pitfalls and negative situations that can result from inappropriate language use.

Numerous researchers and teachers (e.g., Bardovi-Harlig, 1992; Kramsch, 1993; Meier, 2003; Rose, 1994) recommend that learners become amateur ethnographers, collecting their own data through actual examples of speech acts occurring in their daily environment. For learners in foreign language situations, media such as television or movies can serve as a rich source. Hymes (1969) posits that education should be comprised of both ethnography and research on the influences of culture on language, since these endeavors can complement each other. Radio, television, and films are media that display naturally occurring speech acts. For example, television broadcasts that include news shows, political debates, talk shows, or situation comedies get students involved in discussing direct and indirect ways of disagreeing, asking questions, making requests, and so on.

A set of commercial television sitcoms can be used to clarify differences in cultural patterns for common everyday social interactions. Commercial television is a rich source for bringing unconscious cultural codes to the level of conscious perception. Washburn (2001:22) has pointed out the particular usefulness of television sitcoms for developing pragmatic awareness.

Sitcoms present many models of appropriate pragmatic language use among various characters of differing status, familiarity, gender, and in varied settings, such as at work, at home, in public places, and at formal gatherings.

Washburn discusses how to choose appropriate sitcoms as a teaching tool, offering concrete suggestions for developing and incorporating pragmatic activities into the second language classroom. Rose (1994) suggests that videos are a powerful tool for developing pragmatic awareness, particularly in foreign language teaching situations where learners have little or no exposure to the target language outside the classroom. He offers suggestions and outlines several activities for incorporating video into foreign language classrooms. Kramsch (1993:211–223) describes using television commercials as a tool for sharing information about the culture of the target country. Commercials can also be used to raise pragmatic awareness. For instance, Kramsch discusses an American Coca-Cola commercial that highlights (among other information) differences in social role expectations, topic appropriateness, and conversational style.

A caveat to be added is that not all types of activities are suitable for all learners. Students from cultures that value indirect discourse strategies, harmony, and group consensus will find it difficult and uncomfortable to participate in certain language activities, such as debates. Change is not only "not easy" but should be weighed against the importance of maintaining one's own cultural interaction patterns. What we are advocating is creating awareness, not forcing radical transformations of one's self.

Questions for Study and Discussion

1. Discuss the statement "Language exists within the context of culture." How does this statement relate to your personal situation?

2. How do speakers negotiate meaning?

3. Describe what communicative misunderstandings are and some circumstances under which they occur. Provide one example from the text and one from your own experience.

4. What are speech acts? What is meant by illocutionary intent? What original examples can you provide?

5. Discuss organizational competence and pragmatic competence. Give examples of each.

6. What are some factors that influence speakers' choice of communicative style or register?

7. Discuss how high-context and low-context styles influence communication.

8. What role does pragmatics play in conversational exchanges?

9. What are some ways speakers can develop their pragmatic awareness? Which way(s) do you consider most effective? Why?

III. Practice: What Activities Show Us

A. In the Limelight (25–30 minutes)

Communication does not occur in isolation; it occurs within a context and potential range of variables, such as setting, status, gender, and age. These variables are crucial when determining how speakers use language to convey an intended meaning. Awareness of these variables is critical in conversational interactions.

Purpose: To practice distinguishing different variables of conversational interaction

Procedure:

1. Randomly divide into two groups. Group 1 will be the "observers," and group 2 will be the "participants."

2. *Observers:* Arrange yourselves so that you can observe the participants as they discuss their topic. Only observe; do not comment or partake in the conversation in any way. You may wish to take notes during the discussion. Consider the following variables.

   - Who dominates the discussion?

   - How does turn taking take place (length of pauses, interruptions, etc.)?

   - What types of fillers do speakers use?

   - When do speakers use pauses and hesitations?

   - How close do the participants sit to one another?

   - What kind of eye contact takes place?

   - Who avoids speaking, and who tends to jump in?

   - What variables in human identity seem to be involved (e.g., gender, age, social status)?

   - What is the effect of the topic on the discussion?

   Participants: Hold a topical discussion for 15 minutes. You may choose your own topic or take one from the following list. If the discussion lags, begin another topic.

   Possible discussion topics:

   - Your favorite/least favorite things about the United States (or any other country)

   - Which teacher most influenced you in your life and why

- The advantages/disadvantages of living in an urban/rural area

- The hardest thing you have ever done

- Your most embarrassing/happiest moment

- The problems/successes/challenges of the (American) educational system

- The status of women in relation to men

- Your first day at school/in a foreign country/driving a car

3. Discuss step 2 as a full group.

Sample Questions for the "Observers":

- What factors influenced the dynamics of the discussion?

- What cultural variables impacted on these dynamics?

- Was it difficult not to be able to partake in the participants' discussion? Why or why not?

Sample Questions for the "Participants":

- Do you agree/disagree with the observers' observations?

- How did it feel to be under observation as you participated in the discussion? Did this influence your participation?

Sample Questions for the Full Group:

- What did you learn about communicative interactions from this activity?

- What did you learn about yourself as a speaker/listener?

- What differences did you notice between those from different parts of the United States, those from different English-speaking countries, and native and nonnative speakers of English?

Alternative:

1. If the full group is very large, divide into four groups: two groups of "observers" and two groups of "participants."

B. Meet and Greet (10–15 minutes)

Speech acts refer to what speakers do with words and to the reasons for their utterances. Using pragmatically inappropriate language often results in being considered rude or even ill mannered. There are important differences in how and when speech acts are expressed, and an awareness of these differences is essential for effective communication.

Purpose: To examine how one particular speech act is enacted

Procedure:

1. Stand up. Push all chairs and tables out of the way so participants can circulate freely.

2. Circulate and introduce yourselves to different people. Talk to each person for a few moments.

3. Stop after 5 minutes.

4. Discuss the interactions as a full group.

   Sample Questions:

   - How did you go about introducing yourself?

   - What words did you use? What nonverbal cues did you use?

   - How did you decide how you were going to introduce yourself? For example, what variables, such as gender, intimacy, and so on, influenced your form of greeting?

   - How did you "end" each greeting and move on to the next partner?

   - After the initial greetings, what topics did you discuss? What pattern do you see to the topics (discussion of this question can be facilitated by listing the topics on the board)? Why do you think this is?

   - What did this activity teach you about culture and communication?

Alternative:

- Videotape the activity. Have students review the tape and discuss it as a full group, using the sample questions from step 4.

 I, A

To adapt for the language classroom,

Follow-up:

1. With a partner, prepare a written dialogue for a role play using meeting and greeting routines.

2. Present the role play to the class.

C. Critical Incidents (15–20 minutes)

The following critical incidents are exercises focusing on an area of cross-cultural conflict or miscommunication. The situation described in each incident presents a problem related to differences in the norms governing sociocultural communicative interactions, or the "rules of speaking." There are no right or wrong answers in this exercise; the point of the exercise is to stimulate thought-provoking discussion based on the incidents. The goal of considering critical incidents is to increase an awareness of and sensitivity to cultural differences and, in this case, to develop an understanding of cultural influences on language behavior.

Purpose: To expand an awareness of differences in communicative behavior

Procedure:

1. Prepare different sets of two to four critical incidents. How many sets you prepare will depend on the total number of participants (e.g., for a group of 12 participants, prepare four sets).

2. Work in groups of 3–4.

3. Pass out the sets of critical incidents, and ask participants to brainstorm possible solutions.

4. As a full group, discuss the critical incidents, possible solutions, and the cultural values underlying the areas of cultural conflict.

5. Write your own critical incident. Share this with a partner or the full group.

Critical Incident 1

You are at a welcome party organized by the ESL program at your school. You meet several very nice international students who have just arrived in the United States. After a few minutes of chatting, they ask you such questions as "What is your salary here?" "What is your father's occupation?" "Why are so many Americans divorced?" and "Why don't Americans respect old people?" As their questions continue, you feel more and more uncomfortable.

Critical Incident 2

An international student is living in a dormitory with many American students. On Tuesday, she is walking to the cafeteria on campus when she runs into one of the American girls from the dorm. The international student says, "Hi!' and the American student says, "Hi! How are you?" The international student stops for a second to tell the American student how she is, but the American student keeps on walking. The international student is confused and disappointed and feels that the American is fake and superficial.

Critical Incident 3

Shirley, a student from Taiwan, met her two new American female friends at a restaurant for lunch. When she arrived, the American friends hugged and kissed each other and Shirley. Shirley felt quite uncomfortable and did not know how to react.

Critical Incident 4

At an international business meeting, the delegations from various countries are gathered to conduct the business at hand. Mr. Gomez and Mr. Valdez appear to be arguing fiercely with each other; their voices are loud, and they are gesticulating emphatically. The Asian delegation is afraid that a fight will break out shortly. Then, all of a sudden, Mr. Gomez and Mr. Valdez pat each other on the back as if they were lifelong friends. This chain of events puzzles the Japanese and Chinese greatly.

Critical Incident 5

An American teacher runs into some of her former students in the university cafeteria. After the initial greetings, one of the students says to her," You're looking much older, and you've gained weight." The American is taken aback and feels rather offended.

Critical Incident 6

Jack, an American, is in Japan. He asks a Japanese man whom he sees on the street for directions. Jack asks in basic Japanese where a certain building is. The Japanese man seems to be thinking very hard for awhile, tilting his head and wrinkling his forehead. Jack expects that this man knows where the place is, but after 10–15 seconds, the Japanese man says, "Sorry, I don't know." Jack is disappointed and a bit annoyed and wonders why it took this man such a long time to say that he didn't know. He could have said no in a second if he really didn't know anything about where this building was. Jack asks another Japanese man on the street. Again he waits for an answer. Five seconds and then 10 seconds pass. "Maybe this man knows where it is," Jack thinks. "Uh, . . . I'm sorry, I'm not sure," says the man. At this point, Jack is very annoyed and frustrated. "These Japanese . . . ," he mutters to himself.

Critical Incident 7

Moon-Whan and Anna were jogging in the park on a hot summer day. Both of them were really perspiring. They had just spent two hours running, and both were thirsty and hungry. After their jog, they went to the house of Anna's friend Erna, where they had hoped to rest for awhile and reenergize before going home. On their arrival, Erna asked the girls whether they wanted a cool drink of iced tea and some cookies. Anna jumped at the opportunity and said yes immediately. Moon-Whan said no. Anna was surprised by Moon-Whan's response.

Critical Incident 8

Students in Professor Padilla's speech class are enthusiastic about their active involvement in learning oral communication skills. They participate in a wide range of skill-building communicative activities. In their eagerness not only to respond to questions but also to engage in dialogue with the professor, they raise their hand and call out "Teacher," "Ma'am," and "Miss" when trying to get the professor's attention to be called on. Professor Padilla squirms as a visible sign of disapproval to this type of address.

Discussion

Critical Incident 1
The international students are clearly operating under different rules of speaking. Cultures differ on what are considered appropriate topics of conversation and on which types of questions may be asked of whom. Questions that may be considered intrusive in one culture may be part of another culture's way of seeking information to build rapport among speakers.

Critical Incident 2
Different languages have different formulaic greetings. In American English, "How are you?" is usually intended not as a question about one's health but simply as a way of greeting another person. The re-

ply expected is another formula (e.g., "Not bad," "Fine,") not a recitation of one's actual health. Similarly, in other languages, other formulaic patterns exist. For instance, one may be greeted in Thai with "Where are you going?" and in Chinese with "Have you eaten?" These are generally not actual information questions but part of formulaic greetings. Until nonnative speakers learn these formulas or patterns of speech, they may misinterpret the communicative intent and form negative opinions about a speaker who uses them.

Critical Incident 3
In many cultures, it is inappropriate to kiss friends publicly as a form of greeting; in other cultures, such kissing is both suitable and expected. Public displays of affectionate greeting can be disconcerting to someone brought up in a culture emphasizing restraint.

Critical Incident 4
Paralinguistic features such as tone of voice, loudness, and the use and frequency of gestures during communicative interactions differ between cultures. Speakers from different cultures with significant variances in such areas may find themselves unable to understand the actual intent of an interaction. The loud argumentation by members of the Spanish delegation impressed the Chinese and Japanese participants as disagreement or fighting rather than as a normal mode of conducting business, but it is in fact the usual way in which the Spanish conduct business.

Critical Incident 5
There are different possible reasons underlying the student's comments. In some cultures, gaining weight and growing older are valued conditions. In cultures where many people face starvation, excess weight is an indicator of prosperity; in cultures where the old are revered, aging is a positive component of the cycle of life. Another possible reason for the student's comments may be that blatant comments on another person's appearance do not hold inherently negative connotations. In the United States and Canada, people frequently compliment one another on personal aspects such as a new hairstyle or item of clothing; however, it is rude and offensive to point out any perceived defects or blemishes in another person's appearance or dress. In other cultures, pointing out anything "negative" about a person's personal appearance is no more than a simple statement of fact, with no animosity, offense, or malice intended.

Critical Incident 6

Japanese tend to avoid saying no in any type of communicative interaction. In this incident, where no must be said, the Japanese speakers soften the no through the use of an initial pause. The pause is followed by an apologetic no, to indicate the person's regret in not being able to offer the requested assistance. This signals to the hearer that the other person is thinking the question over, regardless of whether he or she already knows the answer. Through such response, the speaker avoids being too direct or rude. While Americans may also pause before responding negatively to such a question, the pause time is generally brief and preceded by the backchannel cue "ummm." Moreover, when American speakers do insert a brief pause, the function of this pause is not to delay providing a negative response but only to indicate they are thinking the question over.

Critical Incident 7

In some cultures, such as in Korea and Egypt, politeness norms require that when someone is offered something to eat or drink, it must be refused the first time around. However, such a refusal is often viewed as a rejection of someone's hospitality and thoughtlessness in other cultures, particularly when no excuse is made for the refusal. Americans and Canadians, for instance, expect refusals to be accompanied by a reasonable excuse or reason.

Critical Incident 8

Nonnative speakers are often unaware of the titles to be accorded to those in positions of authority. Frequently, there are equivalent terms in different languages, but their usage differs. In many cultures, anyone engaged in teaching may be addressed simply as "Teacher." In North America, however, a university professor commonly expects to be addressed as either "Professor" or "Doctor," the form of address commonly used for university professors in order to distinguish them from K–12 teachers.

 A

To adapt for the language classroom,

Writing Critical Incidents

- See chapter 2, Activity F, for suggestions.

D. Evaluate Your Voice (homework assignment; 30–40 minutes of discussion)

Communication is comprised of both verbal and nonverbal components. To communicate more effectively, individuals need to be aware of the numerous subcategories of these two components, so that they may use them to their advantage in an attempt to foster better communication.

Purpose: To gain a better perspective on how speakers sound to their listeners

Procedure:

Homework assignment

1. Tape-record yourself while talking on the telephone to a friend or colleague. You will need to bring this tape in to the full group.

2. Record only your side of the conversation. This will provide you with a good representation of what you sound like to others.

3. Listen to your tape and answer these questions. You might also ask someone else you know to listen to your tape and answer these questions.

   - How was your rate of speech? Fast? Slow? Varied?

   - How was your vocal variety? Varied? Energetic? Lethargic? Harsh?

   - Did you alter your stress and intonation, as in "It's been so **long** since we've talked."

   - How did your tone sound? Soft? Loud? Monotone? Nervous? Nasal?

   - Did your voice fade out at the end of your sentences or phrases?

   - Did you use question intonation in declarative sentences?

   - Did you run out of breath or hear yourself sigh?

- Did you hear yourself using backchannel cues, such as *uh-huh, um, yes, oh, really?* If yes, how did these help the flow of conversation? If no, did the lack of these hinder the interaction in any way? Explain. Where might you have appropriately inserted backchannel cues? Which ones might you have inserted?

- Did you emphasize certain words for extra emphasis? What did this contribute to the interaction?

- Did you display any nervous mannerisms such as coughing, throat clearing, or giggling?

- Did you interrupt, or were you often interrupted? Explain how this impacted on the interaction.

Group discussion

4. Present and discuss your findings about your speech in small groups of 3–4. Listen to any excerpts from participants' tapes as appropriate.

5. Discuss your observations and findings with the full group.

Sample Questions:

- What did you learn about yourself as a speaker?

- Are there any generalizations you can make about your group's findings?

- How could you use this activity in a cross-cultural or multicultural teaching situation?

E. Telephone Endings (20–25 minutes)

Although all languages share the ability to convey the same meanings, how they convey these meanings differs. An integral part of any language is its conversational patterns or routines. These are ritualized or rule governed, yet the rules are not necessarily generated by the grammar of the language. These routines are functional and pragmatic in use and vary among languages. It is essential for speakers to share an understanding of both the function of a conversational routine and the constraints on its conditions of use.

Purpose: To demonstrate how everyday routines are governed by sets of rules and how these rules differ cross-culturally

Procedure:

1. Work in groups of 3–4.

2. Develop a set of "rules" for ending a telephone conversation.

3. Write the rules as if writing a manual for someone that does not know how to end a telephone conversation.

4. Share the rules.

5. Discuss the rules as a full group.

   Sample Questions:

   • Who are the speakers? For example, what is each speaker's social role, status, age, and gender?

   • Who initiates the phone call?

   • What sorts of greetings do the speakers exchange?

   • What is the subject of the conversation?

   • Which speaker initiates the end of the conversation?

   • How do the speakers end the conversation?

   • What factors did you take into consideration? Example factors are status, gender of speakers, degree of intimacy between speakers, and purpose of conversation (e.g., social vs. business).

   • What differences are there between ending telephone conversations and ending face-to-face conversations?

   • What generalizations can you make about telephone endings?

Follow-up:

   • Read and comment on the following resource.

   Godard, D. (1977). Same setting, different norms: Phone call beginnings in France and the United States. *Language in Society, 6,* 209–219.

F. Learning to Look (30–35 minutes to introduce the activity; homework assignment; 30–40 minutes for review and discussion)

One of the most difficult things to do in life is to learn to observe or to record the everyday things occurring around us. So much of what takes place in our daily lives is mundane, so much a part of ourselves and our behaviors, that we often never become aware of what we are doing or how we are behaving until something happens to violate that which we (usually unconsciously) assume to be the norm.

Purpose: To help participants become better observers of the world around them

Procedure:

Pre-class preparation

1. Photocopy enough handouts for each student to receive three copies of worksheet 7.

2. Preview movies for scenes that illustrate different elements of communicative interaction. Choose one or two movie clips to use in class. Some movies that are useful for this activity are *Annie Hall, Barbershop, My Big Fat Greek Wedding, The Contender, Dave, Hannah and Her Sisters, A Great Wall, Miss Congeniality, Rush Hour 1* or *2, Twelve Angry Men, White Men Can't Jump,* and *What About Bob?*

Introduction

3. As a full group, discuss the various elements of communicative interactions.

   Sample Questions:

   • What aspects are involved in communication? List as many as possible. Examples are intonation, type of language (formal vs. informal language), and eye contact.

   • What are some ways in which these aspects differ cross-culturally? How might these differences interfere with successful cross-cultural interactions?

   • What factors influence a communicative interaction? List as many as possible. Examples are gender of participants, age of participants, and setting (e.g., restaurant, meeting).

- How might these factors carry different weight in different cultures?

4. Pass out one copy per participant of worksheet 7.

5. Watch the first video clip once through.

6. Complete worksheet 7 with as much information as possible. Refer to the lists generated in step 3. A sample observation sheet has been provided for the 1977 movie *Annie Hall,* starring Woody Allen and Diane Keaton. Although both the hero and heroine of this film are from the same larger culture (the United States), they are members of rather different subcultures. Annie Hall (Diane Keaton) is an all-American girl from the Midwest, while Alvy Singer (Woody Allen) is a Jewish man from New York. There are several useful scenes in this particular movie. The most productive of these is an Easter dinner scene where Alvy Singer has gone with his girlfriend (Annie) to Minnesota to meet her family. Annie's family and Alvy find themselves having difficulties at dinner, most of which are related to differences in conversational style, topic choices, body language, rate of speech, and so on.

7. Discuss your observations as a full group.

Sample Questions:

- What were some of the key participant variables affecting communication?

- What were some pragmatic variables influencing the flow of conversation?

- What were some differences in nonverbal communication?

- How was setting important here?

- What conclusions can you draw about topic choice? About humor?

- This video clip illustrates differences from two American subcultures. Why might speakers be surprised or shocked by such communication difficulties? What examples can you provide from your own experiences?

Sample Observation Sheet

Source:
Annie Hall video clip

Setting:
Easter dinner in family home in Minnesota/Jewish holiday dinner

Participant Characteristics	Verbal Behavior	Nonverbal Behavior
Midwestern family & a Jewish New Yorker	Longer pauses between turns	Relatively wide spacing between members at the table
Jewish family holiday dinner in NYC	Conversational overlaps; frequent interruptions	Little space between members at the table

This page is reproducible.

Worksheet 7. Observation Sheet

Source:		

Setting:		

Participant Characteristics	Verbal Behavior	Nonverbal Behavior

- How can we benefit from using video clips such as this in a cross-cultural or multicultural classroom?

8. View the video clip again.

- What information can you add to the worksheet that you did not pick up on earlier?

- What information that has been pointed out in group discussion do you notice now?

Homework assignment

9. Give each participant two additional copies of worksheet 7.

10. Assign participants to observe two of the following situations, and complete a worksheet for each one.

- a meal with at least four participants

- a scene from a movie filmed in a language other than English

- a scene from a TV sitcom

- a meeting

- a party

Review and discussion

11. As a full group, share your findings. If the group is very large, discuss findings in groups of 3–4 first, then share five of the most important findings of the small-group discussions with the full group.

Sample Questions:

- Describe your observations.

- Why did you choose this situation?

- What struck you the most about this situation?

- What were some significant variables you observed?

- What differences in communication did you notice between the two situations you observed?

- What role did nonverbal communication play?

- What have you learned from this activity?

Optional: Show video clips of any situations you observed with the full group.

G. On the Spot (15–20 minutes)

Communicative interactions are shaped in the cultural context in which they occur. Face and facework are especially apparent in Asian cultures. Unfamiliarity with the concept of and importance attached to facework and with its impact on discourse patterns frequently leads to miscommunication.

Purpose: To experience how we impose constraints on ourselves to save face

Procedure:

1. Read the following list of tasks. Rank each task in the order you would be willing to undertake each one (with 1 as least willing and 10 as most willing).

   _____ 1. Asking teachers how much money they earn.

   _____ 2. Singing "Jingle Bells" in front of this class.

   _____ 3. Asking someone you have just met what his or her political views are.

   _____ 4. Cheering loudly at a sporting event you are attending with your family.

   _____ 5. Cheering loudly at a sporting event you are attending with colleagues.

   _____ 6. Talking nonstop during class.

   _____ 7. Asking for directions after getting lost.

   _____ 8. Describing your most embarrassing moment to the rest of this class.

_____ 9. Sharing personal feelings with members of the opposite sex.

_____ 10. Kissing a person's cheek as a form of greeting.

2. Tally the rankings on the board.

3. As a full group, discuss what factors influenced your ranking decisions.

   Sample Questions:

   • Was it easy to rank these tasks? Why or why not?

   • How did different variables (e.g., age, gender, and status) influence your choices?

   • Which cultural influences played a role in your decisions?

   • How does your ranking differ from those of the other members of the class? Do the rankings of the different members of the class fall into any discernible patterns of influence (e.g., by cultural background, gender, or any other variable)?

 A

To adapt for the language classroom,

Follow-up:

   • Write an anecdote describing your most embarrassing moment. Include an explanation of why the incident was so embarrassing to you, a description of how you felt, and what you wish you had done differently.

IV. Further Readings

Articles

Boxer, D., & Cortés-Conde, F. (2000). Identity and ideology: Culture and pragmatics in content-based ESL. In J. Hall & L. Verplaetse (Eds.), *Second and foreign language learning through classroom interaction* (pp. 203–220). Mahwah, NJ: Erlbaum.

This article provides readers with a provocative examination of pragmatics and language learning within the context of content-based language learning courses.

The authors take the position that the development of communities within different language learning contexts forces learners to negotiate meaning, thereby promoting their pragmatic competence. The authors' discussion of various aspects of communicative behavior in language classrooms skillfully illustrates their contention that pragmatic knowledge must be gained through authentic, rather than simulated, interactions.

Holmes, J., & Brown, D. (1987). Teachers and students learning about compliments. *TESOL Quarterly, 21,* 523–546.

In this article, the authors offer varied examples of misunderstandings that occur when exchanging compliments in different cultural contexts; furthermore, they analyze these misunderstandings as examples of pragmalinguistic and sociopragmatic failure. They include exercises designed to help learners develop the ability to recognize compliments and to use them properly.

Kasper, G. (2001). Classroom research on interlanguage pragmatics. In K. Rose & G. Kasper (Eds.), *Pragmatics in language teaching* (pp. 33–60). Cambridge: Cambridge University Press.

The author of this article provides a review of data-based research on pragmatic learning in second and foreign language classrooms. The questions addressed in this review include what we know about classroom learning of pragmatics and what research approaches and techniques have been used in studying pragmatics in the language classroom. Readers interested in what classroom-based research has been done and what it has shown us in learning about the advantages and disadvantages of incorporating pragmatic teaching into the classroom will find this article a worthwhile read.

Scheu-Lottgen, U., & Hernandez-Campy, J. (1998). An analysis of sociocultural miscommunication: English, Spanish, and German. *International Journal of Intercultural Relations, 4,* 375–394.

By observing a range of aspects of communication that can vary from culture to culture, the authors of this article illustrate contrasts in modes of and expectations in how speakers signal conversational intent. This is a useful article for readers seeking additional information on the interplay among variables such as context, power, distance, and politeness.

Washburn, G. (2001). Using situation comedies for pragmatic language teaching and learning. *TESOL Journal 10,* 21–26.

This article offers a thoroughly practical discussion of how to incorporate pragmatics into language teaching through the use of television. The author discusses how to choose appropriate shows, supplies guidelines for developing activities based on the language found in a show, and provides specific examples to help teachers develop their own classroom activities.

Books

Agar, M. (1994). *Language shock*. New York: William Morrow and Company.

The author of this book takes readers on a fascinating exploration of the relationship between language and culture. The book is written with the layperson in mind and requires no background. It is a good introduction to the relationship between culture and language. Agar's perceptive observations and anecdotes expose how strongly language and culture are linked, illustrate people's understanding of sense of self (self-identity), and reveal the effects of these factors on communicative behavior.

Boxer, D. (2002). *Applying sociolinguistics: Domains and face-to-face interaction*. Philadelphia: John Benjamins.

For those interested in learning more on the different aspects of talk in different social contexts, this is an excellent introductory work. The author reviews current research in various domains, including talk in familial, educational, and religious contexts. Boxer also addresses methodological issues of conducting research and discusses how various types of research will address different research questions. This text is easily accessible to anyone with little or no background in sociolinguistics but with a genuine interest in how people use language.

Brown, G., & Yule, G. (1983). *Discourse analysis*. Cambridge: Cambridge University Press.

The authors of this book present an expansive overview of the varied approaches to the study of discourse. Using a descriptive linguistics approach, they show how forms of language are used in communication. Their primary interest is in examining how language is used to communicate for a purpose in a context. A wide variety of discourse types are discussed, to enable students to apply these to any language context they encounter.

Gass, S., & Neu, J. (Eds.). (1996). *Speech acts across cultures: Challenges to communication in a second language*. Berlin: Mouton de Gruyter.

This edited volume deals with three areas of speech-act research: methodological issues, speech-act realization in different languages, and applications of research to teaching. The contributors include Andrew Cohen, on the production of what he terms "speech act sets"; M. Geis and L. Harlow, on politeness strategies; Diana Boxer, on using ethnographic interviewing; and Graham, on negotiation. This book offers many different articles, all well written and easily accessible to readers without any linguistic background.

Hinkel, E. (Ed.). (1999). *Culture in second language teaching and learning*. New York: Cambridge University Press.

This edited volume is a compilation of substantial essays on the impact of culture on pragmatics and language learning. The emphasis throughout the book is on the relationship between language and communication. It offers an introduction to research from a variety of disciplines, describes different aspects of culture that influence both second language learners and teachers, and strikes a balance between research and classroom applications. Language teachers should find this text of great benefit.

Scollon, R., & Scollon, S. (2001). *Intercultural communication: A discourse approach* (2nd ed.). Malden, MA: Blackwell Publishers.

This book serves as a practical introductory guide to the main concepts and problems of intercultural communication and is presented within the framework of interactive sociolinguistics. The authors highlight the discourses of Westerners and Asians, men and women, and corporations and professional organizations, as well as intergenerational discourse.

Spencer-Oatey, H. (Ed.). (2000). *Culturally speaking: Managing rapport through talk across cultures.* London: Continuum.

This book offers readers an excellent compilation of essays. Notable authors in the field, including J. House, G. Kasper, and E. Gudykunst, here examine fundamental issues, concepts, and methodological approaches in the study of pragmatics. Also included are several empirical studies investigating cross-cultural communication.

References

Adler, P. (1972). Culture shock and the cross-cultural learning experience. In D. Hoopes (Ed.), *Readings in intercultural communication* (Vol. 2, pp. 6–21). Pittsburgh: Regional Council for International Education.

Adler, P. (1975). The transitional experience: An alternative view of culture shock. *Journal of Humanistic Psychology, 15* (4), 13–23.

Adler, P. (1986). Culture shock and the cross-cultural learning experience. In L. Luce & E. Smith (Eds.), *Toward internationalism* (2nd ed., pp. 24–35). Cambridge, MA: Newbury House. (Reprinted from *Readings in intercultural communication,* Vol. 2, pp. 6–21, by D. Hoopes, Ed., 1972, Pittsburgh: Regional Council for International Education.)

Agar, M. (1994). *Language shock.* New York: William Morrow and Company

Aijmer, K. (1996). *Conversational routines in English: Convention and clarity.* New York: Longman.

Albert, R. (1983). The intercultural sensitizer or culture assimilator: A cognitive approach. In D. Landis & R. Brislin (Eds.), *Handbook of intercultural training: Issues in training methodology* (pp. 186–217). Elmsford, NY: Pergamon.

Albert, R., & Triandis, H. (1985). Intercultural education for multicultural societies: Critical issues. *International Journal of Intercultural Relations, 9,* 319–337.

Allport, G. (1958). *The nature of prejudice.* New York: Doubleday.

Althen, G. (1988). *American ways.* Yarmouth, ME: Intercultural Press.

Andersen, P. (1999). *Nonverbal communication: Forms and function.* Mountain View, CA: Mayfield.

Andrews, M., & Boyle, J. (1995). *Transcultural concepts in nursing care* (2nd ed.). Philadelphia: Lippincott.

Anthony, P., & Vinson, C. (1987). Nonverbal communication in the courtroom: You don't say. *Trial Diplomacy, 39,* 35–37.

Apte, M. (1977). "Thank you" and South Asian languages: A comparative sociolinguistic study. *International Journal of Sociology, 3,* 67–89.

Atkinson, D. (1999). TESOL and culture. *TESOL Quarterly, 33* (4), 625–654.

Augustin, E. (Ed.) (1993). *Palestinian women: Identity and experience.* London: Zed Books.

Austin, J. (1962). *How to do things with words.* Oxford: Oxford University Press.

Bachman, L. (1990). *Fundamental considerations in language testing.* Oxford: Oxford University Press.

Bandon, A. (1993). *Filipino Americans.* New York: New Discovery Books.

Bardovi-Harlig, K. (1992). Pragmatics as part of teacher education. *TESOL Journal, 1* (1), 28–32.

Barna, L. (1998). Stumbling blocks in intercultural communication. In M. Bennett (Ed.), *Basic concepts of intercultural communication: Selected readings* (pp. 173–189). Yarmouth, ME: Intercultural Press.

Barnlund, D. (1989). *Communicative styles of Japanese and Americans: Images and realities.* Belmont, CA: Wadsworth.

Beebe, L., & Takahashi, T. (1989). "Do you have a bag?" Social status and patterned variation in second language acquisition. In S. Gass, C. Madden, D. Preston, & L. Selinker (Eds.), *Variation in second language acquisition: Sociolinguistic issues* (pp. 103–125). Clevedon, Avon: Multilingual Matters.

Bennett, C., & Hirschhorn, R. (1993). *Bennett's guide to jury selection and trial dynamics in civil and criminal litigations.* St. Paul, MN: West.

Bennett, M. (1977). Transition shock: Putting culture shock in perspective. *International and Intercultural Communication Annual, 4,* 45–52.

Bennett, M. (Ed.). (1998). *Basic concepts of intercultural communication: Selected readings.* Yarmouth, ME: Intercultural Press.

Bernstein, B. (1971). *Class, codes, and control: Theoretical studies towards a sociology of language.* London: Routledge and Kegan Paul.

Berry, A. (1994). Spanish and American turn-taking styles: A comparative study. In L. Bouton (Ed.), *Pragmatics and language learning* (Vol. 5, pp. 180–190). Urbana-Champaign: University of Illinois, Division of English as an International Language.

Berry, J., Poortinga, Y., Segall, H., Marshall, H., & Dasen, P. (1992). *Cross-cultural psychology: Research and applications.* New York: Cambridge University Press.

Bird, C., & Shopen, T. (1987). Maninka. In T. Shopen (Ed.), *Languages and their speakers* (pp. 59–111). Philadelphia: University of Pennsylvania Press.

Birdwhistell, R. (1970). *Kinesics and context.* Philadelphia: University of Pennsylvania Press.

Birdwhistell, R. (1974). The language of the body: The natural environment of words. In A. Silverstein (Ed.), *Human communication: Theoretical explorations* (pp. 203–220). Hillsdale, NJ: Erlbaum.

Black, J., & Mendenhall, M. (1991). The U-curve adjustment hypothesis revisited: A review and theoretical framework. *Journal of International Business Studies, 22,* 225–247.

Block, R. (1978). Untangling the roots of modern sex roles: A survey of four centuries of change. *Signs: Journal of Women in Culture and Society, 4,* 237–252.

Blohm, J. (1991). Introduction to cross-cultural communication. Washington, DC: Youth for Understanding International Exchange.

Blum-Kulka, S., & House, J. (1989). Cross-cultural and situational variation in requesting behavior. In S. Blum-Kulka, J. House, & G. Kasper (Eds.), *Cross-cultural pragmatics: Requests and apologies* (pp. 123–154). Norwood, IL: Ablex.

Boudreau, F. (1986). Sex roles, identity, and socialization. In F. Boudreau, R. Sennott, & M. Wilson (Eds.), *Sex roles and social patterns* (pp. 63–83). New York: Praeger.

Boudreau, F., Sennott, R., & Wilson, M. (Eds.). (1986). *Sex roles and social patterns.* New York: Praeger.

Boxer, D. (1993). *Complaining and commiserating: A speech act view of solidarity in spoken American English.* New York: Peter Lang.

Boxer, D. (2002). *Applying sociolinguistics: Domains and face-to-face interaction.* Philadelphia: John Benjamins.

Boxer, D., & Cortés-Conde, F. (2000). Identity and ideology: Culture and pragmatics in content-based ESL. In J. Hall & L. Verplaetse (Eds.), *Second and foreign language learning through classroom interaction* (pp. 203–220). Mahwah, NJ: Erlbaum.

Boxer, D., & Tyler, A. (1996). A cross-linguistic view of sexual harassment. In N. Waner, J. Ahlers, L. Bilmes, M. Oliver, & S. Wertheim (Eds.), *Gender and belief systems* (pp. 85–97). Berkeley: Berkeley Women and Language Group.

Brislin, R. (1981). *Cross-cultural encounters: Face-to-face interaction.* Oxford: Pergamon.

Brooks, G. (1995). *Nine parts of desire: The hidden world of Islamic women.* New York: Anchor Books.

Broome, B. (1999). Palevome: Foundations of struggle and conflict in Greek interpersonal communication. In L. Samovar & P. Porter (Eds.), *Intercultural communication: A reader* (8th ed., pp. 115–125). Belmont, CA: Wadsworth.

Brown, G., & Yule, G. (1983). *Discourse analysis.* Cambridge: Cambridge University Press.

Brown, H. (2000). *Principles of language learning and teaching* (4th ed.). White Plains, NY: Addison Wesley Longman.

Brown, I. (1999). *Culture and customs of the Dominican Republic.* Westport, CT: Greenwood Press.

Brown, P., & Levinson, S. (1978). *Politeness: Some universals in language usage.* Cambridge: Cambridge University Press.

Brown, R., & Lenneberg, E. (1954). A study in language and cognition. *Journal of American Social Psychology, 49,* 454–462.

Brynes, F. (1966). Role shock: An occupational hazard of American technical assistants abroad. *Annals of the American Academy of Political and Social Science, 368,* 95–108.

Bumiller, E. (1990). *May you be the mother of a hundred sons: A journey among the women of India.* New York: Fawcett Columbine.

Burgoon, J., Coker, D., & Coker, R. (1986). Communicative effects of gaze behavior: A test of two contrasting explanations. *Human Communication Research, 12,* 495–524.

Cacioppo, J., & Petty, R. (1983). *Social psychophysiology: A sourcebook.* New York: Guilford Press.

Calloway, B., & Crewey, L. (1994). *The heritage of Islam: Women, religion, and politics in West Africa.* Boulder, CO: Lynne Riemer Publishers.

Caudill, W. (1973). General culture: The influence of social structure and culture on human behavior in modern Japan. *Journal of Nervous and Mental Disease, 157*(4), 240–257.

Chen, G., & Starosta, W. (1998). *Foundations of intercultural communication.* Needham Heights, MA: Allyn and Bacon.

Cheng, L. (1991). *Assessing Asian language performance: Guidelines for evaluating limited-English proficient students.* Oceanside, CA: Academic Communication Associates.

Cheng, L. (1994). Difficult discourse: An untold Asian story. In D. Ripich & N. Creaghead (Eds.), *School discourse problems* (2nd ed., pp. 156–170). San Diego: Singular Publishing Group.

Chomsky, N. (1986). *Knowledge of language: Its nature, origin, and use.* New York: Praeger.

Clyne, M. (1994). Cultural variation in the interrelation of speech acts and turn-taking. In M. Pütz (Ed.), *Language contact and language conflict* (pp. 205–222). Amsterdam: John Benjamins Publishing Company.

Cohen, A., Olshtain, E., & Rosenstein, D. (1986). Advanced EFL apologies: What remains to be learned? *International Journal of the Sociology of Language, 62,* 51–74.

Coltrane, S. (1988). Father-child relationships and the status of women: A cross-cultural study. *American Journal of Sociology, 5,* 1060–1095.

Condon, J. (1974). *Semantics and communication* (2nd ed.). New York: Macmillan.

Condon, J., & Yousef, F. (1975). *An introduction to intercultural speech communication.* Indianapolis: Bobbs-Merrill.

Cook, V. J. (1988). *Chomsky's universal grammar: An introduction.* Oxford: Blackwell Publishers.

Cooper, E. (1986). Chinese table manners: You are what you eat. *Human Organization, 45*(2), 179–184.

Crain, S., & Thornton, R. (1998). *Investigations in universal grammar: A guide to experiments on the acquisition of syntax and semantics.* Cambridge: MIT Press.

Damen, L. (1987). *Culture learning: The fifth dimension in the language classroom.* Reading, MA: Addison-Wesley.

Davis, M. (1990). *Mexican voices, American dreams.* New York: Henry Holt and Company.

Davitz, J. (1969). *The language of emotion.* New York: Academic Press.

DeCapua, A. (1989). *An analysis of pragmatic transfer in the speech act of complaints as produced by native speakers of German in English.* Unpublished doctoral dissertation, Teachers College, Columbia University.

DeCapua, A. (1998). Pragmatic transfer and cultural stereotyping. *Issues in Applied Linguistics, 9,* 21–36.

Delgado-Gaitan, C., & Trueba, H. (1991). *Crossing cultural borders: Education for immigrant families in America.* New York: Palmer Press.

Delpit, L. (1995). *Other people's children: Cultural conflict in the classroom.* New York: New Press.

de Waal, F. (2000/2001). "Reading nature's tea leaves." *Natural History, 109,* 66–71.

Diamond, B. & Moore, M. (1995). *Multicultural literacy: Mirroring the reality of the classroom.* New York: Longman.

Dinh, K., Sarason, B., & Sarason, I. (1994). Parent-child relationships in Vietnamese immigrant families. *Journal of Family Psychology, 8*(4), 471–488.

Douglas, M. (1975). *Implicit meanings.* London: Routledge.

Duranti, A., & Goodwin, C. (Eds.). (1992). *Rethinking context: Language as interactive phenomenon.* Cambridge: Cambridge University Press.

Eckert, P., & Rickford, J. (Eds.). (2002). *Style and sociolinguistic variation.* Cambridge: Cambridge University Press.

Ekman, P. (1972). Universals and cultural differences in facial expressions of emotion. In J. Cole (Ed.), *Nebraska symposium on motivation, 1971,* (Vol. 19, pp. 163–206). Lincoln: University of Nebraska Press.

Ekman, P. (1973). Cross-cultural studies of facial expressions. In P. Ekman (Ed.), *Darwin and facial expression* (pp. 169–229). New York: Academic Press.

Ekman, P., & Friesen, W. (1969). The repertoire of nonverbal behavior. *Semiotica, 1,* 49–98.

Ekman, P., Friesen, W., & Bear, J. (1984). The international language of gestures. *Psychology Today, 18* (5), 64–69.

Ekman, P., Friesen, W., O'Sullivan, M., Chan, A., Diacoyanni-Tarlatzis, I., Heider, K., et al. (1987). Universals and cultural differences in the judgments of facial expressions of emotion. *Journal of Personality and Social Psychology, 53,* 712–717.

Ekman, P., & Keltner, D. (1997). Universal facial expressions of emotion: An old controversy and new findings. In U. Segerstråle & P. Molnár (Eds.), *Nonverbal communication: Where nature meets culture* (pp. 27–46). Mahwah, NJ: Erlbaum.

Ellis, C. (1995). *Culture shock: Vietnam.* Portland, OR: Graphic Arts Center Publishing Company.

Ellis, R. (1994). *The study of second language acquisition.* Oxford: Oxford University Press.

El-Solh, C., & Mabro, J. (Eds.). (1994). *Muslim women's choices: Religious beliefs and social reality.* Providence, RI: Berg Publications.

Enahoro, P. (1998). *How to be a Nigerian.* Ibadan, Nigeria: Spectrum Books.

Esikovits, E. (1998). Girl-talk/boy-talk: Sex differences in adolescent speech. In J. Coates (Ed.), *Language and gender: A reader* (pp. 42–54). Oxford: Blackwell.

Fadiman, A. (1997). *The spirit catches you and you fall down: A Hmong child, her American doctors, and the collision of two cultures.* New York: Farrar, Straus, and Giroux.

Fantini, A. (Ed.). (1995). Language, culture, and world view [Special issue]. *International Journal of Intercultural Relations, 19* (2).

Fantini, A. (1997a). Checking culture/intercultural competencies: The YOGA form. In A. Fantini (Ed.), *New ways in teaching culture* (pp. 36–39). Alexandria, VA: Teachers of English to Speakers of Other Languages.

Fantini, A. (1997b). Developing Intercultural Competence: A Process Approach Framework. In A. Fantini. (Ed.), *New ways in teaching culture* (pp. 40–44). Alexandria, VA: Teachers of English to Speakers of Other Languages.

Feldman, R., & Rime, B. (Eds.). (1991). *Fundamentals of nonverbal behavior.* Cambridge: Cambridge University Press.

Fraser, B. (1990). Perspectives on politeness. *Journal of Pragmatics, 14,* 219–236.

Friday, R. (1989). Contrasts in discussion behaviors of German and American managers. *International Journal of Intercultural Relations, 13,* 429–446.

Furnham, A. (1989). Communicating across cultures: A social skills perspective. *Counseling Psychology Quarterly, 2,* 205–222.

Furnham, A., & Bochner, S. (1982). Social difficulty in a foreign culture: An empirical analysis of culture shock. In S. Bochner (Ed.), *Cultures in contact: Studies in cross-cultural communication.* Oxford: Pergamon.

Furnham, A., & Bochner, S. (1986). *Culture shock: Psychological reactions to unfamiliar environments.* London: Methuen.

Gao, G., & Ting-Toomey, S. (1998). *Communicating effectively with the Chinese.* Thousand Oaks, CA: Sage.

Gardner, R., & Lambert, W. (1972). *Attitudes and motivation in second language learning.* Rowley, MA: Newbury House.

Gass, S., & Neu, J. (Eds.). (1996). *Speech acts across cultures: Challenges to communication in a second language.* Berlin: Mouton de Gruyter.

Gay, G. (2000). *Culturally responsive teaching: Theory, research, and practice.* New York: Teachers College Press.

Gee, J. (1996). *Social linguistics and literacies: Ideology in discourses.* London: Palmer Press.

Geertz, C. (1973). *The interpretation of culture: Selected essays.* New York: Basic Books.

Giles, H., & Coupland, N. (1991). *Language: Contexts and consequences.* Oxford: Oxford University Press.

Giles, H., & St. Clair, R. (Eds.). (1979). *Language and social psychology.* Oxford: Blackwell.

Giles, H., & St. Clair, R. (Eds.). (1980). *The social and psychological contexts of language.* Hillsdale, NJ: Erlbaum.

Gilliland, H. (1995). *Teaching the Native American* (3rd ed.). Dubuque, IA: Hunt Publishing.

Godard, D. (1977). Same setting, different norms: Phone call beginnings in France and the United States. *Language in Society, 6,* 209–219.

Goffman, E. (1959). *The presentation of self in everyday life.* Garden City, NY: Doubleday.

Goffman, E. (1972). *Interaction ritual: Essays on face-to-face behavior.* Harmondsworth, UK: Penguin.

Goffman, E. (1981). *Forms of talk.* Philadelphia: University of Pennsylvania Press.

Goody, E. (Ed.). (1978). *Questions and politeness.* Cambridge: Cambridge University Press.

Grice, H. (1975). Logic and conversation. In P. Cole & J. Morgan (Eds.), *Syntax and Semantics: Vol. 3. Speech Acts* (pp. 41–58). London: Academic Press.

Gudykunst, W. (1998). *Bridging differences: Effective intergroup communication* (3rd ed.). Thousand Oaks, CA: Sage.

Gudykunst, W., & Hammer, M. (1988). Strangers and hosts: An extension of uncertainty reduction theory to intercultural adaptation. In Y. Kim & W. Gudykunst (Eds.), *Theories in intercultural communication* (pp. 35–48). Newbury Park, CA: Sage.

Gudykunst, W., & Kim, Y. (1984). *Communicating with strangers: An approach to intercultural communication.* Reading, MA: Addison-Wesley.

Gudykunst, W., & Kim, Y. (1997). *Communicating with strangers: An approach to intercultural communication* (3rd ed.). New York: McGraw-Hill.

Guirdham, M. (1999). *Communicating across cultures.* West Lafayette, IN: Ichor Business Books.

Gumperz, J. (1971). *Language in social groups.* Stanford: Stanford University Press.

Gumperz, J. (1977). Sociocultural knowledge in conversational inference. In M. Saville-Troike (Ed.), *Twenty-eighth annual round table monograph series on languages and linguistics* (pp. 191–211). Washington, DC: Georgetown University Press.

Gumperz, J. (1978). The conversational analysis of interethnic communication. In E. L. Ross (Ed.), Proceedings of the Southern Anthropological Society: *Interethnic communication* (pp. 13–31). Athens: University of Georgia Press.

Gumperz, J., Gurinder, A., & Kaltman, H. (1982). Thematic structure and progression in discourse. In J. Gumperz (Ed.), *Language and social identity* (pp. 35–52). Cambridge: Cambridge University Press.

Gumperz, J., & Hymes, D. (Eds.). (1972). *Directions in sociolinguistics: The ethnography of communication.* New York: Holt, Rinehart, and Winston.

Gumperz, J., & Tannen, D. (1979). Individual and social differences in language use. In C. Fillmore, D. Kempler, & W. Wang (Eds.), *Individual differences in language ability and language behavior* (pp. 305–325). New York: Academic Press.

Guthrie, G. (1975). A behavioral analysis of cultural learning. In R. Brislin, S. Bochner, & W. Lonner (Eds.), *Cross-cultural perspectives on learning* (pp. 143–155). New York: Wiley.

Haddad, Y., & Lummis, A. (1987). *Islamic values in the United States.* New York: Oxford University Press.

Hall, E. (1959). *The silent language.* New York: Doubleday.

Hall, E. (1966). *The hidden dimension.* New York: Anchor Books.

Hall, E. (1976). *Beyond culture.* New York: Anchor Books.

Hall, E. (1983). *The dance of life: The other dimension of time.* New York: Doubleday.

Hall, E., & Hall, M. (1989). *Understanding cultural differences.* Yarmouth, ME: Intercultural Press.

Hansel, B. (1993). *The exchange student survival kit.* Yarmouth, ME: Intercultural Press.

Hanvey, R. (1987). Cross-cultural awareness. In L. Luce & E. Smith (Eds.), *Toward internationalism: Readings in cross-cultural communication* (2nd ed., pp. 13–23). Cambridge, MA: Newbury House. (Reprint of a 1976 version)

Hayes, N., & Orrell, S. (1993). *Psychology: An introduction* (2nd ed.). London: Longman.

Heath, S. (1983). *Ways with words: Language, life, and work in communities and classrooms.* New York: Cambridge University Press.

Heath, S. (1992). Sociocultural contexts of language development: Implications for the classroom. In P. Richard-Amato & M. Snow (Eds.), *The multicultural classroom: Readings for content-area teachers* (pp. 102–125). White Plains, NY: Longman.

Hecht, M., Andersen, P., & Ribeau, S. (1989). The cultural dimensions of nonverbal communication. In M. Asante & W. Gudykunst (Eds.), *Handbook of international and intercultural communication* (pp. 163–185). Newbury Park, CA: Sage.

Heider, F. (1958). *The psychology of interpersonal relations.* New York: Wiley.

Henderson, S. (1984). Interpreting the evidence on social support. *Social Psychiatry, 19,* 1–4.

Henderson, S., Bryne, D., Duncan-Jones, P., Adcock, S., Scott, R., & Steele, G. (1978). Social bonds in the epidemiology of neurosis: A preliminary communication. *British Journal of Psychiatry, 132,* 463–466.

Henley, N. (1977). *Body politics: Power, sex, and nonverbal communication.* Englewood Cliffs, NJ: Prentice-Hall.

Hilbert, D. (1987). *Color and color perception: A study in anthropocentric realism.* Stanford, CA: Center for the Study of Language and Information.

Hinkel, E. (Ed.). (1999). *Culture in second language teaching and learning.* New York: Cambridge University Press.

Hochshild, A., & Machung, A. (2003) (Rev. ed.). *The Second Shift.* USA: Penguin.

Hofstede, G. (1980). *Culture's consequences.* Beverly Hills: Sage.

Hofstede, G. (1986). Cultural differences in teaching and learning. *International Journal of Intercultural Relations, 10,* 301–320.

Hofstede, G. (1991). *Cultures and organizations: Software of the mind.* London: McGraw-Hill.

Hofstede, G. (1994). The cultural relativity of the quality of life concept. In G. Weaver (Ed.), *Culture, communication, and conflict: Readings in intercultural relations* (pp. 131–142). Needham Heights, MA: Ginn Press.

Holmes, J., & Brown, D. (1987). Teachers and students learning about compliments. *TESOL Quarterly, 21,* 523–546.

Howard, D. (1998). *The Dominican Republic in focus: A guide to the people, politics, and culture.* Northhampton, MA: Interlink.

Hsu, F. (1981). *Americans and Chinese: Passage to differences.* Honolulu: University of Hawaii Press.

Huang, M. (1996). *Achieving cross-cultural equivalence in a study of American and Taiwanese requests*. Unpublished doctoral dissertation, University of Illinois, Urbana-Champaign.

Hur, B., & Hur, S. (1994). *Culture shock: Korea*. Portland, OR: Graphic Arts Center Publishing.

Hwang, K. (1987). Face and favor: The Chinese power game. *American Journal of Sociology, 92*(4), 944–974.

Hymes, D. (1962). The ethnography of speaking. In T. Gladwin & W. Sturtevant (Eds.), *Anthropology and human behavior* (pp. 15–53). Washington: Anthropological Society of Washington.

Hymes, D. (1969). *Ethnography, linguistics, narrative inequality*. Bristol, PA: Taylor and Francis.

Hymes, D. (1971). *On communicative competence*. Philadelphia: University of Pennsylvania Press.

Hymes, D. (1972). Models of the interaction of language and social life. In J. Gumperz & D. Hymes (Eds.), *Directions in sociolinguistics: The ethnography of communication* (pp. 35–71). New York: Holt, Rinehart, and Winston.

Ito, K., Chung, R., & Kagawa-Singer, M. (1997). Asian/Pacific American women and cultural diversity: Studies of the traumas of cancer and war. In S. Ruzek, V. Olesen, & A. Clarke (Eds.), *Women's health: Complexities and differences* (pp. 300–328). Columbus: Ohio State University Press.

Johnstone, B. (1989). Linguistic strategies and cultural styles for persuasive discourse. In S. Ting-Toomey & F. Korzenny (Eds.), *Language, communication, and culture* (pp. 139–156). Newbury Park, CA: Sage.

Judd, E. (1999). Some issues in the teaching of pragmatic competence. In E. Hinkel (Ed.), *Culture in second language teaching and learning* (pp. 152–166). Cambridge: Cambridge University Press.

Kasper, G. (1999). Data collection in pragmatics research. *University of Hawaii Working Papers in ESL, 18,* 71–107.

Kasper, G. (2001). Classroom research on interlanguage pragmatics. In K. Rose & G. Kasper (Eds.), *Pragmatics in language teaching* (pp. 33–60). Cambridge: Cambridge University Press.

Kasper, G., & Dahl, M. (1991). Research methods in interlanguage pragmatics. *Studies in Second Language Acquisition, 13,* 215–47.

Kasper, G., & Kellerman, E. (Eds.). (1997). *Communication strategies: Psycholinguistic and sociolinguistic perspectives*. London: Longman.

Kay, P., & McDaniel, C. (1978). The linguistic significance of basic color terms. *Language, 54,* 610–646.

Keenan, E. (1976). The universality of conversational postulates. *Language and Society, 5,* 67–79.

Kim, Y. (1989). Intercultural adaptation. In M. Asante & W. Gudykunst (Eds.), *Handbook of international and intercultural communication* (pp. 275–294). Newbury Park, CA: Sage.

Kleinke, C. (1986). Gaze and eye contact: A research review. *Psychological Bulletin, 131,* 303–304.

Kohls, R. (1979). Conceptual model for area studies. In D. Hoopes & P. Ventura (Eds.), *Intercultural sourcebook* (pp. 273–284). Washington, DC: Society for Intercultural Education, Training, and Research.

Kohls, R. (1984). *Survival kit for overseas living* (2nd ed.). Yarmouth, ME: Intercultural Press.

Kohls, R. (2001). *Survival kit for overseas living* (4th ed.). Yarmouth, ME: Intercultural Press.

Kolb, D. (1984). *Experiential learning: Experience as the source of learning and development.* Englewood Cliffs, NJ: Prentice-Hall.

Kramsch, C. (1993). *Context and culture in language teaching.* Oxford: Oxford University Press.

Kramsch, C. (1998a). *Language and culture.* Oxford: Oxford University Press.

Kramsch, C. (1998b). Teaching along the cultural faultline. In D. Lange, C. Klee, M. Paige, & Y. Yershova (Eds.), *Culture as the core: Interdisciplinary perspectives on culture teaching and learning in the language curriculum* (pp. 15–28). Minneapolis, MN: Center for Advanced Research on Language Acquisition.

Labov, W. (1970). The study of language in its social context. *Studium Generale, 23,* 30–87.

Landis, D., & Bhagat, R. (Eds.). (1996). *Handbook of intercultural training* (2nd ed.). Thousand Oaks, CA: Sage.

Leathers, D. (1997). *Successful nonverbal communication: Principles and applications* (3rd ed.). Boston: Allyn and Bacon.

Leech, G. (1983). *Principles of pragmatics.* London: Longman.

Levine, R., West, L., & Reis, H. (1979). Perceptions of time and punctuality in the United States and Brazil. *Journal of Personality and Social Psychology, 38,* 541–550.

Lewis, R. (1999). *When cultures collide.* London: Nicholas Brealey.

Luce, L. (Ed). 1992. *The Spanish-speaking world.* Lincolnwood, IL: National Textbook Company.

Lustig, M., & Koester, J. (1993). *Intercultural competence: Interpersonal communication across culture.* New York: HarperCollins.

Lustig, M., & Koester, J. (2003). *Intercultural competence: Interpersonal communication across culture* (4th ed.). Boston: Allyn and Bacon.

Lysgaard, S. (1955). Adjustment in a foreign society: Norwegian Fulbright grantees visiting the United States. *International Social Science Bulletin, 7,* 45–51.

Martin, J. (2002, January 23). Miss Manners Column. *The Washington Post,* p. C10. Retrieved September 19, 2002 from http://www.washingtonpost.com.

Matsumoto, D., Wallbott, H., & Scherer, K. (1989). Emotions in intercultural communication. In M. Asante & B. Gudykunst (Eds.), *Handbook of international and intercultural communication* (pp. 225–246). Newbury Park, CA: Sage.

Mbabuike, M. (1991). Ethnicity and ethnoconsciousness in the New York metropolitan area: The case of the Ibos. In F. Salamone (Ed.), *Studies in third world societies* (Publication No. 36, pp. 83–91). Williamsburg, VA: College of William and Mary, Department of Anthropology.

Meeuwis, M., & Sarangi, S. (1994). Perspectives on intercultural communication: A critical reading. *Pragmatics, 3,* 309–313.

Mehan, H., Lintz, A., Okamoto, D., & Willis, J. (1995). Ethnographic studies of multicultural education in classrooms and schools. In J. Banks & C. Banks (Eds.), *Handbook of research on multicultural education* (pp. 129–144). New York: Macmillan.

Meier, A. (1996). Two cultures mirrored in repair work. *Multilingua, 15,* 149–169.

Meier, A. (1999). Identifying and teaching the underlying cultural themes of pragmatics: A case for explanatory pragmatics. In L. Bouton (Ed.), *Pragmatics and language learning* (Vol. 9, pp. 185–210). Urbana-Champaign: University of Illinois, Division of English as an International Language.

Meier, A. (2003). Posting the bans: A marriage of pragmatics and culture in foreign and second language pedagogy and beyond. In A. Martinez, E. Uso, & A. Fernandez (Eds.), *Pragmatic competence and foreign language teaching* (pp. 185–210). Castelló, Spain: Castello'n Servicio de Publicaciones de la Universidad Jaume I.

Meyers, D. (1999). *Social psychology.* Boston: McGraw-Hill.

Miller, P. (1988). *Nonverbal communication* (3rd ed.). Washington, DC: National Education Association.

Miller, P. (2000). *Nonverbal communication in the classroom.* Munster, IN: Patrick Miller Associates.

Minnis, M. (1994). Toward a definition of law school readiness. In V. John-Steiner, C. Panofsky, & L. Smith (Eds.), *Sociocultural approaches in language and literacy: An interactionist perspective* (pp. 347–390). Cambridge: Cambridge University Press.

Moerman, M. (1988). *Talking culture: Ethnography and conversation analysis.* Philadelphia: University of Pennsylvania Press.

Newstrom, J., & Scannell, E. (1998). *The big book of team building games.* New York: McGraw-Hill.

Nydell, M. (1987). *Understanding Arabs: A guide for Westerners.* Yarmouth, ME: Intercultural Press.

Oberg, K. (1960). Culture shock: Adjustment to a new cultural environment. *Practical Anthropology, 7,* 177–182.

Okabe, R. (1983). Cultural assumptions of East and West: Japan and the United States. In W. Gudykunst (Ed.), *Intercultural communication theory: Current perspectives* (pp. 21–44). Beverly Hills: Sage.

O'Kelly, C. (1980). *Women and men in society.* New York: D. Van Nostrand.

Park, C. (1997). Learning style preferences of Asian American students in secondary schools. *Equity and Excellence in Education, 30,* 68–77.

Parry, K. (1996). Culture, literacy, and reading. *TESOL Quarterly, 30,* 665–692.

Patterson, M. (1990). Functions of non-verbal behavior in social interaction. In H. Giles & W. Robinson (Eds.), *Handbook of language and social psychology* (pp. 101–118). New York: Wiley and Son.

Pedersen, P. (1995). *The five stages of culture shock: Critical incidents around the world.* Westport, CT: Greenwood Press.

Pike, K. (1954). *Language in relation to a unified theory of the structure of human behavior* (Vol. 1). Glendale, CA: Summer Institute of Linguistics. (Reprinted in a 2nd, ed., rev. as *Language in relation to a unified theory of the structure of human behavior,* 1967, The Hague: Mouton de Gruyter.)

Pinker, S. (1997). *How the mind works.* New York: W. W. Norton.

Popenol, R. (1990). Cambodian marriage: Marriage and how it is changing among Cambodian refugees in Philadelphia. In P. Kilbride, J. Goodale, & E. Ameisen (Eds.), *Encounters with American ethnic cultures* (pp. 296–311). Tuscaloosa: University of Alabama Press.

Porter, R., & Samovar, L. (1997). An introduction to intercultural communication. In L. Samovar & R. Porter (Eds.), *Intercultural communication* (8th ed., pp. 5–26). Belmont, CA: Wadsworth.

Richard-Amato, P., & Snow, M. (Eds.). (1992). *The multicultural classroom: Readings for content-area teachers.* White Plains, NY: Longman.

Risager, K. (1999). Language and culture: Disconnection and reconnections. In T. Vestergaard (Ed.), *Language, culture, and identity* (pp. 71–81). Ålborg, Denmark: Ålborg University Press.

Rogers, E., & Steinfatt, T. (1999). *Intercultural communication.* Prospect Heights, IL: Waveland Press.

Rose, K. (1994). Pragmatic consciousness-raising in an EFL context. In L. Bouton (Ed.), *Pragmatics and language learning* (Vol. 5, pp. 52–63). Urbana-Champaign: University of Illinois, Division of English as an International Language.

Ryffel, C. (1997). From culture "teaching" to culture "learning": Structures and strategies for increased effectiveness. In A. Fantini (Ed.), *New ways in teaching culture* (pp. 28–35). Alexandria, VA: Teachers of English to Speakers of Other Languages.

Samovar, L., & Porter, R. (1995). *Communication between cultures* (2nd ed.). Belmont, CA: Wadsworth.

Samovar, L., & Porter, R. (Eds.). (1999). *Intercultural communication: A reader* (9th ed.). Belmont, CA: Wadsworth.

Samovar, L., & Porter, R. (Eds.). (2003). *Intercultural communication: A reader* (10th ed.). Belmont, CA: Wadsworth.

Sapir, E. (1958). *Culture, language, and personality.* Berkeley: University of California Press. (Reprinted in 1964)

Schegloff, E. (1984). On some questions and ambiguities in conversations. In M. Atkinson & J. Heritage (Eds.), *Structures of social action* (pp. 29–52). Cambridge: Cambridge University Press.

Schegloff, E. (1987). Some sources of misunderstanding in talk in interaction. *Linguistics, 25,* 201–218.

Schegloff, E. (1992). Repair after next turn: The last structurally provided defense of intersubjectivity in conversation. *American Journal of Sociology, 97,* 1295–1345.

Scheu-Lottgen, U., & Hernandez-Campy, J. (1998). An analysis of sociocultural miscommunication: English, Spanish, and German. *International Journal of Intercultural Relations, 4,* 375–394.

Schweizer, T., & White, D. (Eds.). (1998). *Kinship, network.* New York: Cambridge University Press.

Scollon, R. (1999). Cultural codes for calls. In E. Hinkel, (Ed.), *Culture in second language teaching and learning* (pp. 181–195). Cambridge: Cambridge University Press.

Scollon, R., & Scollon, S. (1981). *Narrative, literacy, and face in interethnic communication.* Norwood, NJ: Ablex.

Scollon, R., & Scollon, S. (2001). *Intercultural communication: A discourse approach* (2nd ed.). Malden, MA: Blackwell Publishers.

Seelye, N. (1997). *Teaching culture: Strategies for intercultural communication* (2nd ed.). Lincolnwood, IL: National Textbook Company.

Segall, M., Dasen, P., Berry, J., & Poortinga, Y. (1990). *Human behavior in global perspective: An introduction to cross-cultural psychology.* Boston: Allyn and Bacon.

Sokolovsky, J. (Ed.). (1990). *The cultural context of aging.* New York: Bergin and Garvey.

Spencer-Oatey, H. (1993). Conceptions of social relations and pragmatic research. *Journal of Pragmatics, 20,* 27–47.

Spencer-Oatey, H. (Ed.). (2000). *Culturally speaking: Managing rapport through talk across cultures.* London: Continuum.

Stephen, W., & Stephen, C. (1985). Intergroup anxiety. *Journal of Social Issues, 41,* 157–176.

Stewart, E., & Bennett, M. (1991). *American cultural patterns: A cross-cultural perspective* (Rev. ed.). Yarmouth, ME: Intercultural Press.

Storti, C. (2001). *The art of crossing cultures* (2nd ed.). Yarmouth, ME: Intercultural Press.

Szalay, L. (1981). Intercultural communication: A process model. *International Journal of Intercultural Relations, 5,* 133–146.

Taft, R. (1977). Coping with unfamiliar cultures. In N. Warren (Ed.), *Studies in cross-cultural psychology* (Vol. 1, pp. 145–155). London: Academic Press.

Taft, R. (1985). The psychological study of the adjustment and adaptation of immigrants in Australia. In N. Feather (Ed.), *Survey of Australian psychology: Trends in research* (pp. 150–167). Sydney: Allen and Unwin.

Tajfel, H. (Ed.). (1984). *The social dimension* (Vol. 2). Cambridge: Cambridge University Press.

Tannen, D. (1984). The pragmatics of cross-cultural communication. *Applied Linguistics, 5,* 189–195.

Tannen, D. (1986). *This is not what I meant: How controversial style makes or breaks relations with others.* New York: William Morris.

Tannen, D. (1994). *Gender and discourse.* New York: Oxford University Press.

Tannen, D., & Kakava, C. (1992). Power and solidarity in modern Greek conversation: Disagreeing to agree. *Journal of Modern Greek Studies, 10,* 12–29.

Taylor, L., & Whittaker, C. (2003). *Bridging multiple worlds: Case studies of diverse educational communities.* Boston: Allyn and Bacon.

Tenhula, J. (1991). *Voices from Southeast Asia: The refugee experience in the United States.* New York: Holmes and Meier Publishers.

Thomas, J. (1983). Cross-cultural pragmatic failure. *Applied Linguistics, 4,* 91–112.

Ting-Toomey, S. (1985). Toward a theory of conflict and culture. In W. Gudykunst, L. Stewart, & S. Ting-Toomey (Eds.), *Communication, culture, and organizational processes.* Beverly Hills: Sage.

Ting-Toomey, S. (1988). Intercultural conflict styles: A face-negotiation theory. In Y. Kim & W. Gudykunst (Eds.), *Theories in intercultural communication* (pp. 213–233). Newbury Park, CA: Sage.

Ting-Toomey, S. (1999). *Communicating across cultures.* New York: Guilford Press.

Ting-Toomey, S., & Kirogi, A. (1998). Facework competence in intercultural conflict: An updated face-negotiation theory. *International Journal of Intercultural Relations, 22,* 187–225.

Tobin, J., & Friedman, J. (1983). Spirits, shamans, and nightmare death: Survivor stress in a Hmong refugee. *American Journal of Orthopsychiatry, 53,* 439–448.

Torbiörn, I. (1988). Culture barriers as a social psychological construct: An empirical validation. In Y. Kim & W. Gudykunst (Eds.), *Cross-cultural adaptation: Current approaches* (pp. 168–190). Newbury Park, CA: Sage.

Triandis, H. (1972). *The analysis of subjective culture.* New York: Wiley.

Triandis, H. (1975). Culture training, cognitive complexity, and interpersonal attitudes. In R. Brislin, S. Bochner, & W. Lonner (Eds.), *Cross-cultural perspectives on learning* (pp. 39–77). New York: Wiley.

Triandis, H. (1988). Collectivism vs. individualism: A reconceptualization of a basic concept in cross-cultural psychology. In G. Verma & C. Bagley (Eds.), *Cross-cultural studies of personality, attitudes, and cognition* (pp. 60–95). London: Macmillan.

Triandis, H. (1994). *Culture and social behavior.* New York: McGraw-Hill.

Triandis, H. (1995). *Individualism and collectivism.* Boulder, CO: Westview Press.

Turner, J. (1987). Toward a sociological theory of motivation. *American Sociological Review, 52,* 15–27.

Tyler, A., & Boxer, D. (1996). Sexual harassment? Cross-cultural/cross-linguistic perspectives. *Discourse and Society, 7,* 107–133.

Tzanne, A. (1999). *Talking at cross-purposes.* Philadelphia: John Benjamins.

Ulichny, P. (1997). The mismanagement of misunderstandings in cross-cultural interactions. *Journal of Pragmatics, 27,* 233–246.

Vinson, D. (1982). Juries: Perception and the decision-making process. *Trial, 18,* 52–55.

Ward, C., & Kennedy, A. (1996). Crossing cultures: The relationship between psychological and sociocultural dimensions of cross-cultural adjustment. In J. Pandey, D. Sinha, & D. P. S. Bhawuk (Eds.), *Asian contributions to cross-cultural psychology* (pp. 289–306). New Delhi: Sage.

Washburn, G. (2001). Using situation comedies for pragmatic language teaching and learning. *TESOL Journal, 10,* 21–26.

Watson, O., & Graves, T. (1966). Quantitative research in proxemic behavior. *American Anthropologist, 68,* 971–985.

Webbink, P. (1986). *The power of the eyes.* New York: Springer.

Weinstein-Shr, G., & Henkin, N. (1991). Continuity and change: Intergenerational relations in Southeast Asian refugee families. *Marriage and Family Review, 16* (3–4), 351–367.

Wenzhong, H., & Grove, C. (1999). *Encountering the Chinese: A guide for Americans* (2nd ed.). Yarmouth, ME: Intercultural Press.

White, S. (1989). Backchannels across cultures: A study of Americans and Japanese. *Language in Society, 18,* 59–76.

Whorf, B. (1956). *Language, thought, and reality: Selected writings of Benjamin Lee Whorf.* Cambridge: MIT Press.

Winkelman, M. (1994). Culture shock and adaptation. *Journal of Counseling and Development, 73,* 121–126.

Wintergerst, A. (1994). *Second-language classroom interaction.* Toronto: University of Toronto Press.

Wodak, R. (1996). *Disorders of discourse.* London: Longman.

Wolfgang, A. (1984). *Nonverbal behavior: Perspectives, applications, intercultural insights.* Lewiston, NY: Hogrefe and Huber.

Wolfson, N. (1981). Invitations, compliments, and the competence of the native speaker. *International Journal of Psycholinguistics, 24,* 7–22.

Wolfson, N., D'Amico-Reisner, L., & Huber, L. (1983). How to arrange for social commitments in American English: The invitation. In N. Wolfson & E. Judd (Eds.), *Sociolinguistics and language acquisition* (pp. 116–128). Rowley, MA: Newbury House.

Wolfson, N., Marmor, T., & Jones, S. (1989). Problems in the comparison of speech acts across cultures. In S. Blum-Kulka, J. House-Edmondson, & G. Kasper (Eds.), *Cross-cultural pragmatics: Requests and apologies* (pp. 174–196). Norwood, NJ: Ablex.

Yoshikawa, M. (1988). Cross-cultural adaptation and perceptual development. In Y. Kim & W. Gudykunst (Eds.), *Cross-cultural adaptation* (pp. 140–148). Newbury Park, CA: Sage.

Yule, G. (1996). *Pragmatics.* Oxford: Oxford University Press.

Zaharna, R. (1989). Self-shock: The double-binding challenge of identity. *International Journal of Intercultural Relations, 13,* 501–525.

Zinn, M., & Eitzen, D. (1990). *Diversity in families* (2nd ed.). New York: Harper and Row.

Index